The Other Side of Fear

The Other Side of Fear:

A Backpacker's Memoir

Written By

Jenni Reavis

Unhidden Heroines Book Series, Book 1

Copyright © 2021 by Jenni Reavis

All rights reserved. This book may not be reproduced in whole or in part, stored in a retrieval system, or transmitted in any form by any means – electronic, mechanical, or other – without written permission from the publisher, other than for "fair use" as brief quotations embodied in articles and reviews.

This book is independently published. Some names have been changed to protect identities of characters.

Edited by Kristin Alsup and Jackie Bell
Book cover design by Rose Miller

First printed, April 2021.
Paperback ISBN: 978-1-7361743-1-9
E-book ISBN: 978-1-7361743-0-2

Dedication

To the 19-year-old version of myself who so badly needed the woman I've become,

To the women who struggle to find the pieces of themselves after it,

To the women who continue to suffer in silence,

who haven't yet found the words to tell their story,

who thought if they told it, that nobody would listen,

that nobody would believe them, or that nobody would care,

Who are scared of what others would think if they told,

Who would fear for their lives if they breathed a word of it,

I validate you, I hear you, I believe you, I love you.

You are all heroines.

This one's for you.

"Everything you want is on the other side of fear."

– **George Addair**

Acknowledgements

Thank you Sharianne Carson for making this opportunity possible and for being the living example of the expression, "Empowered Women Empower Women." Also, thank you for taking care of Gracie Ann so that I can live in alignment with my life purpose abroad. Without you and all the ways you have empowered me, none of this would be possible.

Thank you to my social media followers who donated to my GoFundMe campaigns during three years of backpacking; you made it possible for me to go places I otherwise would not have, and your donations also contributed to miracles in the lives of other people.

Thank you, Officer Kelly. Our reasoning stays between us.

Thank you, Leslie Bell, for investing in my path in a way that is now an echo heard 'round the world.

Thank you to Donelle Cole for being such an inspiration with your self-published work *From Living to Legacy: Beyond the Barriers of Mediocrity* and for having so much patience to answer all my questions through my process of writing, organizing, and self-publishing this book.

Thank you to my editors Kristen and Jackie for taking the mess of my manuscript, which was paint splattered on canvas, and investing your talent to make it a beautiful work of art. I could not have done this without you.

Thank you to those who have kept me alive without me even knowing it.

Thank you to all those who shared words of wisdom and encouraged me to be the most authentic version of myself that I can be.

Thank you, Dr. D, for showing me what active listening and empathy are.

Thank you to my fur baby, Gracie Ann, for giving me a reason to hang on, for showing me what unconditional love truly is, for being with me every footstep of this path, and for supervising the writing of this book by laying under my desk lamp to watch my every move. I love you with all my heart.

I am thankful for those who have hurt me along the way because my wounds gave me a reason to dig deeper inside of me in a way that I would not have, and the payoff of that has been amazing.

Contents

CHAPTER 1: VILLA DE LEYVA 1

CHAPTER 2: BRILLE 15

CHAPTER 3: HOSTAL MASAYA 28

CHAPTER 4: SOULFIRE 37

CHAPTER 5: WHEN THE BIRDS SING AT DAWN 48

CHAPTER 6: BROKEN HEART, A FINE ART 58

CHAPTER 7: SEX, DRUGS, AND FUCK YOUR ROCK-N-ROLL 67

CHAPTER 8: INTERVENTION, REHAB, AND ALEX 78

CHAPTER 9: AFTER REHAB 88

CHAPTER 10: THE BIRTH OF MY FIRST BUSINESS 96

CHAPTER 11: MAKE LOVE NOT WAR 102

CHAPTER 12: THANK YOU, MA'AM, MAY I HAVE ANOTHER? 109

CHAPTER 13: SHARIANNE CARSON 117

CHAPTER 14: MY LIGHTBULB MOMENT 127

CHAPTER 15: KEEP RISING 134

CHAPTER 16: TOUCHDOWN IN COLOMBIA 148

CHAPTER 17: JARDÍN 158

CHAPTER 18: UP IN FLAMES 169

CHAPTER 19: GIOVANI 181

CHAPTER 20: YUCCA & CHICHARRON 191

CHAPTER 21: THE ROSE THAT GREW FROM CONCRETE	199
CHAPTER 22: BUCARAMANGA	207
CHAPTER 23: NEVERTHELESS, SHE PERSISTED	215
CHAPTER 24: THE SACRED TEMPLE	226
CHAPTER 25: A 5,000-KILOMETER ROAD TRIP, YEEHAW	236
CHAPTER 26: SANTIAGO, CHILE	244
CHAPTER 27: PERU-ISH	256
CHAPTER 28: ARGENTINA	264
CHAPTER 29: GETTING SOBER	276
CHAPTER 30: UNHIDDEN HEROINES	285
List of Books I Recommend for Further Reading:	300
How to Find and Follow me on Social Media	303

Chapter 1

Villa de Leyva

Living in Medellín in January of 2020, one of my journals began to fill with handwritten bits of my story. I was renting a room in a tiny apartment with a retired couple I met through a friend in Jardín. In the mornings, I walked through local neighborhoods around Belen Rincon to find a Juan Valdez or other coffee shop tucked away, where I sat for hours drinking amazing Colombian coffee, eating pastries, people-watching, and writing.

Until one day, after two months of being still, my soul said it was time to hoist my bag and hit the open road. All I needed was a couple changes of clothes, basic toiletries, my journals, and a few bucks in my pocket. I was free to let the wind blow me wherever my soul pleaded to go.

I threw the basics in my backpack, paid my rent through the end of May so I could keep everything else in my space, and off to the bus station I went. My first stop was San Carlos, a place I heard about from the locals. Few tourists went there because they were likely to visit more common places on the Tourist Trail, such as Guatapé, Medellín, or Jardín.

San Carlos was only four hours east of Medellín, a dreamy town as magical as Jardín. During the four days I spent there, I went for a motorcycle ride to the swimming hole near waterfalls way back in the mountains. I enjoyed a whole day riding on top of a rural bus the locals refer to as a "chiva," riding through rural routes, and ducking tree limbs and power lines.

I knew I wanted to end up in Boyacá, a department of Colombia just north of Bogotá. I wanted to spend a month exploring the Tenza Valley and the small villages scattered along the opening of it. Something mystical was calling me to Boyacá, and since I was starting to catch wind of the pandemic frenzy, I figured it would be a great place to be still for a month, if needed. Plus, I would be close to the big city of Bogotá if anything happened.

I kept showing people the map; I wanted to get from where I was in San Carlos to Boyacá, and every person insisted that the only way to get there was to go directly to Bogotá and take a bus north. But, according to my map, I could see pathways that led from village to city to village along the way, so I planned on bus-hopping or hitchhiking bit by bit until I ended up wherever my spirit shook inside.

The climate through that region was hot and humid, and my bus rides were very strange. Some people were wearing masks, and some were not. At this point, I thought the whole pandemic thing was a big conspiracy and hadn't paid the least bit of attention to the hype. Everyone on the bus looked at me as if I were a swamp monster. The bus was only half-full, and nobody would move their bags for me to sit down. *That's okay*, I thought. *I will stand.*

The bus driver of that bus suddenly turned around and asked where I was going. "Puerto Araujo," I responded. He promptly pulled over.

"Get out here. In the next hour, a blue bus will come from the other direction that will go to where you are heading. I thought you were going somewhere else."

All eyes were on me. *Wait, was I being kicked off for not having a mask? Would anyone else ever stop to pick me up without a mask?*

One single week ago, I would have been able to sit wherever I wanted, and the person next to me would have been intrigued at their first opportunity to talk to a foreigner. Many of the people I'd met along my journey invited me to their homes with open arms, and their kids climbed all over me like a jungle gym.

Hell, I didn't even know if a bus would come at all, and I was now standing on the side of the freeway in the humidity and heat. My bags were sitting on the dusty road next to my feet. The worst bit? I had to pee. How in the world was I supposed to do that? There wasn't any sign of traffic anywhere from either direction, but I didn't dare pull down my pants to pee. I had no idea who could be lurking in the foliage, watching me.

I picked a banana leaf off a nearby tree and used it to pee standing up. That was a trick I had learned long ago traveling in Colombia whenever we got stuck in the mountains for long periods of time. I pulled down my pants enough to accommodate the banana leaf for my pee to shoot down it, and I suddenly started laughing so hard. The world was in a pandemic, and there I was peeing through a banana leaf on the side of a vacant, dirty road, unsure of whether a bus would even come on by, or where I even was.

As I peed and laughed, I cupped my mouth and belted out a rooster call up to the sky. "Kukurukukururkuku!!!" I always had the best time just hanging out with myself. Then, I heard a honk and around the bend came barreling a blue bus that did stop for me.

I got off in a place called Puerto Araujo, where I was told to wait again on the side of the road for another microbus that would take me to a small town called Cimitarra, where I had been told buses stop to pick up passengers to go to Boyacá. I wasn't entirely sure what my final destination would be quite yet–I would wait until I got closer and figured out the availability of microbuses with destinations that gave me a *ping ping* on the inside.

I must have waited there for an hour for a bus before finally giving up. It was getting dark. I didn't want to spend money on lodging, but it didn't feel like I had an overnight bus ride in the future for that night.

I was hot and so hungry, not having eaten since the sun came up when I bought homemade bread from a little lady selling food out of her basket. The climate was stiflingly hot at 110 degrees Fahrenheit, although I was prepared to sleep in a hammock somewhere outside in the heat. I felt dust caked over my lips, lining the inside of my mouth and throat, but I hoisted my bag on my back and set out on foot in the direction of the town's main streets, hoping to find lodging somewhere with running water where I could at least take a shower.

This village was tiny, and I was certain I was the first foreigner the locals had ever seen. My tattered tennis shoes left tracks behind along the sandy path that led me into town. I saw one broken sign with enough letters for me to read that it was lodging, but when I peeked inside, the one dim light in the hallway exposed old, open vacant rooms with stained mattresses and dirty floors. A toothless old woman in a bright purple skirt waddled around the corner, clenching a broom in her hand, and I think we startled each other equally.

"Hospedaje?" I asked.

I only understood enough bits and pieces to put together that there was no running water there. I gifted her a grin, a "No, gracias," and carried on my way. Her neighbor who was out pretending to sweep her porch was kind enough to tell me that if I was looking for a night's stay somewhere, there was one hotel in town a few blocks ahead by the main plaza.

I learned later that this village's population was 1,260 people, which is why the local people stepped outside their tiny houses to see me up close. I can't imagine how foreign

I must have looked to them. Children watched, wide-eyed, peeking around buildings and fixtures. I was relieved to find a place with a room available that had a shower and an AC unit in the wall. As a rule, I don't drink any liquid when I go on long bus-hopping trips because I never know if I will have access to a bathroom (or a safe place to pee without one.) I made note to suck down at least a half a gallon of water that night to hydrate my body and pee overnight while I had access to the bathroom connected to my room. The only bus out of town was the next morning at 5 a.m. It was going to be a short night.

I wandered out to find a hot meal and some water. The main plaza was about 50 meters square with two benches and a chipped statue in the middle. Around the plaza, I found a small grocery store, a hardware store, and one restaurant. At the restaurant all that was left for sale was a bowl of beans with avocados and fried plantains topped off with a bottomless glass of fresh mango juice for the price of one whopping US dollar. I don't know if it was because of my insatiable thirst or because the lady in the kitchen did something different, but of all of the mango juices I tasted in six countries across South America, that was the best I had ever had.

I sucked down glasses until I felt like my belly would pop and chuckled to myself thinking of the scene in Forrest Gump when he drank 40 Cokes at that banquet right before he met the president. I enjoyed them so much that I didn't care that the other people in the restaurant were all staring at me and whispering. I was used to being stared at everywhere I went. The young girl giving me table service was very pregnant, and I thought to myself, "Aannnnddd, the population is about to be 1,261."

I found out later from a Colombian local that they may not have been whispering about me because I was different, but in disbelief that I had wandered in there by myself; that area was still considered a hotspot in regard to guerilla warfare and violence from rebel groups. I never did verify whether that was true, but it didn't matter. I figured there was a reason I passed through there, and I made it out on the bus at 5 a.m. the next morning.

I was going to get off in a town called Chinquinquirá, but the bus driver talked me into going to a town called Villa de Leyva. It was only two hours further, but he was happy to take me that far for no extra charge. He was persistent that I needed to see it and since I didn't have a set plan I was open to the suggestion.

When I got out of the bus terminal in Villa de Leyva, I immediately noticed a huge energy shift. I was getting dirty looks from all around me. I was not welcome there. It was an obvious, unquestionable repulsion. People's eyes were glaring at me over their masks. Everyone had on a mask. I did not, nor did I have any clue where to find one.

There was a group of Germans standing outside of the terminal talking. "Hey, what did you guys think of this place?" I stopped to ask.

"We wish we could tell you!" One of them said back. "We just got here this morning and couldn't find a place to stay, so now we've got to figure out where to go."

"No place to stay, like everything is booked?"

"No. No one will give us a bed because they think we are the reason people in Colombia got sick, like we brought it from Germany, but we have been backpacking here for months." I stood there trying to process their information. This was nuts.

"So, what are you going to do?" I asked.

"Where else they will receive us, we have no idea. We are brainstorming. Maybe we will go on to the next village."

"Do you need me to help you interpret?" I offered. "I'm fluent in Spanish."

"No, no, we can figure it out on our own, thank you, miss. Blessings to you." We blew each other kisses and carried on. As I walked closer to town, I noticed worried people scurrying by me, people whispering and staring. There weren't many people out, and above all there was a heavy quiet.

When I reached it, I learned that Villa de Leyva has the biggest main plaza of any place in Colombia. Not only was I shocked at the vastness of it–but even more so at how empty and quiet it was. It was still daylight out. The bright blue, cloudless sky seemed like it had chosen the wrong day to make its appearance. I would have never matched it to this day or the weight that was growing in the pit of my stomach.

I walked up and down streets, knocking on doors that had lodging signs. Most people didn't even open their doors and it seemed as though I was wandering the streets of a ghost town. Occasionally someone would come to the window to see who was knocking, but when they saw I was a foreigner, they waved me away. Not accepting foreigners. Many of them had signs on their doors saying just that.

No no no, I knew I had a better chance of finding something than the group of friends traveling together. I figured that even if I didn't find an official bed at a place to pay for a night's stay, I could sleep on a bench in the park with the stray dogs to keep me company. I had done that often in Jardín to ward off the loneliness during sleepless nights.

I walked to the end of a long street, intending to turn the corner to walk the street that paralleled the park, when I saw a sign poking out that said, "Hospedaje." When I got closer to knock, I discovered that there were two sets of wooden doors: A big one for grown people, and a small one for children or big dogs to go through. The small door was open, and someone was there. I knocked. Silence. I knocked harder. Silence. I chose to duck into that small space and let myself into the building.

The reception area was absolutely beautiful and there were vacant rooms with bunk beds and elegant features all around the area. There were paintings from local artists hanging on the walls, hand-carved wooden fixtures, and potted plants hanging in perfect spots. I could faintly smell cleaner in the area, which told me that the person attending hadn't heard me because she was somewhere cleaning, probably mopping.

"Holaaaaaa, buenas tardes, disculpe!" I shouted down the hallway. Nothing. I stepped closer to the hallway, cupped my mouth, and yelled again. I finally heard the shuffle of someone's uneven footsteps and out hobbled a plump elderly woman holding a mop. She stared at me wide-eyed from all the way down the hall, clearly with no intention of coming any closer.

"Do you have a place to stay? How much per night?"

She silently stared back with hesitation. Fear sprawled all over her face. She started to slowly shake her head. "No foreigners. They just released a new mandate. I think it's fines or time in jail for housing foreigners illegally, and I can't risk that. I have a special needs son that requires my full-time care."

"Senora, can you show me a printout of the mandate?" I knew she had to have one. I knew that upon releasing it, officials had most likely delivered a printout of it by hand to every doorstep. She was not eager to comply, and she didn't want to take me in. I wanted to find a way to show her that by housing me, she wasn't housing me illegally. I had done nothing illegal. All of this was illogical. She started to interrogate me.

"Where are you from? How long have you been in Colombia? Why are you traveling alone? Where were you before arriving at this village?"

The questions kept raining down on me. I could not tell her that I had been through several places lollygagging about on my adventure. I told her I was renting a room in Medellin with a retired couple and had been since January, and before that, I rented a room in Jardin for two months. I had valid contact information and addresses for both of my places. I showed her the stamp on my passport from where I entered Colombia way back in November.

"I have one room only for you and only for a night or two. Understand?"

Yes! I wondered which of these open rooms around reception she would put me in, but instead, she led me down the hallway, past the kitchen, and onto the back patio. There was another patio along the side fence with three rooms that stood apart from the house. She opened one of the doors to a luxurious room with a queen-size bed, fancy blankets, a dresser, and a private bathroom.

"This is all I have. It's a very nice space, as you can see. Brand new and clean. Fifty-thousand pesos per night." That was way too expensive. When backpacking, I never paid more than 15,000 to 20,000 pesos per night for a bunk bed in a simple hostel with a shared bathroom. I had definitely not budgeted for that.

"Senora, that is way too expensive. Why can I not pay half of that for a bunk bed inside of reception?" Those rooms outside would also be cold at night and had no heaters.

"You cannot be close to the reception in case the police come by," she curtly states. "They make several rounds a day to random places to see if people are hiding tourists."

Jesus, was I now part of the underground railroad system? None of this felt good.

"For that price, I will include breakfast in the morning. You can find something better. Please go look." This lady knew I had nowhere else to go. However, if I left, I risked not finding another place, and if I came back here, she may not open her door for me again, not that she had in the first place.

The next day I can catch a bus to take me to the next town.

I paid her for a night, dropped my stuff, and went to find something to eat. There were some businesses open with vendors inside, beckoning me to come in. I was the only person wandering the streets. The prices were extremely expensive, people desperate to make what they would while they could. Out of all the vendors who were trying to flag me into their shops, I chose the one who had an aura of kindness around him, quietly standing in the doorway of his place with his hands tucked in his pockets. When our eyes met, he gave me a sincere smile.

"Do you sell food?" fell out of my mouth without even intending it to.

He looked up at the vacant spot where stains gave evidence of a sign that used to hang there and then said, "We had to remove the signs since we have been so slow the past few weeks. We are going to shut our doors by the end of the week. How did you know that I sell food?"

He led me into the dining area and made me pollo ajiaco, one of my favorite dishes that I had tried every single place it was offered so that I could compare how it differed in different regions. I was intrigued to try it made from his hands, since he was from Venezuela.

We visited for a long time over our soup, and I found out that he, his wife, and four kids had fled the crisis from Venezuela two years ago and used every last penny of what they had to start this restaurant, and now they were going to lose everything because of economic crisis from the pandemic.

"But we are still so happy," he said. "We Venezuelan people have suffered so much tragedy already. These hard times will seem like a joke to us, and we will overcome everything because of what we have already survived." The resilience of these people never ceased to impact my life in every place I went.

His wife joined us. "You know they enforced a strict curfew effective tonight at 9 p.m.?" She asked me. "Do not get caught outside between 9 p.m. and 6 a.m. or they will fine you very big. They are looking for every possible way to exploit tourists, and the media is creating all kinds of fear that white foreigners are responsible for this whole pandemic. Be very careful. Always look around you. We know what it is like to be an unwanted foreigner. We can't imagine doing it alone like you. You are welcome here, and if we can help, please message me. Take my number."

Her words told me what my intuition already knew. *Something much worse was on the way.* I felt the ominous presence of a big monster, a new monster, one I hadn't ever seen. I had slayed so many monsters, but it was time to be brave. I had reached level 1000 of Zelda.

She continued, "As a matter of fact, I have a friend here who's also alone. I feel like you need to meet her. I am going to give you her number and send her yours. Who knows how long you might be here."

Who knows how long I might be here?

I was catching a bus out the next morning. I didn't like the vibe of this place or anything happening in it at all. I was okay to be stuck somewhere for a week or two, even a month, somewhere I felt good, somewhere I could happily write. More than ever, I felt the urgency to continue working on the story I had begun to patch together from handwritten pieces. I just wanted to write.

I explored the streets a bit more on foot, so thankful for a full tummy. The sun was down by six as usual, and I plopped down on a bench, looking at the beauty of the plaza under an endless black sky divinely decorated with stars. The geographical area surrounding this place was more desert-like, allowing a sacred night space for stars to show their glory.

I will come back here another time. Tomorrow I will ask my intuition where to go next. If things close, I don't want to be here.

My thoughts were interrupted abruptly when three police officers appeared in front of me from my right-hand side, startling me out of my hazy night-gazing. "Show us your passport," one demanded. My heart began to pound in my chest. The round of interrogations began. While one scanned my pages looking for my entry stamp, another fired questions. The third just watched me and listened to my answers. I was hesitant to tell anyone I was traveling alone because the kidnapping risk was sky-high, especially by corrupt law enforcement officials. My tongue kept sticking to the roof of my mouth as I watched the officer roughly thumb through my precious document. I watched every movement. That passport was my lifeline. It could disappear in one instant.

I told them the lie that I was on my way to Bogotá, where my friends and husband were waiting for me. They asked where I was staying. I made up a woman's fake name and assigned her house to the location of street signs that my mind had taken a snapshot of earlier while I was exploring (not the first time my photographic memory saved me from a difficult situation). "She lives on that street in the house with the blue door," I said matter-of-factly.

"How did you know to stay with her?" The quiet officer asked. The other two were looking at each other and making a mental note of every bit of info I was giving.

"Well, she is a long-time friend of the lady I was staying with in Medellín," was the first thing that came to my mind. "I have all of her information, her full address, document ID number, cell phone, etc. Feel free to call her. She is happy to verify anything you have doubts about." My heart was pounding so hard. I was terrified they could see the pulse jumping out of my neck. I didn't want to find out what would happen if I got caught lying.

The three looked at each other and then looked at me. I looked all three of them back in the eyes, refusing to break eye contact until I had my passport in my hands. The officer with my documents handed them back reluctantly and then said, "Curfew is at 9 p.m. to 6 a.m. It is now an obligation to wear a face mask. Do not break rules or there will be strict consequences." They vanished into the night as quickly as they had appeared.

Once I got back to my room, I took a shower and laid down to watch Netflix, only to discover that the Wi-Fi didn't even reach my room. I was used to living without Wi-Fi, or a lot of things for that matter, so I sat at the back patio to smoke my Marlboro Red under the stars and listen to the quietest night I had heard in months. It was so quiet that it hurt my ears.

It was trying to tell me something, but I couldn't make out the words. It was very similar to the heaviness of a quiet that would fall over Oklahoma City right before a tornado outbreak that would destroy everything in its path. There's nothing you could do about it except feel it, wait for it, and ride out the storm, unsure of whether you would see life on the other side of it or not. I felt that this was going to be very similar.

The next morning, the owner knocked on my door to have me come eat breakfast. On the table outside was breakfast with eggs, fresh fruit, bread, and juice made from scratch. The sun was out, and the sky was a beautiful crystal blue. I figured I would go to the bus station to inquire about tickets first and then come back to gather my things. Stepping outside of the lodging, though, was a different world.

The storm was approaching. People hushed, frantic, scurrying about in the streets, staring at me with angry eyes above their masks. When I got to the bus station, all the doors were closed, and I was stopped by two police officers outside the front door. They requested my documents and started the interrogation. Finally, they told me, "The bus station is closed. No transport will run until after April 12th." April 12th! It was March 23rd! That was almost three weeks! I could not pay the price this lady was charging for a room for that long.

Quarantine was in effect at midnight. The president had mandated a 19-day lockdown to be in effect starting at midnight. I would be allowed out for one hour in the morning every other day according to the last digit of my passport number. Any foreigners who violated the mandate would be subjected to an expensive fine or face time in Colombian jail. We had one full day left of freedom, and I was standing in it.

Chapter 2

Brille

As I shuffled along, back to the park, dazed and anxious about my newly budding reality, I received a text from the girl who the lady at the restaurant had told me I needed to meet.

"Yenni, this is Brille, Mariana's friend. You know the Venezuelan people who fed you at the restaurant yesterday? Do you have time to meet?"

I felt tremendous relief because I wouldn't be alone. There was a reason why the universe had connected us, especially in such an interesting way. She happened to be just around the corner, and we nearly collided crossing the street on our way to meet each other. We were friends immediately. We hugged and clung to each other like tomorrow would not come, and we had no idea if it would with how things felt.

I had never been so happy to hug a stranger, and when we looked at each other in the eyes, we knew we had met before in some other lifetime. I had a new sister. She looked like a real doll, tiny and petite, with long dark hair and perfect makeup. She was wearing a skirt with new knee-high boots and a black sweater showing one slender, feminine shoulder.

She asked if I would like to see her coffee shop. Sure! We only had one full day of freedom before 19 days of confinement; little did we know then that the 19-day mandate would be extended for five months. On our way to the coffee shop, we were confronted by three policemen who started their routine with me. Documents and 100 questions.

"They are dogs," Brille whispered to me as they walked away. "Do not trust them. Do not tell them you are alone. They hate you. They are not here to protect you, and don't believe what they say. Make sure you know things for yourself."

Her coffee shop was tucked away down the street on the other side of the plaza Church. There was a beautiful arched wooden door with stunning stonework carved around it. It almost looked like a scene from a movie set in medieval times. Once inside, I saw that this was a place where several small businesses were located. There was a small garden in the middle of the space with a table and chairs. It looked like it should have fairies. It was such a magical little nook. She showed me her coffee shop and her beautifully packaged products.

"Do you have cigarettes?" she asked. I pulled out my new pack of Marlboro Reds. She made us a coffee and sat down at that cozy table neighboring the garden. She began to tell me her story as I sat intrigued. We pulled cigarette after cigarette out of my open pack and smoked as I sat there wide-eyed listening to her story.

She and her American husband had ended things horribly on a vacation in Mexico. After an escalated argument, he left her there, and she hitchhiked and backpacked her way back down through Mexico and Central America until she made it to Colombia. She had shown up in this village without a peso in her pocket and volunteered at a hostel in exchange for shelter. She always dreamt of starting her own coffee shop, so she started fighting for that dream, doing one small thing at a time. Now she not only had that coffee shop, but exported her coffee brand in large quantities to places all over the world. She told me how much she struggled and suffered, knowing she had not been a good wife and had so deeply regretted not giving her husband what he deserved. She wanted him back, and she had their love story printed on the back of her bags of coffee. Her hope was that somehow this coffee would cross his path wherever he was in the United States and that he would read this story and come find her. She was still in love with him. In fact, they were still legally married, yet she had no way to reach him.

I already knew that she had suffered before she ever told me her story. There was something about her depth that told me everything. I understood it because suffering had done the same thing inside of me. We discussed how crazy the current dilemma was and she said she would walk me outside before parting ways so that we could begin preparing for our lockdown. We were smoking our last cigarette under the stars when she turned to me and said, "I feel like I have a message for you from the universe. May I tell you?" I wondered what she knew about my life. We just met, and she did most of the talking.

"You have been traveling for a long time. I see many months, at least three years you have been on a wild adventure." The following June marked three years since I had arrived in Medellín on that one-way ticket, and it still seemed like only yesterday. My face didn't give her any feedback. I told her to keep going.

She continued, "Your travels have changed you. Every single place where you have gone held codes that changed you. You have been silently collecting data this whole time. I see that you have begun a project. You have started to write a book. If you haven't started yet, you will. I see it as a birth. You will create a masterpiece. I see the birth of this book opening a canal for many more to come through because you are now aligned with your purpose. Your path traveling may at times have seemed random, yet each place and event has played a role in aligning you with it. Now it is time to take a great rest from traveling and write. If you don't do that, your travels from this point forward will not serve the same purpose. They won't be satisfying and you will always feel as though you are spinning your wheels."

My heart was racing. She didn't know me and definitely did not know about the tattered journal in my backpack where I had begun to scribble pieces of my story out by hand at hidden bakeries in tucked away neighborhoods in Medellín. I listened. I swallowed down my pounding heart and gave her a nod that confirmed I had heard her.

She continued, "The world needs your story, Jenni. Your purpose is to travel. Don't worry about getting stuck. I also see you giving conferences and helping thousands and thousands of women later on down your path. I see lots of flags around you, which means you will cross many borders and have connections with people all over the world. Your work will be available in many languages. Jenni, it's time to be braver than ever. For me, too. Okay, I will text you. We must prepare for what is coming, Jenni. The worst has yet to start."

That I had definitely felt. She gave me a tight hug and then clicked off in her fancy boots. I watched her petite silhouette disappear into the night as I stood amazed at how intricately the universe had laid everything out just for that exact moment. I hadn't even planned to come to this village – deciding at the last minute when the bus driver convinced me that I would make this place my next destination. Out of all the restaurants where I could have eaten, I'd felt an impulse to go to the one where the Venezuelan couple connected me to Brille.

I raced back to where I was staying and told the lady that transport was closed. I would need to stay there a few more days. Could she give me a better price? No, she indeed would not. She also told me she wasn't okay with me using her kitchen to cook. "There will be food service open for delivery, and I will still include breakfast," she informed me. Food in that touristy town was very expensive and there was no way I could afford to call food in every day. She said she would allow me to boil eggs if I wanted, but no cooking. I went to the store and bought a dozen eggs and a loaf of homemade bread, a $3 investment that would provide something for the next few days.

Jesus. I hunkered down in my room with my boiled eggs, bread, plantain chips, and bottled water. I thought about the police officers I had lied to about staying with a friend and that house with a blue door. I thought I'd be gone by now. I didn't have Wi-Fi in my room which meant no Netflix, no meditation music while I slept, no YouTube videos, and limited functions of my WhatsApp messages. The next morning, I discovered that my "included breakfast" had been converted to boiled eggs and a piece of bread left on the chair next to my room. For the price she was charging me I should have had three meals per day included, eating at a table with her family.

When I tried to use the Wi-Fi in the reception area to download Netflix episodes to watch in my room, I discovered that it was too slow to even stream, so I decided to go to my room to sleep. *Sleep at noon on a bright, sunny day?* I thought. My nerves were wound too tight. I had gifted my books in English along my journey traveling and I had no internet. I took a sleeping pill and faded away. Actually, I did that the next two days as well just to make time go by and to kill my anxiety.

When I woke up on Friday morning, I had a message from Brille asking if she could come by to take me to the grocery store since it was our day allowed outside. I also had an urgent intuitive message: **You are sinking into a depression. Nobody else will pull you out. Leave the place where you are and go somewhere that empowers you.**

I got dressed, ate my boiled eggs and bread. On my way out the door, I walked past the kitchen to see the family eating a home-cooked meal at their table. I was so hungry. The owner was spoon-feeding her special-needs son - a 30-year-old with cerebral palsy. He was fully dependent on his mother to feed him, change adult diapers, and bathe him. During the day, she would park his wheelchair outside where he would grunt and moan and coo to the birds all day long, sometimes laughing and shouting.

Brille was waiting for me. She had been worried about me and said that my light looked dim. We turned the corner to walk toward the store a few blocks away where the locals bought groceries for the cheapest price, when suddenly she glanced behind and around us, grabbed my arm, and pulled us into a door that she knew was unlocked. It appeared to be a place that had formerly served as a coffee shop, with the coffee bar against the back wall and open tables for customers.

She yelled something upstairs, and down came an older woman. "Hello, I'm Brille's friend Martha. May I serve you both a coffee? I don't have any desserts available or else I would offer you something sweet." Brille informed me that this is where she was currently staying upstairs in the spare bedroom. They had been friends for years. We sat there smoking and drinking coffee while I told her about my past couple of days.

When we left, we pulled the door shut behind us and rounded the corner, and two cops on motorcycles pulled up next to us. "Oh fuck," I said. "I already know they're going to stop us." Of course, they certainly did. They asked for both of our documents. They wanted to verify that we had permission to be on that street that particular day, and of course wanted to see my passport stamp from when I entered Colombia. Any foreigner who had arrived in Colombia within the 14 days before the quarantine began was required to be completely quarantined with absolutely no access to go into public for any reason, and anyone caught violating that would immediately be put into jail. They told us we were free to go and reminded us we had one hour to go buy essential goods and immediately return to our homes. There and back only, understood? They did not inquire, this time, about where home was for each of us.

When I got back to my lodging, I used the Wi-Fi in the reception area to look for another place to stay in the area. Ironically, someone from one of my travel pages on Facebook had messaged me suggesting that if I needed a place to stay, they recommended Green Garden Hostel there in the village. It was only a left-hand and a right-hand turn away from where I was currently staying. I messaged the owner on WhatsApp, and he responded almost immediately. He seemed so warm and kind and also stated that in the hostel were a few other stranded foreigners, and that they would all happily receive me as part of their family. I told him I would sneak out late at night when the owners of my place went to bed.

I had my stuff ready all day, just waiting until Matilda and her family finally retreated to their rooms. They walked around me in silence as if I weren't even there. It was the most awkward, unwelcome experience I'd ever had in Colombia during the year-plus I'd spent traveling there. I didn't want them to have any clue about my actions. They would figure it out soon enough when they found my room vacant.

Finally, at 11 p.m., everyone disappeared. I messaged the owner of the Green Garden Hostel that I would be on my way. He responded that under no circumstances should I go out by myself because of the consequences I risked by breaking quarantine as a foreigner. He insisted he come get me and help me with my bag. Again, I marveled at how the universe had sent an angel directly to my path. The streets were dead empty and the silence was deafening. We walked in silence, hearing the crunching of our shoes on the gravel, my heart pounding. There were streetlights that cast shadows, and I wished I could be like Peter Pan and detach from it until we reached the hostel. At any moment, I felt a police officer would come around the corner or jump out from the shadows. If I were walking by myself and it happened, they could take me to jail, take my passport, and I would have no contact with the outside world for god knows how long.

Oh my gosh, I was embraced by an entirely different reality once we got through the gates of the hostel. The other guests were a group of six people from France and one guy from Belgium who had just met one another traveling and had been hanging out there together for a week. They were making homemade pizza to throw in the brick oven outside and were drinking red wine, which was profusely offered as a welcome. As a sacrificial offering to my dedication to sobriety, I clung to my, "No, thank you." I knew that just one glass would open the door for many more, and right now it was more imperative than ever to keep a clear sober mind.

The next day, I woke to interesting news: authorities were going to lift the quarantine restriction on Monday, only to allow travelers to make it to Bogotá to catch international flights. We would have permission to leave this awful village and things could be better in a bigger city, but we only had permission to fly. I would have to leave

Colombia and return to the USA. The decision broke my heart. This wasn't how I wanted to leave. I didn't feel ready. What about my laptop and things that were still in Medellín? I didn't have much time to really think hard about it. I had to make a decision and go with it. If I didn't use this opportunity on Monday to leave this place, who knows how long I would be stuck in that village.

Then Brille called me. "Honey, one of the cops that stopped us yesterday just came by here looking for you. One of the neighbors saw you with me and tattled that you came here to drink coffee, and they want to find you for breaking quarantine. The cops thought we were hiding you here, and when we showed that you were not here, they left angry. I told them I didn't know where you were, but please keep a lookout."

Fuck, I had to get out of this terrible place. I rounded up everyone from the hostel to see if we could join good vibes. Nobody else had heard that we had permission to travel to Bogotá the following Monday. There would still be no public transport, so we would have to find a private driver to take us from the village to the city.

"If anyone wants to leave Monday, we must buy airline tickets today, Saturday," I said. That would give us all day today and tomorrow to find a driver who could get us across the border of Cundinamarca to the airport in Bogotá as well as time to get our packing done. Yes, there were three other people who wanted to leave, and we got on our phones that very moment and found flights. With such a heavy heart, I bought an outgoing ticket for the following Monday back to the United States, leaving at 4 p.m. It was done, and it had cost just about everything I had left with a couple hundred left over. Oh my, what would life in the States be like in the midst of all this? I had made calls and texts to let worried people back home know I'd be on my way soon.

There was a French couple at a hostel around the corner who was also coordinating a humanitarian flight on private transport the following Monday. On Sunday evening, they came over with their belongings on their backs so that we could all plan to escape this nightmare. Well, someone from the village had secretly taken pictures of this French couple walking along with the bags on their back, and they posted the pictures on a social media page that was for that village only with the message: "Look how much our governor disregards our safety. He is still letting in these disgusting people. Who agrees that we should find who is hiding these tourists like rats and take matters into our own hands?" Pictures of them walking with their packs on their backs made it look like they were recently arriving, which wasn't the truth, as they were just changing hostels. They had actually been backpacking in Colombia for months.

The post went viral, shared over 300 times by local people, and there were hundreds of comments such as these among so many others:

"They should all be taken out to the desert and left there to survive. Disgusting."

"They're killing us by bringing disease, so they too should die."

"I hope they catch the disease they brought to us and die."

"Start setting hostels on fire to see where they escape from."

"Hostel owners should be held accountable for harboring criminals."

"Disgusting pigs, get rid of them. They're not welcome here."

I found it ironic how welcome we were whenever businesses wanted us to come with our foreign money to purchase stays at hostels, food, beers, and tourism packages. Now, we were stranded in a time of terror and they had no hand to offer help. No solace, no comfort, no shelter, no kindness at all to share. They threatened us. They knew nothing about us except that our skin color gave us away for being foreigners, and for that we were hated. This whole situation taught me in a whole different way to what extent fear destroys everything.

We were all sitting on the front porch of the hostel in disbelief as we read all these hateful messages about us when two motorcycles pulled up, and four men with neon green vests started banging on the gate. It was the police. The owner answered, opening only enough space to see them but blocking them from seeing us. Someone had snitched that he was illegally hiding tourists there. They were looking for an American girl with a flower tattoo on her neck and a French couple both with long hair who had been rumored to arrive at the hostel earlier in the day.

I was the only one in the group who spoke enough Spanish to understand what the police were saying. "They're looking for me and them," I said, pointing in the direction of the French couple. One of the French girls was outraged. Lucy stood up and yelled in English, "Oh, but we haven't done anything wrong! Tell him to come in here to face us. If they take one, they take us all! We will not be treated as criminals!" The other guys calmed her down. The hostel owner defended us, declaring that he followed protocol, we had done nothing wrong, and he would not allow his guests to be harassed. After much arguing, the police finally left. The owner was Colombian and knew his rights as a business owner.

We had a wonderful, last meal together which Brille had bravely snuck through back streets to be a part of. Before she left, I gifted her one of my blank journals that said, "Do everything that scares you the most" sprawled across the front of it. We gave each other one last tearful hug goodbye, and she disappeared into the late night.

The next morning our private car arrived at 7 a.m. sharp. I lay awake all night in my bunk with a million thoughts running through my head that ranged from, "What if the local people really set this place on fire and I never even make it out?" to, "I'm not ready to go back to the States" to, "What about my laptop and clothes still in Medellín?" I prepared to leave everything behind.

It was only a four-hour drive south from Villa de Leyva to the airport in Bogotá. On that drive alone, we went through four different checkpoints where there were military officers armed with AK-47s and police officers in combat gear. They reviewed our documents and interrogated us at length (as had all the others the past seven days). Sheesh, seven days and 168 hours is all it took for the whole world to go up in flames.

When we got to the airport, I was in for another surprise. There was a long line of desperate travelers waiting to be let in. We were surrounded by people frantically talking - mostly in French and German. I did not see any other Americans anywhere. When we finally got to the security officials who were checking ticket itineraries and passports, the three friends I had arrived with were admitted...but I was not.

"We have no outgoing flights to the United States," stated the woman officer.

"But I just bought my ticket yesterday," I insisted.

"We have no outgoing flights to the United States. And we won't until after April 12th when the 19-day quarantine lifts."

I stood there blinking my eyes, trying to understand what I was being told. I was convinced that I must have been misunderstanding what she was telling me in Spanish. "How is this possible?" I asked her. "I just booked my ticket yesterday, and the departure time is today at 4 p.m.," I repeated myself, thinking maybe *she* hadn't understood *me*.

"It looks like someone sold you a fraudulent ticket. I am so sorry. We cannot help you. Contact your embassy. I know for sure we have no outgoing flights to the USA today, nor do we have any more scheduled. We will not have any until after the 19-day lockdown." My group had stopped and turned to wait for me. My stomach had already sunk hard to the ground. I waved them goodbye. Their faces told me they wanted to understand why I couldn't come through, but they didn't have time to find out what was wrong. Their flights were leaving, and their families were waiting.

I couldn't feel my legs. My whole body felt numb. Where would I go? What would I do? I waded through the thick crowd of angry Europeans making demands of airport officials. I made it to a point a few feet away from the crowd and dropped my bag to the ground, where I also sat down. *What a shitshow*, I thought. Some of them had tickets and some didn't. Some had been sold tickets the airlines had double-booked and were arguing over whose ticket was valid. Everyone considered themselves equally entitled to their flights and were pushing, shoving, and arguing. It reminded me of the scene on *Titanic* where everyone knew the boat was going to sink and were fighting over who got lifeboats, knowing there was only room for a few.

I sat down on the dirty pavement next to a trash can, lit up a Marlboro, and watched the heavy rain pour down.

Finally, a sky that matched the day.

Chapter 3

Hostal Masaya

Obviously, traveling taught me about myself and about life, but what it taught me the most is that nothing goes as planned yet no matter what, everything will be okay. I had started to do a wonderful job at truly believing everything was working in my favor, and curveballs didn't shake me up so much. It was all a part of the adventure. However, I struggled to be positive, sitting there on the littered pavement, watching this big mess of frantic people.

I was grateful in that moment that Brille had insisted on taking me to get data put on my phone during our last time together so I could communicate without being dependent on a Wi-Fi network. I couldn't imagine how much more scary the situation would be if I couldn't use my phone to make calls or send texts. I searched for hostels and hotels in Bogotá and learned that the few still open for business were not accepting foreigners. I felt my stomach growl, and it seemed to complement the chill in my bones from the cold, rainy Bogotá climate. I was once again exhausted at a soul level.

A cab pulled up, and two guys got out. They saw I had a cigarette and therefore had a lighter, so they asked if they could join me for a smoke. I have always loved the 8-minute chitchats over a cigarette with strangers. I have had many divine encounters like that whenever I least expected. They were from Belgium and Romania and were there to catch their humanitarian flight back home. My nerves were too shaken to really talk, so I listened to their crazy experience getting shuttled out of the village where they had been stranded.

The Romanian guy let his friend do all the socializing, but as they were finishing the last drag of their smokes and loading their bags on their backs, he chimed in, "If something happens today, preventing you from flying, you should try Masaya Hostel for a place to stay. We just came from there. The owners are keeping their doors open for foreigners. Good luck." And off they went.

I was reminded that the universe always shows up. Sometimes we just have to wait a little bit longer. I hopped in a taxi and off to Masaya I went. Once I got my things stuffed in my bunk there, I noticed I had received an email from the United States Embassy notifying of a humanitarian flight sent by United Airlines for the following Saturday. I had used most of my remaining funds for the fake ticket, so I couldn't book any more flights, but my mom insisted I use her card to reserve my seat. See, in the United States, a "humanitarian flight" doesn't mean it's free.

So, I would be at Hostal Masaya for a few days. It was absolutely amazing. The beds were warm and comfortable; the architecture was beautiful. There was a big group of German and French people there waiting to catch their humanitarian flight. I usually sat with my earbuds in, studying German, eavesdropping on their conversations to see what words I recognized. We all shared the same co-ed bathroom in the main hallway, so whenever I would shower, the bathroom would be full of naked German people using the mirrors and waiting their turns for the toilet stalls.

My anxiety was extraordinarily high because of how everything had happened and the uncertainty of everything. I wanted to drink so bad, especially when every night all the Germans would sit on the outside patio drinking bottles of wine and rum. They always offered me a cup, but no matter how bad I wanted it, I kept saying no. If I could make it sober through a martial law lockdown in a foreign country, I could make it sober through anything. Also, studying another language aided in dissipating my anxiety.

I was in a small room that had two bunk beds, or four beds total, and I shared my room with two German girls and another girl named Anastasia who was born in Russia but had migrated to Germany with her family when she was younger. She spoke five languages and loved to help me with the grammar parts of my German lessons. She didn't get along with the girl above me who usually sat in her bunk talking loudly on her phone with her bunk shade pulled down. Actually, nobody got along with that girl in the bunk above me. Anastasia loved letting her know it. They would start to argue in German or Russian, and Anastasia always had the last word.

On Thursday night, I received an email from United Airlines that my scheduled Saturday flight was canceled. My mom would call to figure out a refund or a reschedule. I felt powerless and scared. The embassy informed me that although Saturday's humanitarian flight through United had been canceled, they would offer another one through Spirit Airlines on the Monday after, but I had to submit an application of interest and wait to be contacted. I immediately submitted my application. The following Sunday night, I was sitting downstairs with my German friends learning new words when I got a call from a guy at the embassy. Did I still want a seat on the plane for the following day? Yes! He instructed me to be at the U.S. embassy there in Bogotá at 6 a.m. sharp the next morning. I shared my news with the group, who toasted in my favor and wished me luck on my journey back to the states, and then I ran off to shower and pack.

I went to sleep with my suitcases totally packed, dressed to travel early. I was sitting on the couch at dawn the next morning after a sleepless night, listening to the quiet of the hostel, wondering what would be in store for me at the embassy, what going through the airport would feel like in the midst of this chaos, and what would be waiting for me in the states. Thankfully, I had an impulse to check my email and discovered that in the middle of the night I'd received another email saying my flight for that day was canceled. *Canceled*. Four hours after I had hung up the phone with the immigration official calling to confirm my seat, packed my things and bid tearful farewells, the flight had *canceled*. The email stated I could submit another application for the next humanitarian flight that would leave on Wednesday.

At that moment, I decided that I would submit one more application, and if the door didn't open for a flight, I was going to stay.

There must be a reason why I haven't been allowed to leave. Maybe I still have a purpose to fulfill here. Maybe my anxiety is coming from resisting that.

I never got a call back for that flight the following Wednesday, so I was staying!

That same Monday that my flight canceled, most of the people in our hostel caught their flight back to Europe, leaving behind just a small handful of us to share the whole hostel space. There was Lucas from France, who put together our daily workouts on the patio every afternoon. There was Slavko, an actor from Venezuela who had just been a star in the movie *Two Autumns in Paris*, and there was Alex from Zimbabwe who ran his own graphic design business online - he worked on his computer night and day. Two young French guys and a French couple showed up and stayed for a while. Christian, Andres, Kelly, and Marta (and Marta's kids, whenever she brought them) were the employees there who took turns rotating two weeks on and two weeks off.

When the big group left to go back to Europe I was left in my room all alone, which for me was absolute bliss. Even though public transport was completely shut down, shipment companies were still in service. Consuelo, the lady I rented a room from in Medellín, was kind enough to pack all my things in two boxes and ship them to me - right to my doorstep of our hostel. One night after everyone went to bed, I pulled a square table into my room from the lounge outside and made my room a cozy nook with a place to sit and work in the silent privacy of my own, glorious space.

In one of those boxes was my precious laptop, so I was immediately able to start getting in some hours for the online company I had worked for on and off for two years (tutoring English). I unpacked all my things and organized my whole room, making it all mine just the way I needed it to be to feel sacred, safe, and welcoming. It was time to start writing my book. In the afternoon, I taught for two or three hours, and in the morning and night times were all mine to dive into the process of writing. What had initially seemed terrible would turn out to be a time full of so much love and many treasures with new people crossing my path that would turn out to be life-long friends.

I was usually the first one awake, and I would make myself a big, healthy breakfast with a big cup of Colombian coffee. I took it outside to enjoy by myself on the patio, usually with my journal. One day, my morning solitude was cut short when a handsome, bearded guy who I had never seen before appeared in the doorway upstairs and came down to join me. He was looking for the best place in Bogotá to hunker down for a few months and focus on editing his documentary.

This guy was different from any human I had ever met. He was really rough around the edges and didn't really get along with anyone, which I was capable of understanding, and it was the trauma we had both been through that brought us together, I believe. But he said words that forever marked me. After I had also shared some of my story and I told him about my book project, he said, "Don't put anything less than your whole heart into it. Do whatever you have to do to make that possible. Set boundaries, throw your phone away if you have to, and whenever you get blocked in your writing process - 'cause you will - remember why you wanted to do it. Be as real as you can and fuck everyone else. Do you, be you, and never look back, Jenni. This is your work, your life, your signature for the world. Nobody else has lived your story, and nobody can do your path like you. Never be scared to be unapologetically the most authentic version of yourself that you can possibly be. Whoever doesn't like it can fuck off." One day, he mysteriously disappeared just as quickly as he had appeared on the first day he joined me for breakfast. I always wondered where he went or how his documentary work was going.

My time in lockdown, although seemingly hopeless and terrifying in many ways for the whole world, turned out to be something absolutely pivotal for me in a wonderful way. Although it was devastating to have my opportunities for rogue backpacking adventures stripped away, for the first time in my life, I was *still*. I thought that I had already been still when I first started traveling on that one-way ticket nearly three years prior to where I found myself in lockdown. The pace of Colombian life was so different from the pace of life in the United States, but this was a new kind of still, one that made me realize that I had never ever been truly still for an extended period. Especially not sober.

I no longer had the distraction of a rogue exploratory adventure on the *outside* of me and had nothing but time on my hands to begin a rogue exploratory adventure through the depths on the *inside* of me. I had already responded to the deep cry from my soul that had been begging to give birth to this book, when I had begun piecing together handwritten scratches of my story in those hidden nooks of my Medellín hood. I felt this was a huge turning point. The words that Brille gave me in Villa de Leyva reverberated in me every day.

Life in the streets of Bogotá in the midst of a global pandemic was a stark contrast from the cozy nook I made for myself in my room at Masaya. The economic situation in Colombia was a rocky one in the process of recovery after fifty years of political violence before the pandemic hit, but with everything getting shut down because of COVID, it was a life-or-death situation for many in terms of hunger and violence. The weight of hopelessness and desperation in the air outside the hostel was so heavy that it felt hard to breathe.

The lockdown procedures were extremely strict, only allowing one person per household to leave for essential items like food or medicine for one hour on the days that coordinated with the last number of their passport, per government mandate. People broke into homes just to steal food and I heard rumors that in the area, police officers were raiding hostels and holding foreigners hostage for ransom. My expat friends from other countries like Bolivia and Argentina told me that the situation was the same where they were quarantined.

There were police and military officers on every corner stopping every passerby for interrogation, which sometimes made me feel more safe and sometimes more in danger. They asked me the same questions as the officers had asked me in Villa de Leyva when the pandemic first hit. They always asked me what hostel I was staying in, and I always lied. I couldn't trust anyone. Face masks were mandatory everywhere, even just walking down the street with nobody else around. Any foreigner caught breaking the new country-wide mandates would be subject to an outrageous fine or placed in Colombian jail, or both. At the grocery store, there was always a long line of people waiting to go in, spaced six feet apart per stickers on the ground, and upon entry I got sprayed down with disinfectant to the bottoms of my feet and was obligated to use hand sanitizer.

I only ventured outside into that reality once a week. I taught English online a couple of hours a day which gave me the opportunity to connect with adult students from around the world. They shared their perspectives of the pandemic in Japan, Oman, Turkey, Algeria, Brazil, China, Saudi Arabia, Morocco, and Vietnam. The feelings of vulnerability, urgency, fear, and desperation were mutual with every one of my students, but that allowed us to connect more intimately as humans than I had ever experienced while teaching.

Outside of my time teaching, I knew it was time to start putting my soul into my book. I had no idea where to start. I was so scared of revealing myself at such a vulnerable level, but the mysterious bearded man's words resonated in me. They made me think. Why did I want to write this book? What was my why? I had once heard an influencer say, "Whenever you make it to the other side of something really hard, you have the responsibility of sharing your testimony about it with others to help them." That was my *why*. So, I continued writing.

After two months in lockdown at that hostel in Bogotá, I got let go from my online teaching job. Although they never gave me an explanation, I feel that it has everything to do with me sharing the link to my YouTube channel with my students, *haha*. I was forced to make a very difficult decision because I knew that without income I couldn't stay. I decided to let my dad help with a plane ticket for a humanitarian flight back to the states.

I never imagined leaving Colombia like that, but I chose to accept it and be open. I only had a few days to say my goodbyes, close things that needed to be closed, leave behind things that needed left behind, and pack. I didn't feel good about going back and I was so scared that once I got there, I would be stuck somehow. Although I had no idea what would be on the other side of this new veil, just as I hadn't known what was on the other side of so many, I felt ready to push through it and be open to anything waiting for me on the other side.

As I finished packing, I took quiet time to finish reading a memoir on my laptop Kindle. It was called, *A Girl in the Woods: A Memoir*, by Aspen Matis. In her book, she shares an intimate account of being sexually assaulted her first semester of college, dropping her classes, and embarking on a very dangerous hiking adventure on the Pacific Crest Trail from Mexico to Canada. It was no coincidence that at the end of her book, upon being invited as a guest speaker to tell her truth at the university that she had left behind, she said, "The bravest thing I ever did was leave there. The next bravest thing I did was come back, to make myself heard."

Yes, indeed it was, and indeed it would be. The next day, I boarded my flight back to Oklahoma City, and I began the nine months it would take to unravel my story for this book.

I gift to you....my story.

Chapter 4

Soulfire

"She had a peculiar habit of setting fire to anything that didn't feel like freedom."

– Mira Hadlow

The first time soulfire burned inside me, I was 15 years old. It was 2 p.m. on a Monday as I walked into my first Spanish class.

As a little girl, I was enamored by my grandma's travel stories and knew my destiny included seeing all the countries she told me about, including the ones she never got to visit. I put the Spanish channel on the TV and danced around speaking gibberish, and in the hours I spent alone in my room I made up secret languages with my imaginary friends.

That lightly-glowing ember ignited into all-encompassing flames during my first real language class. From that moment on, I would never forget the feeling of my soul's true passion blooming within me.

The walls of my classroom were lined with flags from Spanish-speaking countries around the world, showcasing the color patterns of the flags on bulletin boards which held framed quotes in Spanish. Posters featuring stunning images depicting each unique culture brought traditional native dances and clothing to life in front of me. I'd never seen a native woman making her culture's traditional food from scratch, and I wanted to learn everything about these beautiful women.

I studied the women in the photos with their worn hands and speculated at the immense wisdom they must carry, their stories, how many things they have created from talents passed down from generations of elders, all from the love they have shared, taking care of so many others. While my grandma told me her travel stories, I remembered the times she would make her food from scratch, too.

"Let me show you how to make homemade noodles," she would beckon. "One day you'll have a husband and a family to make noodles for, and you will need to know how to cook, clean, and sew."

"Naw, I will marry someone who does all those things for me," was my response.

She always laughed like it was the funniest thing she ever heard.

I was in a small, private school at the time I walked into that language classroom. My parents transferred me there when I'd had a "mysterious" psychotic breakdown during my 8th grade year, one that led to my first suicide attempt, which landed me in a mental hospital before being sent to live with my grandparents in another state for the remainder of the school year. When I came back from there, they announced that they had enrolled me in a private Christian school so that I could be more closely monitored and have a change of scenery.

I found religion while attending school there, which helped me in that time of my life. It was a place I could hide; it provided me with a shield to protect myself from the wars waging around me, and it helped me focus my mind on something other than the pain I carried inside.

That shield helped protect me when my dad left right after I started the new school. He'd been gone on "business" for a few days but hadn't been in contact with anyone. My mom was worried sick something had happened to him, but suddenly one day his silver impala showed up in the driveway. He told my brother and me his news over ice cream at Sonic: he didn't love our mom anymore and didn't want a family anymore, so he and mom had decided the best thing for everyone was for him to move to Lawton to be closer to a job assignment for a while.

Just like that, he dropped us off back home and drove away with his suitcases in the back seat. I found out, however, when I answered the phone that was ringing off the hook, that my mom was not part of this decision. There had been no conversation about it. In fact, it was me who told my mom that Dad had ghosted us.

When my father came back for my brother, religion shielded me from the screaming match on the front lawn. My brother watched from the backseat of the car while I stood alone on the front doorstep, and our eyes remained locked until my dad's Impala turned the corner.

My mom worked a low-paying, part-time job at the church, and it wasn't long before our utilities got cut off. My mom did the best she could with the paycheck she had, and we learned how to stretch cheap meals as far as possible.

A couple at our church happened to be looking for part-time employees to staff their BBQ truck, so it was the perfect time for me to snag my first after-school job. It was just a few months before my 16th birthday. Every day after school, I raced home, changed clothes, raced back to work, and closed down the restaurant by 9 before I headed home to start my homework.

As anyone who's been involved in the American education system knows, it's during this time in an adolescent's life when the school expects students to begin choosing a career path. For me, those career decisions were looming. What did I want to do with my life? What did I want to study? I never felt like I was smart. My brother was the smart kid, always in advanced math and science classes, always recognized for his grades. I was never interested in school until I found Spanish, but I didn't want to teach it. I wanted to learn languages while I traveled, but there was no career path with that included.

How was I supposed to know what I wanted to do if I'd never been out in the world? Why did I have to sit behind a desk as a slave to a system I didn't feel passionate about to chase a paycheck, hoping one day I could buy myself the freedom to do what I really wanted? If we as humans were meant to stay in one place forever, wouldn't we have roots instead of feet?

My grandma announced she'd take my brother (who was a grade below me) and I on a trip to celebrate our graduation and encouraged us to agree on a place we could both be happy. I only wanted to be as immersed as possible in Spanish, all day every day, with a new culture I could explore, and my brother wanted to lie on a beach. My grandma decided that spending a week on the island of Cozumel, Mexico was what everyone needed.

That trip changed the course of my life, and I knew it would the moment we stepped out of that airport and arrived at our hotel. The island people were beautiful; I was enchanted. I hadn't yet even experienced speaking with anyone in their native language! While we were there I made friends with Flor, who sold pottery from a cart by the hotel pool, sitting on her stool for hours every day in the sun. We chatted for hours in Spanish, and she would take me with her to places in her neighborhood so that I could see what life was like for the locals away from the world of tourism.

By the end of the week, Flor and I were friends, and she asked me for my email address, which helped her introduce me to her son who was my age. Of course, I was ecstatic about the opportunity to make a real friend from the island but also to have a native Spanish speaker with whom to practice my language skills once I got back to the states.

I tried to reason with my grandma about why I should stay. Her answer was NO. My rebuttal went something like, "How could anyone sacrifice their whole life doing something that didn't feel this good and put off this feeling for decades? Why should I have to wait to experience these dreams until my 65th birthday? What if I wasn't guaranteed life until that age? What if I only had a year or two left to live my life? Why did I have to suffer something I didn't like in order to feel worthy of doing something I *did* like? Why couldn't I live my happiest life while my body was young and my soul vibrant? Why did I have to do things the way other people did them?" Surprisingly, she remained unmoved.

After boarding our plane, my stomach sunk further and further into a hole as we traveled back home, back to the mundane routine of sitting in classrooms and being pressured about the life decisions I needed to make for my future. Or, perhaps, I needed to choose which color of jail cell I wanted to walk into and stay for the next 40 years.

The way I felt that week I was on the island: that is what I wanted to do with my life forever.

However, I thought maybe I should give the 'approved' path - the one my parents, teachers, and friends all talked about - a shot, so when I graduated high school, I enrolled in basic college classes and worked two jobs. I worked every position possible and was happy to pick up as many shifts as I could whenever they became available. I knew paying for college would be my responsibility since I wouldn't have financial aid, so I worked as many shifts as I could to save for my tuition and books.

I made it through one fall semester with impeccable grades and a more positive experience than I expected as a college student. But it felt like I was in prison. One day, right after having taken finals for that first semester, I was browsing the classes that had opened for spring enrollment, when I heard this cry in me so strongly. *I don't want to do that.*

I listened. *What DO you want?* I asked myself.

I wanted to know what life would be like to live in Cozumel for a while. I wanted to live there and work just as the local people did, to have friendships, a nightlife, dance to Latino music, and eat authentic Mexican food. I wanted to live simply, and more than anything, I wanted to listen to and speak Spanish all day every day. Lalo, Flor's son from Cozumel, and I had kept in touch ever since I had left months before. We had gotten to know each other fairly well through chatting online several times a week.

I decided I would not enroll in spring classes. I would work like crazy to save money to go live on the island, and I wouldn't tell anyone except for Lalo my secret plan. I continued to pick up shifts at the restaurant and also got a job at the local Albertsons grocery store, where I rotated between working the customer service counter and stocking shelves. I was tired a lot from working so many hours, but then I would connect to the soulfire that burned in me whenever I thought about stepping into my true passion in just a few short months. I was then immediately energized.

My first one-way ticket across borders alone was when I was 19 when I stepped out of the airport into the humid island air of Cozumel. I was going back through a door I'd left open, going back to harvest seeds I'd planted before. I stayed with Lalo and his family on the outskirts of town, sharing a one-room house made from cinder blocks with five other people. At night we hung hammocks at angles across the room to accommodate space for everyone, and in the morning we put the hammocks away.

However, Lalo and I would often go lay on the rooftop under the starry island sky until the hot sun touched our faces to wake us the next morning. The rooftop was also where we hung wet laundry, and I can still breathe in the smell of that Mexican laundry soap that always smelled like home to me.

I was fearless and fierce, a fair match for the wind that blew off the ocean and tasseled my long, braided hair behind me when I rode on the back of a speeding motorcycle, flying down a highway which ran along the coast. I knew I'd found a happiness to claim as my own for the rest of my life. This happiness fit my true self like a tailored glove fits on the hand it's made for.

I looked everywhere for a job there, but much to my dismay I discovered I couldn't get a job without a work visa, which I hadn't considered before leaving the states. When I realized I wouldn't be able to bring in money, I decided it was time to live my life to the max and explore as much as possible with Lalo before I had to leave.

Lalo and I went as hard as possible, adventuring while we could. He and his family took me to private beaches only the locals knew, where we caught fresh fish and grilled it over a campfire on the beach. He had a friend with a speedboat take us to another island close by where we explored ancient ruins. Lalo took me to a neighborhood party where we all danced to live music all night. We took the ferry for a 45-minute ride across to the mainland, where we explored more ruins and hidden places. We shot pool in every bar where locals play on the island.

Lalo and I got our first tattoos together, which were matching palm trees with sunsets around them in a small circle design in the middle of our right thighs. His mom cooked us homemade dinners from scratch several times while I stayed with them. My hair was so long, it hung to my waist, and Lalo talked me into getting cornrows. So, my head was full of braids and still hung beautifully, nearly to my waist. I would put on a bandana that matched whichever outfit I picked out each day, and we rode motorcycles all over that island with my braids just a-blowin' in that wind, wind I will never, ever forget the smell of. I belonged to it, and I was an heiress of its freedom.

Until, one day, I had only enough money left for a ticket home. Lalo and I gave each other a tearful goodbye as I disappeared into the airport security room. I was in for a surprise when the immigration officers began requesting a little piece of paper that I had been given when I entered the country. I realized then I had thrown that paper away the day before while packing, not knowing I would need it. The men behind the glass window did not find nearly as much humor as I did in my predicament, and they pulled me into a room with more officers.

Why was I in Mexico alone? Where was I staying? How could I prove my date of entry? How was my Spanish so good? They said they would not let me get on any flight without showing them proof of when I entered the country.

"That's perfect for me, because I don't want to leave anyway," I told them.

I never got nervous or scared. I thought the whole thing was hilarious, and I was secretly hoping they wouldn't let me get on my flight to go back home. I didn't want to go back there anyway.

No such luck. I boarded my flight, and I cried the whole way back home. The thought of plugging myself into the system there and being a hamster on a wheel made me wish that the airplane would take a nosedive into the ocean right then and there. I wanted more than that for my life.

While I bawled, I promised myself I would find a way to keep living this dream. I would do everything it took to find this place of happiness. I promised myself I would find something that made my light shine like it shone when I was there traveling. I wouldn't let anyone or anything dim it. I promised myself I would be fearless and take risks and work as hard as I had to make my dream a reality.

I got back in perfect timing because my mom was transitioning from her one-bedroom to a two-bedroom apartment. I returned full-time to my job at Albertsons, and I also enrolled in full-time classes again.

One day after work, I had this wild hair to go to the animal shelter to get an estimate on how much it would cost to adopt a kitty. I couldn't afford everything right then but wanted an estimate so that I could set aside for it from my next few paychecks.

"Excuse me, miss, are you here to adopt a cat?" Came a voice from behind me in the parking lot as I approached the shelter door.

I turned around to see the young couple who had stopped me. I explained I was just there to get a price on adoption fees and that I needed to save some paychecks before I could invest in everything a new pet required.

They said they'd found a grey Russian Blue kitten on their farm. Its mother was missing, and their son was allergic to cats. They were there to drop her off at the shelter but asked if I would be interested in taking her. They said they would take me to the store to buy everything she would need. They gave me their phone number because they were willing to pay for her to get spayed and vaccinated later. I had to say yes; it was fate. They bought all her supplies and even left me with a $20 bill to get her food and litter over the next two weeks. She was so tiny she was barely eating real food.

It was love at first sight for us. Peas and carrots we were from that moment on. At night, she curled up on my shoulder and fell asleep nursing on my earlobe, until one day, I came home with a stuffed lamb I had found on an Easter display while stocking shelves. Something about it reminded me of her, so I brought it home. She quit nursing on my ear and forever after nursed on her lamby. I named her Gracie Ann.

Those people had to be angels, crossing my path with this baby. Why had they insisted that I take her when they could have dropped her at the shelter and the shelter would cover her expenses? I didn't understand then that it was divine intervention.

Right before I'd left for Cozumel, I was working the customer service desk when I'd met a handsome Latino man who came in to send a money order. He asked me out before I left, and I told him that if I made it back to the states that I would. He saw me stocking shelves one day and held me to my promise. We went out a few times but broke things off after a few dates.

Other than our few dates, I went out dancing to Latino discotecas with my Mexican friends and did volunteer interpreting and translating. Most of all, I daydreamed about the soulfire I experienced during my time in Cozumel.

It was me and Gracie doing homework, housework, and singing kitty karaoke. We always had a great time, and she thought everything I did was great. I had no idea just how much she would be my saving grace for the chambers of terrors that would open for me less than a year after experiencing my island paradise.

Chapter 5

When the birds sing at dawn

"I'm gonna fucking kill you," he growled through his grinding teeth, his fingers in a death grip around the steering wheel.

After I'd tossed and turned all night, I left my friend's apartment at 5:30 a.m. to go shopping for a few basic things. Maybe killing an hour at the store would help me get my mind off the bad news from the week before which had broken my heart.

In that moment, I had no idea that an ex-boyfriend had stalked me there.

I've never been the kind of person to freak out in the face of emergency. A still, calm voice inside told me to start taking mental photographs of my surroundings, trees, street signs, houses nestled off in the distance, anything that could help me bring the cops back to this place, given I survived whatever was about to happen.

His eyes were dark and angry, darting from right to left looking for entrances on each side of the road. He was driving so fast, getting further from town with each passing second, heading toward big empty lots of fields and foliage. Unexpectedly, he whipped a left turn into an entrance of country lots for sale. Tears began falling; they were silent on my cheeks.

I felt pebbles under my toes on the truck's floorboard. Hadn't I left the house in flip flops to go to the store? At some point when he abducted me and stuffed me into his truck, they must have fallen off. If I hadn't gone to the store, or if I hadn't worn flip flops, would this still have happened? If I had shoes, could I have kicked him or ran away? Of course, this was somehow my fault.

Would these moments be my last? Would it be a slow death? Would it be fast and painless? I am only 20 years old and haven't lived my dream yet!

He took another left turn so hard that the truck only had two tires on the ground. I couldn't stop thinking of things I'd said and done, and now I wouldn't be able to redo any of it.

Gracie! She wouldn't understand why I was missing. *Jesus, who would take Gracie?*

With another hard, left turn, he threw the truck slightly up on two side tires again, but this time the tires found grass. We were off the road, and now he revved the engine as we flew through a field. He plowed the foliage and drove full speed right through a barbed wire fence. I heard the metal spikes of the wires make awful screeching noises as the fence dug into the brand new Ford truck. I haven't heard a sound like it since then.

This truck had been his whole world, his pride and joy. He saved for it for years and dutifully washed it at least twice a week. If this is what he was willing to do with his precious truck, what was he about to do to me?

The glass cracked where the fence had come to rest, and it started to spider web across the whole windshield. He killed the engine and demanded I get out.

I did not. I sat there shaking with my eyes closed. In my head flashed the clip from Forrest Gump when Jenny was with Forrest praying in the field.

Please God, make me a bird, so I can fly far, far away.

The time it took him to walk around the truck and get to my door seemed like an eternity. With no idea what was coming, I only knew I was barefoot, that he was insanely strong, and that I was out in the country, away from any sign of life.

Fighting him would mean losing. If I fought back, he would get even angrier and do something worse than what he currently had planned. My truck door opened, and he leaned across to pull me out. I did the only thing I could think of and bit him so hard on the shoulder that I felt his skin break. He didn't even wince. It was like he could feel nothing.

He used a handful of my hair to yank me from the truck and then pulled me around to the back. He opened the tailgate and dropped his shorts to the ground.

"Suck my cock," he instructed.

His cock was at half-mast. Jesus! How could anyone be excited in a moment like this? He was turned on! I closed my eyes and pretended I didn't hear him, although I knew the backlash would come.

"I said, 'suck my cock.'"

He shoved my head down onto his cock. In my mind, I used a trick I learned in my childhood whenever I needed to escape a painful reality and let my mind transcend to another place.

He took a handful of my hair again and stroked himself several times, then pulled me up so I could catch a quick breath. He directed me into the truck bed. I was scared and knew I couldn't get away barefoot. He was going to get his way regardless. I lay down with my ass on the edge of the truck bed, as he used both hands to rip away my shorts and panties.

Then he raped me.

I could feel his breath all over my face; it smelled like soured alcohol. Apparently, he'd been drinking all night.

Where had he been? What had triggered him to do this? Who was he with? Had he done drugs? He had never done drugs or even spoken of drugs during the months of our relationship. Everything about him now indicated that he was a stranger.

"Look at me," he said.

Silent tears streamed down my face. As hard as I tried to access that far-away place, I couldn't. I then realized seeing me cry was pleasing him.

Was he going to kill me after the rape? Did he have a gun or a knife? Would it be a bloody death?

He got mad that I had dried my tears and stopped suddenly.

"You're not even worth the fucking effort."

And just like that, it was over with.

Was he going to leave me here? Was he going to kill me now?

I scooted down out of the bed of the truck as I looked for my shorts. I felt the wet grass and stones beneath my feet as I found them a few feet away. I still had no idea where I had lost my flip flops.

He was fumbling around on the ground with his shorts caught on his foot. His impairment was obvious, and suddenly I had a vision of me killing him. Could I get in the truck and run him over?

Oh my god, this was it. I would win. It was over. I was as terrified as I was torn, bleeding, bruised, and barefoot, scratched and shaking like a leaf, but the keys were on the floorboard. I pulled myself inside the truck and locked the doors. I bent over to get the keys.

With trembling hands, I tried to find the key that fit in the ignition, but there were five keys on the ring that all looked similar to me.

I found the one, and as soon as I slid it into the ignition, the truck roared to life. He popped into view at the driver's side window wearing a menacing grin. As he reached inside the window to unlock the door, I realized I had remembered to lock the doors but not roll up the windows. He opened the door and forced me to scoot over.

I had this awful sinking feeling in my stomach, like acid eating me alive. How could I be so stupid? I had made everything worse. Now he was really pissed.

I wanted to run, but I had no shoes. I had to be strategic about how I handled every little detail. My eyes were scanning the nooks and crannies of his truck. Maybe he had a utility knife tucked in a pocket somewhere. I imagined what it would feel like to stick it in the side of his neck. All I needed was a blade a little shorter than an inch to puncture his jugular, and I could kill him. I never imagined I would be capable of murder. I learned in that moment that we never know what we are capable of until the moment we are presented with a rare set of circumstances. He pulled out in the truck and pulled back onto the main road. We were sliding around on gravel again.

"Why did you do this to me?" I asked, staring at him.

He only stared ahead, through the broken windshield, grinding his jaw back and forth.

He finally said, "Because I hate you, and I want you to fucking hate me forever."

I couldn't bear any more, and I didn't care if I made him mad enough to kill me. If he killed me, I wouldn't have to live through the aftermath he had just created.

We roared down a stretch of Garth Brooks Boulevard, heading back toward Yukon when I finally saw headlights on the road. If I threw myself out of the truck, I knew I could survive the impact of the road. It would pale in comparison to the damage that was now inside of me.

I started to open my passenger door, but he noticed and immediately grabbed my shirt and bra and twisted them around his hand. I tested how secure his grip on me was as I tried to thrust myself feet first out the door. I couldn't escape his death grip. Maybe I could get somebody's attention.

"Stop doing that."

I used my left hand to jerk his steering wheel, making him swerve into the other lane where there was a car coming toward us at just the right moment. Oscar overcorrected the wheel, nearly losing control of the truck. The driver laid on his horn and swerved around us, but Oscar knew he had been seen, and the game was over.

We were back to town at this point, approaching the main traffic light in front of the Walmart. He took a sudden left turn into the parking lot, and he stopped about 100 feet from my car.

"Nobody will ever believe you. I hope you hurt for the rest of your life." He said as he let go of my shirt.

I sat there for a moment, dazed and dizzy. He peeled out in his truck as I slid from the truck seat. My legs were rubber. Worms slithered inside from my bones, and they devoured me from the inside out.

I was alive.

I was alive. Why did he let me live? I didn't want to be alive. I didn't want to face my new reality.

How was my car so far away? Could I carry myself there? I saw a lady sitting in her car, simply eating her Braum's breakfast. The smell of grease from her hashbrowns made me even more sick to my stomach. When she looked at me, she took a drink of orange juice to wash down her hashbrowns, and she smiled at me. She glanced down and noticed my bare feet, which caused her to scan me from head to toe. She was trying to figure me out. I didn't want her to look at me. I didn't want anyone to see me ever again.

One barefoot step after another brought me to my car, which was exactly how I had left it. The door was still standing wide open, and my keys were laying on the ground by my tire. My groceries were in the passenger seat. The bag was untouched right where I left it, the shampoo, lip balm, and eggs perfectly intact.

I, however, was not perfectly intact. I was shattered. A monster truck had driven through my life and demolished every part of me as well as the surrounding areas.

How could a dozen eggs survive an F5 tornado?

If I didn't call the cops right in that moment, I never would. If I didn't make that call, he would get away with what he did, maybe come back to finish what he started, and most likely would do it to someone else. I had to make contact immediately while his DNA was still on me.

Who do you call after you get raped? I think most girls would call their mothers, but I didn't have mine, which is what had left me tossing and turning on a friend's couch before heading to the store just a couple hours before.

That left my dad. I hated that he was my only option. I loathed being so vulnerable with someone while I was in the midst of tragedy, especially someone who had already left innumerable and deep wounds over the years. While I knew I needed to be somewhere I felt safe, I had no such place. I didn't have anyone else to call, and maybe he could help make decisions.

I felt completely alone in the world. *Just one small thing at a time. One breath at a time. Find your cell phone.*

Where was my cell? I saw it sitting in my cupholder right where I left it. I opened it and hit "talk" to see my call record, then the green button to dial my dad's number.

He answered in a perplexed tone, saying "Hello," knowing it was very odd to receive a call from me at 7:30 AM on a Saturday. "Hello?" He said again.

I couldn't speak. What could I say? How could I say those words?

Just give facts. Push enough wind through your throat to make noises that form the words, one word at a time.

"Jen, are you okay?"

I gulped and pushed air through the sandpaper in my throat.

In a shaky voice I said, "I was just raped."

"What? By who? Where are you?"

"Oscar. In the Yukon Walmart parking lot."

"Have you called the cops?"

"No."

"I'm on my way."

My dad and the police showed up. My dad paced back and forth as the police asked me dozens of questions. They recorded my whole story.

The officers asked me if I wanted to press charges and said that if there was enough evidence for a trial, that would mean I would testify against him in court. Was I willing to do that? Knowing it was a terrifying concept, I said yes.

I knew where to find Oscar. He lived with a coworker just a couple miles away. I gave the cops the address. One of the officers and my dad went to interrogate Oscar, and the other police officer took me to Midwest Regional Hospital to gather evidence, including a rape kit.

There were two nurses in my hospital exam room, one to give me the exam, and the other mostly to be with me. She held my hand and asked me questions, although there was never sincere empathy from either of them. She held my hand as a part of her job description, but not because her soul connected with mine. I lay on the exam table like a lamb on a slaughter block.

The nurse told me to take a deep breath, and suddenly I felt a sharp pressure go up through my cervix into my pelvis from whatever the nurse was doing. I wondered what the fuck he had done to me to make it hurt so bad.

"Sweetie, take a deep breath. I have to do this for evidence. I promise I am almost done."

How was I even here?

I couldn't breathe. For Christ's sake, I left my friend's apartment for lip balm and eggs after a sleepless night, and now I was being scraped for evidence to press charges against my rapist.

There was no semen for evidence, because he had never ejaculated, but there were other scrapes, bruises, and cuts to document. They finished and let me dress while everyone waited outside.

My dad and police officers were back, but the officer who had delivered me to the hospital was gone, replaced by a female cop. I remember her and her blonde hair pulled back like it was yesterday.

She took me to another room where I gave my story again to both her and the other officer. Her empathy impacted me because she connected with me in a more intimate way than anyone else had. She felt me. Despite her hardened exterior, I could feel that my story was personal to her.

For that ten minutes I didn't feel totally alone. This was the third time I had given my story, and when I finished, they all compared stories to ensure all the details meshed.

The police officer who had gone with my dad to find Oscar told me Oscar answered the poundings at the door and that he denied having seen me that day. The officer said he would submit the report and be in touch with the

DA if I wanted to testify against him. Was I still willing to press charges?

Yes. My answer was yes. And just like that, we were done. It was time to go "home," which at that time was a couch at a friend's house.

I never did find my flip flops.

Chapter 6

Broken Heart, A Fine Art

Six days before my kidnapping and rape, my whole world had already been blown to smithereens when I found out that my mom and the guy I had been dating were having an affair behind my back. He had moved into my room temporarily since his lease was up and we were waiting on our apartment to be ready in Edmond, close to UCO so that we could live together and I could walk to campus for classes.

After I found out, I was frantic to get out of the apartment before she got home. I didn't ever want to see her again. I packed an overnight bag with random clothes, mostly work uniforms. My mind and heart were racing. Did I have to keep going to work? How was I supposed to function to do anything? I wasn't sure where to go. All I knew is that I had to disappear.

My best friend Lisa was studying out of state at the time, and I hadn't heard from her in months. I ran through a list of options where I could go until my apartment was ready, and suddenly my friend Nancy's name popped into my head. She lived close with her kids. I knew she had a couch and would be happy to let me crash on it for a few days. I texted her and immediately had a place to go.

God, I hoped my apartment would be ready soon. I had no idea what to tell Nancy.

Before I left, I bent down to scoop up my cat – my fur baby – Gracie Ann. I promised her I would be back for her soon.

When I arrived at Nancy's, she greeted me with open arms. She knew I was upset, but I did not know how to talk to her or anyone about the betrayal that had just occurred. Was I so unlovable and unfuckable that my boyfriend resorted to sleeping with my mother? It was a humiliating secret I would keep all to myself for a long time.

Nancy let me stay silent about my problems and let me know I had called just in the nick of time. The next day she and her kids were headed to Dallas for a week of summer vacation. I would have the house to myself and that's exactly what I needed; a place to shed my tears alone.

After Nancy left, I realized I had left behind a few essential items at my mom's. So, after a sequence of sleepless, tear-filled nights, just six days after being betrayed by the person who had taught me about integrity and purity, I found myself at Walmart, then kidnapped and raped.

Although Oscar had denied seeing me, after my rape exam the police returned to his house and questioned him again. They found barbed wire in the wheel well of his truck and a bite mark on his left shoulder. Additionally, they collected the surveillance videos from the Walmart parking lot, which showed my abduction. They had collected enough evidence to take him into custody and hold him in jail until we went to trial.

***

My story had made the front-page news in the Yukon paper, and I was not yet out of Yukon. I was putting gas in my Ford Focus on the following Monday - two days after the rape - when I went in the store to pay for my gas and saw it. There, right on the counter next to a display of impulse buys, was a stack of papers and Oscar's face staring right at me. His mug shot, his furrowed brow, and eyes dark and angry looking into the camera, while he was dressed in an orange jumpsuit.

I felt my heartbeat start in my wounded crotch, although I wasn't sure if it was from the actual rape or the exam that was done afterward. I felt cold and lifeless on the inside, reinforcing what I had realized when I got home that Saturday afternoon: something had changed inside of me. Something had died.

"Look mom and dad, I made the paper!" I thought. They would be so proud. Grabbing several copies of the paper and a pack of gum, I slid my purchases across the counter to the cashier.

"Quite a story, huh?" Said the young chick behind the counter, smacking on her gum. "In Yukon? The world has gone crazy. That kind of stuff only happens in big cities. At least we know this monster is behind bars. Poor girl."

I didn't respond. I didn't even look up or acknowledge that she was there. I wanted to tell her to shut up and stop smacking her gum. What the fuck did she know about what happened in Yukon? She couldn't even talk without smacking her stupid gum.

I imagined how many thousands of papers had been printed and were on display in every store and gas station in Yukon. Luckily, my name wasn't in the paper – just his. There was no doubt in my mind that word would leak out about who the victim was, and when it did, my life there would be over.

I had to get out of Yukon.

***

Four days later, I *finally* heard from the apartment manager in Edmond. I went back to my mom's apartment when nobody was home and gathered my personal things.

I didn't have much, and the most valuable item was my baby kitty Gracie.

I'd only brought a few changes of clothes, a couple pairs of shoes, and a little basket of earrings and makeup when I left my mom's. I had always been a simple girl, and I remember realizing it during my trip to Cozumel where I had been content and fulfilled while living out of one simple suitcase.

The apartment manager Randy received me kindly before taking us upstairs to my new place. He studied the small heap of belongings I pulled out of my car.

"Do you need help carrying anything up?" He was petting Gracie until she looked back with dark eyes. He was enough of a cat lover to know that meant, "Touch me again and you get shanked."

"This is all I have."

"What about a bed? A Mattress? Pillows, furniture?" I had taken a big fuzzy blanket from my mom's couch when I went back for Gracie. I just shrugged my shoulders.

He was silent for a moment, studying me. I was silent in return.

"I have an apartment I use for storage where I keep things left behind by tenants. I can see if there are things there that you need. The mattress there isn't new, but I only keep the things that are in great condition, so it's clean. I have an extra pillow if you need one."

I agreed that I would let him look, mostly because I didn't have any other option. That night he came up with a mattress and pillow where Gracie and I would sleep on the floor.

"This will get you fixed up tonight, kiddo, at least to sleep. In the next few days, we will see what else we can find."

Finally, I had met someone kind. We would grow to be great friends in time. In fact, he was the only person I had in my life at all during that period, and I would later understand that he was divinely placed onto my path to oversee me during this awful time in my life.

***

The next day, the DA called. The trial was set. I was going to see him–my rapist. I would once again tell my story, only this time it would be in front of a full courtroom and jury of strangers.

My dad called twice the week before the trial, sharing with me that my mother wanted to support me and that in times like these girls need their mothers. I told him to tell her no. She wasn't welcome at my trial, wasn't welcome to know where I lived, or even be anywhere near my life.

The day of my trial, I wore a pink sweater and black flats. I took the stand, and Oscar was ushered into the courtroom in handcuffs, wearing the orange jumpsuit I'd seen on the front page of the Yukon paper. He sat down with his attorney and looked straight at me with a smug, shit-eating grin on his face. He had said I wouldn't have the courage to file a report, but I did, and here we were facing each other before a jury. He said nobody would believe me if I spoke, and now we would find out if that was true.

I had to speak. I had to tell my story in front of all those people. My dad was there with the youth pastor from my high school years, the jury was listening and ready, and the rest of the people in the seats were all strangers staring back at me. It was time to do what I came here to do. I always wondered who the strangers were and why they came to my trial. I never found out.

The District Attorney questioned me first, and I gave my testimony. It was then that Oscar's attorney cross-examined me.

"Did you and the defendant once date?" Yes.

"Did you ever have sexual relations during the course of that relationship?" Yes.

"Then how is this occurrence a rape?" How could I prove it was against my will?

But his last question was the worst.

"Ms. Reavis, is it true that you were raped by a man from your church in the past year?"

My heart dropped and the room turned upside down. I felt my chest start to close and the walls of the courtroom began closing in on me. Yes, it was true, the previous rape had happened.

Oscar was the only one I had ever told, one night after too much wine while we were dating. Then, I put the conversation and the trauma both in a box and hid it really deeply within myself. I never went back to that church. Little did I know that when I went to trial to face my kidnapping rapist ex-boyfriend, I didn't have to talk about just one rape in front of a courtroom of strangers that day. I had to talk about two.

Oscar was laughing in front of me. The only thing I could muster to answer the attorney's question about why I hadn't reported the previous attack was a quiet, "I dunno" while I stared at my hands, folded in my lap. I found myself wishing the judge would hang me so that I wouldn't be humiliated any more.

"No more questions, Your Honor." Courtroom adjourned.

All I wanted was to lie on the used mattress on the floor of my musty apartment and listen to Gracie purr in my ear. The softness of her fur always fixed everything.

***

The two jobs that I had when I moved to Edmond were only summer jobs, and they ended when I moved into my apartment. This was the first time I was completely on my own, and on top of all the trauma I had just endured, I was also facing tremendous financial pressure to figure out how to pay for my apartment and the bills that came with it.

Since Randy was the only one working for the apartment complex, he asked his boss about hiring me to help him clean and fix up the complex, which had been in foreclosure, and there was a lot of work to do to get the units rented out. Luckily, his boss said yes, and we began our new adventure.

To this day, working with Randy at that apartment complex was one of my favorite jobs. I found a fullness and joy that came with working for myself. Even though I still technically worked for a guy in California who owned the property, I was in control of my own work schedule.

Randy and I had so much fun together, and I soon learned that I loved to get dirty, do heavy work, and use my hands every day. Randy was a genius when it came to, well, everything related to fixing. He taught me how to lay tile, how to change out the plates for light switches and outlets, how to install plumbing and flooring. He would take on the main role of the job and teach me what he knew while I assisted him. He taught me how to paint and clean professionally to a military standard. He had learned that when he spent six years in the U.S. Army.

One time, I organized a potluck for all the tenants where everyone brought a traditional dish from their native country so that we could all experience something from each culture. Most of the tenants at that apartment complex were international students from Kenya, Ghana, Iran, Saudi Arabia, Japan, Turkey, China, Morocco, and Kuwait.

Together, Randy and I built a tightly knit community there. It was safe for both Gracie and me. I always left the doors open to my apartment and to whatever apartment I was working in so that Gracie could wander back and forth. She was a part of everything that I did, even while I cleaned and painted. She would often just hang out in the apartment I was working in, sprawled out on the floor to nap or snooping in the new nooks and crannies.

Sometimes, others in our apartment complex kept treats just for her and would have her come hang out inside if she asked to go in their spaces. She was the apartment complex mascot.

After a long day of work, I would get back up to my apartment to make Gracie and me dinner. While the job didn't pay very much, and Gracie and I were hungry often, Gracie always got fed before I did, and we were together no matter what. We ate together, and she loved everything I cooked. Every day, I promised her I would work hard to offer her the life she deserved. "One day I will build you a kitty castle," I promised her.

For the time being, I felt like I would be okay stuffing all my broken pieces down deep inside as long as I could just work all day, every day. I truly loved working with Randy, and it was rare that we weren't having fun. When tenants moved out, they often left useful things behind. Within just a couple of months, my apartment was beautifully furnished with a full kitchen, a dining table with a bench, a soft, imitation-leather couch, a TV, a stand with shelves for my books, and lamps. I had an assortment of different plates, coffee cups, and silverware, but I liked it that way.

One night, Randy came over for dinner and saw THE newspaper laying on the kitchen table.

"Jesus Christ, what the fuck is wrong with people?" He said in disbelief after skimming over the article. "This crazy motherfucker just ruined the life of an innocent person."

"Yeah, that girl was me," I confessed. He choked on his sandwich.

"You are the victim from this article?"

I told him the horror story of testifying in front of all those strangers.

Randy promised that I would be safe no matter what the verdict from the jury was.

I hoped that was true.

Chapter 7

Sex, Drugs, and Fuck your rock-n-roll

"I don't think we have a strong case, Jenni," the district attorney confessed to me. "The surveillance video was too far away to really see it in enough detail to confirm that you were kidnapped. The forcible sodomy was your word against his, and since he didn't ejaculate inside of you, there isn't enough DNA from the rape kit to have a strong case. I just want to let you know that it is very possible that he will walk."

I was at Randy's, petting his seven cats when I answered the call. Now Oscar would kill me for sure. How was this possible? Tears flooded down my face. Randy noticed and turned off the TV.

"What about the skin under my fingernails? What about my cervix being fucked up, and the scratches and bruises all over me, and the wire in his tires?"

I heard the D.A.'s sigh over the phone. "Look, as a father myself, I can tell you that I am outraged. I am just telling you what I know. If he walks, you have the VPO filed against him. Let's still hope for the best."

Oh, yeah: the Victim's Protective Order. Sure, like that would protect me. I hung up the phone and told Randy what I'd learned. While I knew he would help me feel safe in every way that he could, he couldn't protect me from my nightmares. Nobody knew the fear flaring inside from just walking around a corner. A VPO wouldn't save me from the possibilities that ran through my head each time I closed my eyes, and it wouldn't protect me from waking up every day with the rage and pain I carried from both my mother and my rapist. I hated being inside me. Every time I slowed down, I could feel the acid eating its way through my body and coursing through my veins. The very next day, the D.A. called me again. I obviously expected to hear that Oscar had been released. The universe gave me a very surprising green light instead.

The day before, right after our phone call, Oscar had called his lawyer requesting a meeting. He broke down and bawled in front of his attorney, said he'd had an attack of conscience, and that he was guilty. He confessed to his crimes. They gave him 15 years with the possibility of getting out after 10 with parole. He was charged with kidnapping, forcible sodomy, and first-degree rape. He would be away in prison for at least 10 years.

"You are very lucky," the D.A. told me. "Had Oscar known it wasn't a strong case, he wouldn't have pleaded guilty. God gave you a miracle, young lady."

Yeah, thank God for His wondrous fucking miracles.

***

Right after the conviction, I went to a campus psychologist since as a UCO student, I got two sessions for free. I couldn't afford to pay anyone else, and I definitely did not have the fight in me to delve into the process of finding one. Doing seemingly simple tasks was impossible in my state of existing.

I was only in this campus psychologist's office for about 10 minutes, gazing silently at all the books lining her office wall-to-wall. She wore a beige suit and beige high heels with old school pantyhose.

"Have you ever survived a rape or any kind of sexual trauma?" I asked her.

"No," she responded reluctantly, caught off guard by the direct question. "But I do have a Ph.D. in psychology with a specialization in helping women who have been through sexual trauma."

She could kick rocks out yonder with her fancy books and fan her face with her doctorate diploma for all I cared. Someone with only a degree could not help me, and I knew I would never trust her. I could only imagine being able to connect with someone who had come out on the other side. I stuffed everything down deep, hoping maybe one day I'd meet someone who could help me. I got up and walked out without saying another word and never looked back. I wouldn't seek help again until my self-destruction led me to a hellish rock bottom later. Even though I had enrolled in a couple of advanced Spanish classes for that semester, there was no way, psychologically, that I could handle going to classes. I didn't even have the mental fortitude to process where to go in order to withdraw from them. So I didn't, and that was the first semester that I flunked–a far cry from my usual 4.0 GPA.

***

My dad came by a couple of times to take me to the store to buy groceries. I wasn't really sure what to talk about with him. I wasn't emotionally safe enough with him to tell him the truth about my condition, not when I was growing up and not at this awful time, although I appreciated that he took me for groceries. My gratitude was cut short when he hit me with his long list of questions about why I failed my classes, reminded me that his paying my car insurance was contingent upon my being enrolled in a degree program, and lectured me about how I needed to figure out where I was going with my life.

He then reminded me that his offer for help still stood, which was that I could come stay in his spare bedroom so I could focus on classes and not work so much to pay rent and reminded me that it was my choice if I wanted to take the hard route. *Yes, dad, everything has always been my fault.* The last straw was when he told me that my mom had been trying to contact him about me because she wanted to see my new apartment, to share this difficult time with me, and that he did not want to be the middleman.

I marveled at how it was possible that another human could fail to understand me so completely, and him being my father. I added about five more reasons to my list of one thousand to not allow him access to my life again. I rode in silence, listening to his compassionless, empathy-void, condition-invoking offers, placing more stones in my internal wall, which revoked entry for any more pain.

***

Randy and I got so many apartments ready in the two months that we worked together that all except two were full. The owner decided that Randy could manage things on his own, but that I could keep helping as a part-time gig. I accepted the truth that it was time to find a full-time job. It was obvious to me that if I stopped moving, I would sink, and then Gracie and I would be homeless. I found a full-time job at a busy medical clinic in Edmond, working as a bilingual receptionist.

Randy gave me a gift during our time spent together. He taught me how to run. I told him I had always hated running. I was a slow runner, and when we were obligated to run for a gym class in school I was always the last one. It was miserable. He told me that he was also a slow runner, that it's okay to run at my own pace, and then he taught me a counting pattern he'd learned in the military that would help me gauge the rhythm of my foot pattern as I ran. He even ran with me to help me find my pace. One day, I ran one whole mile, and eventually I was able to run 4 miles, and before too long I was able to run ten miles without stopping. This empowered me to keep surviving and keep pushing forward.

Around the same time, I found an advertisement for a degree program at a local community college for Interpreting and Translating Spanish. I motivated myself to enroll in classes for the spring 2007 semester. I thought as long as I could be where I spoke Spanish and engage with the local Latino community, I could connect to my heartbeat somewhere. If I could keep myself busy every waking hour of my day, I wouldn't have time to think about or feel anything inside.

With the way federal-based student aid works, I was still considered a dependent on my mom's taxes. Since I had cut her out of my life due to her betrayal and we were no longer in contact, I couldn't use her information for my financial aid. I worked extra hours to save enough cash for my tuition and books. It was just Gracie and me in this big, cold, cruel world, which I had convinced myself was against me. *I trust nobody*, I thought. *The people who should have cared about me and protected me the most in my life have hurt me the worst.*

***

A couple of months into my new job, the fragments of my trauma were still festering inside of me and started to manifest as severe anxiety, PTSD, and depression. I didn't know at the time what PTSD was, but my understanding came later.

Now that my rapist was behind bars, the misery of living the aftermath began. I had night terrors and would wake up in cold sweats, having panic attacks, and would hover over the sink breathing into a paper bag. With or without sleep aids, I could be awake for days, so I would nearly overdose on sleep aids, desperate to get some kind of rest. Both extremes drastically impacted my ability to function at work.

Dealing with the short-term memory loss associated with my condition, it was nearly impossible to learn new tasks at work; my co-workers and patients took the brunt of my shortcomings. They explained things over and over, but nothing would stick in my mind.

Something as simple as running to a convenience store for cigarettes and smelling someone who smelled like my rapist would send me into a blackout. I was terrified that my mom or her new boyfriend (my ex) would find out where I worked and walk through the front door. I never felt safe. I never felt safe leaving my apartment or driving to work. I couldn't go to the store or leave work and drive home. I never felt safe while awake or to go to sleep. When I was conscious, it wasn't safe, and it wasn't when I blacked out. I had nowhere to go. I wasn't safe anywhere on the outside of me, and it damn sure wasn't safe to be inside of me.

***

I was at work, making copies in the copy room one day, and out of nowhere I had a rape flashback. I was in that field, and the air smelled like it did that day out in that vacant lot. I was on my back getting raped, and the smell of his sweat and sour alcohol breath were all over my face.

"I'm gonna fucking kill you"

The words were ringing in my ears, harmonizing with the printer.

"Jenni."

I suddenly came back to present reality. Where was I? I was in the copy room at work. Someone needed me, and I had to do my job. Wait, what was my job?

"Jenni," said the voice again. I looked up at the door where a co-worker was poking her head around the corner. "We can't pull our next patient back until we have those privacy forms. Any day would be great. Also, we have a Hispanic patient on hold waiting to talk to someone in Spanish. She's been on hold for a while."

Oh, shit. How could I speak Spanish to a patient right now? I picked up the stack of papers which were finished printing. They were warm in my hands.

I had just gotten raped all over again. My walls were closing in, my throat was closing up, everything was closing. I felt worms crawling through me, all over me, both inside and on the outside of me. Those fucking worms. I needed to get sick. I ran to the bathroom, choked on tears and vomited before convincing myself I could face the public. I wiped my face, then put on a smile because no one could know my secret.

When I got to my desk, my cell phone was vibrating around in circles, indicating I was missing incessant phone calls. It was my mom. I hated her. Between the phone calls from my mother and the frequent flashbacks of my day in that hot summer field, it was too much at once. I blocked her.

I stopped eating. I felt sick every day anyway, but also my eating felt like one thing I could control in a world of chaos. Every day I felt like I had acid inside of me, in my heart, stomach, head, even in my blood. I hated sleeping because of the demons that waited for me there, but I hated being awake because my reality was a nightmare, too. I became accustomed to hunger pains for days and watched my body slowly melt away.

Soon I found release, where so many do, in the bottles of booze I brought home after work. I had finally found a way to numb the pain inside. As a previous version of myself, I had never liked the taste or effect of it, but now seemed like the perfect time to try again. My initial experiments became a habit, and soon it was a ritual. Every night when I got home, I would light candles, swig cheap vodka from a plastic bottle on my empty stomach and cut myself while listening to dark music.

I imagined that from each new cut, I was bleeding from the inside out. Maybe if I cut myself enough, deep enough, eventually all my anger and pain would bleed its way out. I wore long sleeves under my scrubs at work to cover my wounds.

I went to work hungover every day, but even I knew I could only maintain this behind-the-curtain reality for so long.

***

My best friend Lisa found her way home to Oklahoma City from college without a place to land. She and I had met in high school years before when she sat down next to me in home economics class and asked me to borrow a pencil. We were best friends from that point forward.

She was staying on my couch, gathering the pieces of her life, and devastated from her own traumas. It was overwhelming to share space with someone else in need, but it was also a comfort that she was there. In some way, knowing that someone depended on me to stay alive kept *me* alive.

We were the only family that we had, and as long as we stuck together, maybe we could make it out alive. I tried to give her what I myself needed the most: a shield from the cruelty of life's blows. Stepping into the role of a caretaker was one that I knew well, and it gave me something to grasp to avoid sinking deeper into a hole.

It was Christmas break in 2006 when Lisa and I moved into a new place together. Since I had flunked my fall 2006 semester and found the new degree program at OSU-OKC, I planned to start classes there in January. Moving close to the new campus made sense and we found a cheap apartment in an area with a horrible reputation, but it was all we could afford. It was a couple of blocks away from the part of Oklahoma City most known for drugs, parties, and strip clubs around every corner.

One night, I met some guy online and had him over to the house so that we could party. I didn't know at the beginning of the night that this was the day I would have my first experience using ecstasy. Once drinking had become my new normal, just drinking daily became not enough. I began to say yes to anything and everything.

Ecstasy delivered me to a magical land with no anguish attached to it. My current reality and all the monsters in it ceased to exist. For twenty bucks, I grabbed enough ecstasy for my magic carpet ride to last all weekend long. Rolling on a fun Friday night turned into a weekend-long party, which evolved into the thought that I clung to for dear life just to get me through my weeks. Eventually, I was using it almost every day.

I loved me when I was on ecstasy. When it hit my system, it was like putting on a new pair of glasses and looking at the world. These glasses fit perfectly, and I needed a pair that matched every outfit. Breaking in new accessories means wearing them as much as possible until they become a part of you, and that's what I did. I "wore" my new drug every minute I could.

I was losing a lot of weight; you might even say I was skinny. Spending hours looking in the mirror, I loved seeing my cheeks hollow, and I adored my new feminine, slender shoulders.

My shoulders looked like those of a slender, elegant lady in a diamond commercial, with glowing skin draped only in an exquisite, slinky black dress. These were the shoulders a dapper gentleman would drape his jacket around to protect his lady from the cold as he guided her around the dance floor of an opulent ballroom. When I was fucked up on ecstasy, I was the elegant and respectable woman who a prince would swoop in to save, not the kind of loser who men rape and whose boyfriends fuck their mothers.

When I was high, I would put on all my makeup and dress up, dreaming about how it would feel to live that elegant woman's life. What would it be like to wake up inside of her life? I pretended to be my favorite actress with millions of dollars, or that I was singing for an audience of a million people waiting on the edge of their seats for me to sing one last song. I was Adele. When I did ecstasy, I could teleport myself to any reality I wanted, live any life I wanted. At the time, I wanted to be anyone but me, which is why I hated coming down. The comedown felt like moving from a mansion nestled in my favorite piece of paradise to a tiny trailer in a meth park crawling with roaches. Each one got worse, so bad that they left me in darker places than where I had started.

Miraculously, I still made it to my classes, and I loved school. Translating difficult material and learning new things from my instructors tickled my soul's passion.

During one of those classes, I met Dr. Dearner. She was kind and passionate about imparting her knowledge as a translator. Her Ph.D. was in Linguistics, and she was a professional translator in six languages.

In class, I daydreamed about Cozumel. I knew that my life purpose was to travel and love people from different cultures, but that radical adventure I had taken at 19 already seemed like a lifetime ago. It seemed impossible just to get out of bed now, forget about finding the courage to go travel abroad again. That dream was a smoldering ember deep within me, but I wouldn't be able to blow life on it for a long time. Gracie at my side and classes were the only things keeping me alive. I always showed up to class drunk, high on something, and so exhausted, but I always showed up.

Chapter 8

Intervention, Rehab, and Alex

A few months later, I was in my bed sick, coming down from a bender that lasted more days than I could even remember when Lisa stepped into my room. She sat down on my mattress (I still slept on the floor), but I didn't look at her.

"You're sick." She said. "Jenni, I can't watch another person die from drugs and alcohol. Make a choice. Choose change, and I'll be with you on the journey. Choose change, or I leave."

I had already gotten fired from my job for showing up late, showing up drunk or high, and I was never capable of fulfilling my work duties because I was so tired. For months I just had endless, meaningless sex and lived strung out on drugs.

Choosing between life and death at that point seemed too big for the power inside me. All I felt was empty, so far away from any kind of reality. Being sober and present was unbearably painful, but to stay checked out had grave consequences. What I wanted was to be high and fade away little by little, eventually just becoming dust the wind could carry away to some new faraway place, new land, new adventure. How had I even gotten to that rock bottom?

She was waiting for an answer. Did I want her to call my mom? Did I need help making a choice? Was I willing to go to rehab?

I hadn't spoken to my mother in a year, and I couldn't afford rehab. I took a few days to think about what I wanted to do, staying in my dealer's dingy apartment, chain smoking menthols, getting fucked up, and getting fucked. People came in and out, buying their dope, some staying to smoke, snort, shoot, or swallow, and then they left.

What if I just let go of everything and stayed here? Could I turn tricks and do drugs all fucking day long every day? If I stayed numb, I wouldn't feel it anyway. What's the point of keeping a job anyway–to pay bills? Naw, I couldn't anymore, couldn't care. Humans are the only species who have to pay to live, and I wanted more out of life than to chase a degree plan for a phantom job opportunity. Who knew if the phantom job could pay for bills and give me a better quality of life anyway? Nothing about being a hamster on a wheel seemed like a better quality of life to me.

When I didn't come home for a few days, Lisa called my mom without waiting for my answer. I felt like it was a huge betrayal at the time, but later I was able to understand that it was an act of love. She saved my life. When she talked to my mom, she spilled the beans about everything. Of course, Mom had been wondering for months where I was living, what I was doing. My mom, in turn, called my dad. That's when I got the voicemail from my dad reminding me that his name was on the title of my car, and since I was involved in "nefarious behavior," that could reflect on him poorly. He was coming to take my car.

***

It turns out, my mom reached out to my dad for financial help getting me into a rehab program. When he told her he was done trying to help me and turned her away, she then reached out to some of his family members who had resources to help me. She got me checked into a 30-day program at a place called Valley Hope, in the middle of nowhere about an hour north of Oklahoma City.

To say rehab was an intense experience is putting it mildly. I was already numb and dead on the inside, but I had always been the tower of power for everyone in my life, including for my mom my entire childhood. To be in her passenger seat, sick as fuck, being hauled to rehab, was beyond surreal. The landscapes whizzed by, and I had no will to live, really. I knew I was at a crossroads but didn't really have the strength to choose a path, nor did I care.

After check-in, I surveyed my room. The nightstand held brochures about addiction with the name of the place printed all over them. "Valley Hope," it read. *Hope, my ass.* While I might not have known it at the time, I learned more about drugs and addiction while being inside Valley Hope's walls than I did outside of them. I hated it, but at that point, I hated everyone and everything, mostly myself.

During my first 24 hours there, I became one with my bunk and refused to leave it. I slept and wrote and ignored any sign of life around me. I hated food and hated eating. I hated people talking and the sun shining through my window. I loathed their advice about where to go and how to live my life, like they knew anything about *ME*.

Just let me do things my own way, fuckheads.

I knew that my own way was killing me, and I knew I needed an intervention, and I hated that, too.

After 24 hours of hiding under my covers, my assigned counselor knocked on my door. She informed me that there would be group therapy every day and three meals per day, and thus far, it seemed I was blowing off both. If I continued to do so, I wouldn't meet the expectations required to checkout from my program after 30 days. Surprise, I hated her, too.

I tried the group counseling, even tried to speak when it was my turn. I looked around and realized it had been a year since that awful week in July when my life shattered into a million pieces. My life consisted of being strung out on drugs, and there I was in a figurative train wreck of a rehab full of rednecks with meth mouth. How the fuck did I get here? How do I get out? How was I supposed to talk about what I had gone through with these people?

When it was my turn to share, I had a full-fledged panic attack and ran. After that, I sat quietly in group sessions so the lady in the corner with her glasses perched on her pinched nose and stained blouse could check this box off her list.

I went to the cafeteria and pushed food around on my plate long enough for my babysitters to check their box that I had eaten. When people at my table got up to go outside for some post-meal smokes, I went with them. I was still quiet, even upon being beckoned for conversation from the group. I ignored the cues from others and stared at the ground. I just wanted to smoke with them and listen to their crazy stories. The two girls who were there for meth addiction went down to the fence line to smoke dope.

One of the two was already dead, though. I could see it in her eyes. It was only a matter of time before her physical body gave out. She looked terrible, and I couldn't stop staring. Her yellow skin, teeth rotting out of her head, eyes sunken in. She was here because of a court order to attend rehab. The second girl was addicted to ketamine.

She looked just as bad as the meth girl with big purple track marks up and down her arms, feet, and neck. Death had taken her, too, but it looked different. She was only 25 and already looked so old, like she was rotting from the inside out. I wondered what kind of wounds she was hiding that allowed death to take her at such a young age.

I knew what some of mine were and how they hurt. Hers had to be worse.

Another patient shared about her opiate addiction, which started with a sports injury and a prescription for Lortabs. At her lowest point, she sent her son to play with his friends, with instructions to raid the medicine cabinets in their homes for pain killers.

I chain smoked my menthols and listened to them brag about their crazy drug stories when I realized that someone was violently vomiting in the background during our entire conversation. I started to ask what that was about but was spared the act of opening my mouth when someone mentioned the new intake coming down off heroin.

Fuck. I had never been around heroin or anyone on it. I had only seen that in movies. One thing I was certain of, I had never heard someone so fucking sick in my life. What could make someone SO sick? I realized that was what Lisa saw in me, too, and why she was so scared. Death was creeping onto me. That's why I felt only cold and hard on the inside. I'd been numbing everything so that I wouldn't feel myself get eaten alive.

***

The next morning, while playing with my eggs, I noticed this beautiful creature sitting at the end of my table. His shiny, curly hair cascaded down around his face while he faced a sketch pad on the table.

Did he want to have breakfast with me? No. He was the person who had been so sick coming down off heroin. We instantly connected and spent the next three days without leaving each other's company. In spite of his outer beauty, there was no sexual attraction between us. Our connection was purely an emotional and spiritual thing. We were supposed to cross paths.

He was 28, only three classes short of finishing his degree in music. He played both the guitar and piano, and his voice was the voice of an angel. He had spent a college semester in Spain, so we spoke only in Spanish, something that made us both so happy.

I imagined how beautiful it would be to meet someone like him while exploring the streets of Spain. What had opened the chasm between the beautiful life that he had lived and the life he was living right now? It wasn't long before I found out. In a car accident two years before we met, his fiancé--his pregnant fiancé--had died. The same accident left him with chronic back pain and deep emotional pain. He used the prescription pills for his back pain to treat both, but that eventually converted to an addiction to heroin.

I loved staring at his curls. They were glossy and caught the light just right when he pulled them back in a ponytail. He shared memories of his fiancé, how she was his first love, pregnant with his first child, and even the huge argument they'd had the night of the car accident. The pain was his motivation to stay numb. Of course, he wanted to hear my story, but I was usually just quiet. I liked listening because then my mind wasn't on my own. I hated being sober. It hurt.

Also, I was very leery to let him in on my secrets. I was sure he wouldn't like me. I hated me, and surely if he knew what was inside of me, he would see all the same reasons to hate me as well.

It was my fifth day in rehab, and we were lying in the grass looking at the stars, which filled the Oklahoma summer sky.

"I will never quit heroin." He said matter-of-factly while clearing his throat. He sighed and looked over at me.

His quiet, determined statement ricocheted off every blade of grass around my head.

I thought maybe I had misunderstood.

"Huh?"

"I'm only here because I ran out of money for dope. Here they give me pills to help the chemical comedown. There's no way to come down without help." He said these words as he studied my face, searching for feedback or a response. I gave him none on the outside, although the thoughts were a whirlwind inside my own head.

"So, then what?" I persisted. "Are you gonna be 50 doing this same dumbass shit?"

"Nope," he quietly responded. "I will either be dead or in prison by then. Those are my only options. Quitting isn't one of them because I can't imagine my life without heroin. I would rather die."

I remained quiet, letting those powerful words resonate.

"Have you ever seen anyone shoot up?"

I shook my head.

"A friend came to see me earlier and brought me some dope. Do you wanna watch me shoot up, Jenni?"

Something intrigued me about seeing him do it. I couldn't imagine being desperate enough to stick a needle in my arm.

"Sure," I responded under my breath.

He hopped up and gave me a hand to pull me up. At Valley Hope, men and women stayed in separate bunks, so we hiked together toward his dorm.

"Jenni, my family hates me. I've stolen everything I can from anyone I can to get dope. My parents just paid this bill, desperate for any attempt to save me. They think someday I will quit, that someday they will save me. My love for heroin is far greater than any pain I cause to anyone else. It is a monster that has overtaken me, Jenni.

I hate myself for how much pain I have caused people, but doing it numbs it all."

I lit up a menthol for us to share and listened to our shoes crunch the grass. I knew I shouldn't be there. Getting caught in a boy's dorm would put a mark in my chart, and I already had so many from skipping meals and group activities. He snuck me in a backway and calmly told me he knew his roommate was at dinner and then would be visiting with a family member, so we had at least an hour. I wondered if his roommate's visitor was also bringing him a fix like Alex's friend had done earlier.

Once inside the dorm, he pulled me into the bathroom and shut the door. He used a little tool from his pocket to unscrew the towel rod next to the sink. His setup was hiding inside: a syringe and heroin. He pulled a shoelace from his shoe and took a spoon out of the coffee mug next to the sink. I wondered if he had strategically placed that mug and spoon there hours before, in anticipation of this secret moment.

"I've already lost everything that was once important to me in my life," he explained while preparing his rig. I watched him mix heroin and water in the spoon and ready it in the syringe, thumping out excess oxygen.

"You've never reached this point. You aren't like me. It's not too late for you. You still have a way out. You weren't meant for this. You can still save yourself."

He sat down on the toilet and showed me where to tie the shoelace on his arm. He found the perfect vein and shot up.

I felt heaviness hit me like a weighted body suit. It pressed down on my chest and clenched my throat. His eyes rolled back into his head as he slumped against the back of the toilet, his head thumping against the wall. Had he overdosed? I didn't think so. I backed out of the bathroom slowly, taking in the horror of the scene that had occurred directly in front of my eyes. I sat on the bed and watched him twitch.

He never meant to be here, and it had happened one decision at a time, one lie at a time, and death was taking him a little more each time. The room was full of death and darkness in that moment. The movie *Final Destination* came to mind, thinking about when death would creep in and kill people in random ways.

How many lies was I away from being at that point? He didn't think it was too late for me, but was it? If I really wanted my life to end, did I want to do it like that or in a quicker way? I realized in that moment I didn't want either. I watched Alex and realized that it was time to fight for my life.

I texted Randy immediately. "Can you please come pick me up? Valley Hope in Cushing. Overnight disappear."

He responded, "Be there at 3 a.m."

I snuck back to my dorm and was grateful to find my roommate was gone completely. *She must have checked out*, I thought to myself. I showered, packed my suitcase, and made my bed up exactly how it was when I found it the first day I arrived. At 2:30 a.m., I snuck out the back of the building with my bag on my back and hid in a grove of trees that surrounded the first entrance to the property.

When I saw Randy's headlights, I motioned for him to stop, ran, threw my bags in the back of the truck, and disappeared into the starry summer night.

I have thought about Alex throughout the years. We stayed in touch for about a year. When I bailed rehab, I left him a note with my cell number, and then I heard he was staying on his dealer's couch, serving as a drug mule in exchange for drugs. When we talked on the phone, he would tell me how many guns had been shoved in his face, that he had been forced to commit murder for his dealer, about all the close calls he'd had with the police.

One day, he stopped answering my calls. I am not sure whether he died or was finally in prison, and I will probably never know. But, I carry the lesson he gave to me in my heart always. His stories would save my life years later when I would face addiction again, alone in a foreign country.

Chapter 9

After Rehab

Randy rescued me that night, and he took me home to his house for a few days. It was a perfect place at that moment. He lived in a small town 30 minutes north of Oklahoma City on a 2-acre lot a few blocks away from the main part of town. It was nature, it was quiet, and it was peaceful, or at least in comparison to what I'd been dealing with lately.

There wasn't time to get comfortable at Randy's, though. He'd been notified that he only had a few days to find a place to live, as the owners were foreclosing on the property. I had to figure out what to do with my life. My soul needed a safe place to rest for a long time, but I had nowhere to do that. If I stopped moving, life would run me right over, and life had proven to me that I couldn't depend on anyone else to carry me.

Almost a year after that hellish week, here I was starting from scratch with no car, money, or job, just painful pieces scattered inside me that were an even bigger mess from so much endless partying and meaningless sex with strangers. I knew I needed to start seeing a therapist or someone to help me with the things that were such a mess inside. It wasn't just about choosing not to do drugs; it was really deep roots of pain that led me to the path of doing them. I needed to address those roots, but I didn't have time or money for any of that. If I didn't start working, I would be homeless. I would have to take time to feel later.

Nobody knew where I was, tucked away at Randy's house. My dad kept calling. "Where are you?" he demanded.

Suddenly he cares.

"I still have your car. Your brother is using it right now while he is in town on summer break because his car is in the shop. Just give me the word, and I will get it back to you." He also told me that family members who helped pay my rehab expenses were demanding to know if they would get any money back since I quit early. Nobody really cared about my disheveled, devastated state. They wanted their money. Valley Hope had called me when they figured out I was missing and told me that they would be willing to give a partial refund if I gave up the name of the person who had drugs on their property. There was no way I was going to snitch, so there was no refund.

I never wanted to accept anything from my dad ever again. Not only were his gifts always attached to conditions, but now I knew that he would easily take them away whenever he didn't approve of what I was doing, usually in the moment when I needed help the most. He insisted that I come live with him. I wouldn't pay rent, and I could have my car. From his house I could work, save money, and take classes. He always insisted I needed to walk this path with my life, as if that would magically fix everything. I told him I would think about it to get him to go away.

I needed a place to stay regardless. Lisa was going her own way, and Randy was unstable. My dad wasn't an option I was willing to take. I didn't have any friends with houses or an extra couch where I could crash safely. That left my *mom*.

My mom was insistent I stay with her. She wanted a place in my life and felt entitled to it after jumping through hoops to help get me into rehab. She was finally settled into the house she purchased when I found out about her betrayal with my then-boyfriend. She had officially moved into the house shortly after my life fell apart. Actually, my ex-boyfriend was a professional painter with high-end clients in the richest neighborhoods around Oklahoma City. He had done the fancy paintwork in her new kitchen and living room.

***

I remember discovering their affair after I left work late one night. I called both their phones, but neither answered. It occurred to me that he could be helping her work at her new house and simply lost track of time. Maybe they had the music turned up and couldn't hear their phones. I drove to the house and was alarmed when both of their cars were there, the house was completely dark, and still no one answered any of the doors or phone calls. I was locked out.

I assumed they must have gone to the neighbor's or something. When the truth came out, I felt incredibly stupid. It was obvious now they had been there and ignored me, being in the full bliss of each other, christening the new house in erotic ways. I knew they were because that's what he and I did whenever my mom was at work. I hadn't used a condom with him, and I imagined he didn't use one with her either, a closeness I never imagined sharing with my mom. I wondered if he even washed his dick off before switching us out for the other.

I didn't want to live there. I never wanted to visit there ever again, not once in the history of forever, not only because of the terrible memories of that house, but Yukon would forever be the home of my rape. The town plastered with newspapers hosting my story on the front page. The whole package was a barrel full of triggers for me, and I had no clue how I would manage to stay sober from drugs.

***

Lisa had found a job at the OnCue gas station on the corner of Reno and MacArthur. She could get me a job connection there if I wanted, which sounded much more appealing than turning in piles of applications to places all over town. For the time being, I stayed at my mom's and decided I would let all the toxic trauma triggers be motivation for me to work as hard as I could to get the fuck out of there. As much as I dreaded doing it, all I needed was to get my car from my dad's house.

A few days later, I got a call for an interview at OnCue, so things were working out perfectly. I got the job, I got my car back, and now it was time to hustle hard. The store manager had recently fired several employees at once for stealing, so I had a guaranteed set schedule of 40 hours during the week, plus as many extra shifts as I wanted to pick up.

OnCue not only gave me a sense of self-worth and empowerment to be independent again after rehab, but it gave me the structure to stick to a healthy routine. The more I worked, the less I was at my mom's house, or in Yukon for that matter.

I spoke just as much Spanish on my shifts as I did English, and I loved helping resolve conflicts through interpreting. It reconnected me with my beloved Latino culture. My customers and my work family were the reason I woke up every day, happy to go to work. They were my security blanket, seeing the ones who came in every single morning for a 24-ounce coffee, a pack of Camel blues, and a honey bun. Having their cigarettes ready and starting their day off with a positive word and a smile made me feel important to their day, and they did the same for me.

One of our regulars who I will never forget is Garvin, a homeless veteran who would wheel himself through the back door of the store. He had lost his legs somehow, but he never had proper treatment to take care of amputations. The stubs were rotting off with gangrene, and they were covered in maggots eating his flesh alive. He would panhandle long enough to come inside for the tall beer and a cheap pack of lite smokes that his cup cull of change would buy, and he slept in a nook between two businesses right there at Reno and MacArthur.

He was always so happy and would usually say something ornery to try to flirt with me, with a stubbed out half-cigarette dangling from his toothless mouth. I would banter back with him. "Garviiiiiiiinnnnn, you must be drunk already! Where in the world have you been partying without me?!" The manager hated him coming in because he stunk and obviously would ward off customers with those green and purple maggoty stumps that he whipped around in his wheelchair.

Sometimes, when it was my turn to stock the grill, I would sneak the old food that was supposed to go in the trash into a paper bag to bring to him in his hidey hole. When my shift was over, I would bring the stale food and a couple of big ass beers, and we would sit there and talk about life. He was so funny, full of stories and sadness.

What I gathered from his stories is that his injuries were military-related. When he came back from his mission abroad, he also came back fucked up in the head because of everything he survived, and he didn't get help. He drank about it, which eventually caused him to lose his family, which made his addiction worse, which eventually left him homeless.

Neither of us realized at that moment how much we had in common. The maggots that were eating him alive on the outside were like the ones I had felt on the inside. Our stories connected in abstract ways. I was able to listen to him and understand him in a way that most didn't because of my own suffering. I was able to see the aftermath of what happens inside of a human if healing doesn't occur, but I couldn't think about that then. I didn't have time to heal or feel. I had to keep hustling hard or else I would be homeless, too.

Three months into my time at OnCue my district manager pulled me into the back room to ask me whether I would be interested in a level II supervisor position at a store on the south side of the city. The area was mostly Hispanic, and they desperately needed a bilingual supervisor to help the store manager on the second shift.

I jumped at the opportunity, not only for the new challenges it would give me, but also because of the slight pay increase and benefits it would give me. It also came with a set schedule agreed on ahead of time, which would allow me to be consistent with taking classes to be working toward my degree. I learned how to do inventory and do store orders for merchandise. I enjoyed managing, and the employees who worked during my shifts loved being a part of our shift. We were a family.

I was still allowed to pick up extra shifts if I wanted, which I did, and I spoke Spanish the whole time I was at work. My dream of traveling was still tucked away, even though the tiny ember was barely glowing, at least it was still warm in there somewhere. Connecting with the Latino culture at work helped me tremendously.

My morale was considerably higher compared to where I was mentally just three months prior. It seemed so long ago that I had been on death's doorstep in rehab. I remained sober from drugs and had drinks every now and then, but I had a bigger drive in me this time around. My wounds were still there, for sure, but I had a renewed vision for living my life.

My favorite professor, Dr. Dearner, reached out to me, concerned that I had not continued my enrollment in the degree program. Since I was working so much overtime at OnCue, I decided I would be able to afford the spring semester, so as soon as the spring schedules opened, I enrolled and paid my tuition up front.

Now, it was time to find my way out of Yukon and out of my mom's house. OnCue offered free beverages for public service professionals such as firefighters, police officers, and EMT drivers. I became friends with most of the cops and sometimes helped them interpret for different conflicts. They were in the store often between calls and would hang out in a small group at the end of my counter. About a month into my new role, one of my regular cops shared some interesting information.

"Obama is offering a stimulus for first-time home buyers. If you have good credit, you should consider looking into buying your first home. My wife's a realtor. You have a set salary here. There's a high chance you could get approved for a home loan. Just food for thought." He tossed his wife's business card on the counter before leaving with the other officers to go take a call.

After having my experience abroad, I had never considered buying a home, at least not in the United States. I knew that I at least wanted to finish my associate degree before I left the country again and that I would need to work as hard as I could until then and try to save for a life abroad. Buying a home now seemed like something way too big to bite off.

But was it? I wouldn't know unless I checked it out, and I found out that I did indeed qualify for a home loan. I began looking at houses, and I found a home close to my store for a great price. It was a three-bedroom, two-bathroom house planted on a corner lot with a huge yard that had beautiful landscaping left behind by previous owners. The payment was right in the range of where I wanted it to be for my income and my budget.

I knew that by signing the paperwork, I was committing to working so much that I would never see the light of day. But, I feared that I would regret it if I did not try. I finally had security with my job. I wanted security with my living arrangement after so many instances of being on the brink of homelessness.

I decided to take the leap. I was going to be a homeowner. I was prepared to do everything it took to stay afloat. I felt like I was taking my power back in some way, and for that, I had this inner victory party about my decision.

But, on the day of my signing, the whole drive to my broker's office, I could not shake the feeling that I was making a huge mistake.

Chapter 10

The Birth of my First Business

Things sailed along for a steady year. I took classes and picked up extra shifts. My dad and his new wife got a new SUV, so I took over the loan on their Jeep Liberty they had for sale. It was my first "new" vehicle, and also my first time having a monthly vehicle payment. I didn't feel comfortable financially between the mortgage payment, car payment, and other bills. My salary was overstretched. But, having a steady job and a home, I was stable in another way. I had earned a 4.0 in school in spite of what I was suffering through. I had stuck in school, and I felt like I was climbing my way out of a hole by staying away from drugs.

I started going out with a guy who came into my store often just to see me throughout the week, and I finally gave in to his invitations to come to church with him. I was willing to give it a chance, hoping to have some kind of refuge from the storm that still brewed deeply within and reared its ugly head during rare moments. I actually stopped long enough to be still, alone. Being in a Latino church with him with everything in Spanish and by meeting Latino families from different Spanish-speaking countries kept me connected to that place within me where soulfire burned. It wasn't nearly as bright anymore, more like an ember with a faint glow, but I couldn't let it go out.

Things at work seemed really good. I loved the challenges that came with management, and I loved my work family (Amanda, Candy, and Morgan). I developed friendships with regular customers, like Judy and Angela, David, Ron, Danny, and Wanda who came in every day. I had a set schedule, which made it possible to be consistent with my class schedule. For the first time in my life, I had a set schedule, a set salary, and a personal environment to call home that empowered me to be successful. My regular customers and my team members at work were my family.

My mortgage payment had slowly crept up because of my homeowner's insurance premium, so to make up for it, I rented out the back room in my house to one of the girls who worked for me on my shifts. She had a newborn baby and needed an economic place to go so that she could get away from the toxic relationship with her baby's daddy. We had a lot of fun and formed a friendship that would last over our lifetimes.

Things were flowing seamlessly until my boss started sexually harassing me. At first, he made subtle comments that I thought were a misunderstanding. I had maintained my habit of going for long walks and jogs in the mornings before work. Even with people all around, he would say, "I love it when you wear those khaki shorts," (just softly enough that no one else could hear it), or "Those jogs are really paying off."

One time, when our truck came in, he told me I was the only one he trusted to put away the big stuff in the back room. I caught him lurking in the shadows watching me climb up and down a stool to organize the top shelf. He told me he intentionally did that so he could watch me stand on my tippy toes.

The last straw was after a 10-hour shift one Sunday night. I was ready to get home and study for an exam I had the next day at noon. A new night employee no-showed their shift. Under store policy, it was always the store manager's responsibility to cover no-shows, but when I called my boss, he told me that he wouldn't come in. He informed me he would arrive at his normal time at 6 a.m., and I had two options: One, I could stay to cover the shift myself, or two, I could leave the night manager to fend for himself.

I chose to stay because I did not have the heart to put a member of my work family in a dangerous situation of covering a night shift himself. I knew something big needed to change, but I wasn't sure exactly what to do. When my boss arrived at 6 a.m. for his usual Monday morning shift, he had that week's schedule ready. He had changed my hours, putting me on the schedule literally for that same Monday, meaning I would go to class, take my exam, hope for some kind of nap, and have to come back the same afternoon. He had also changed my schedule for the rest of the week, making it impossible to attend classes.

That's when the camel's back broke. We had this full-blown argument in front of other work members and customers, and everyone was quietly gawking, waiting to see what would happen. The show's grand finale was me saying, "Go fuck yourself" and sailing my middle finger over my shoulder as I grabbed my belongings and walked out the back door.

I sat in my jeep stunned, enraged at the situation. When I woke up the next day, I had free time for the first time in a long time. I had been living in my house for a year by then, and not once had I ever had time to just sit on my back patio to enjoy my morning coffee.

Shit, I had quit my job. I had a mortgage payment and a car payment to make. My management salary wasn't great, but it was more than I would make starting a new position elsewhere. I already barely made ends meet.

I decided to take a couple of days to thoroughly clean my house, take a bubble bath, and just be still. Actually, I realized I had been working hard for 10 years of my life, since I was 15. I hadn't ever taken days just for me, except those magical weeks I was abroad, alone, bubbling over with sacred soulfire. Even though I had been in a more "stable" situation than ever before, was it really? Oklahoma is an "at-will" employment state, which means someone can get fired at any time for any reason. I had been working so hard for so long, investing my time and talent into the success of others.

By the time I left OnCue, I'd been dating and attending church with Jose for a few months. While I was enjoying a moment of freedom with my first day "off," my text notification sounded. Now was as good a time as any to tell him everything, so he came over for coffee.

"We could start a lawn business," he said brilliantly. He worked in retail but pointed out he could help on his days off, keep his income from his day job, and I could do the full-time part of the lawn care business as the owner. Growing up, I had always loved working outside and getting dirty. I decided to take the leap.

"We want to start a lawn business," I announced to Ron as we walked in. Ron owned a lawn shop a couple streets down from where I worked at the gas station. He was one of my regular customers.

He stood there studying me for a second, surprised at my news. "You're off in the middle of the week, and you want to launch a new business. Does this have anything to do with why I haven't seen you at the store the past few days?"

I didn't see any purpose in investing energy in talking about old shit. It was old, and none of it mattered anyway. I had to go forward; I told him just that.

"But do you even have any customers?" he insisted.

I didn't feel like I owed anyone any more information. "Look, I'm not here for any opinions. You sell lawn equipment. That's what I need. Can you help me, or can you send me to someone who can?"

He started to laugh. "A woman who doesn't take shit from anyone. I love it. Let me run your credit to see if you qualify for a Toro card." All the financing for the business would have to come through me. Jose had no credit and no savings.

Toro was the brand name of a commercial lawn equipment company. He ran my info through the computer and reported I had a $10,000 limit on a Toro card, and since I was a first-time buyer, my balance was interest-free for a year. He pointed out that my jeep had a hitch that could pull a lawn trailer. My God, the universe was on fire.

Jose picked out all the equipment we would need to start, which we would store safely there until we got a trailer. At Lowe's, we discovered we could open a line of credit with the store, one which was large enough to purchase everything else we needed: a shed, tools, and a lawn trailer. This morning, I was drinking coffee on my back patio, and now, a couple of hours later, I was a business owner.

My mom did some graphic art jobs on the side, so I asked her to make flyers in vibrant neon colors that had my business name and cell phone number on it. "Jenni, does this have anything to do with why you aren't at work on a weekday afternoon?" The next day she brought a box of flyers. I was so proud of those flyers. "Jenni's Lawn Care," they read, with my cell phone number and services offered.

Jose brought his friend Nico over to help build a big gate in the fence that opened up to the cul-de-sac and a shed where we could store all of our equipment and tools. Jose suggested that he just move in since his day job could help cover household expenses while we built our business. I gave him the green light to do it, although there was a sinking feeling in my gut that told me something was not right. I'd had several red flags with him, none of which I'd heeded. I did a great job at explaining them away, but not a better job than he did. I figured I was overthinking it and decided to be positive and hope for the best.

I was able to finish my spring semester and ease into our first lawn season, which started slow but then exploded overnight. It was as if everyone opened their lawn flyers from their doors at the same time and wanted a bid. I had no idea how to bid jobs or how to run this business, but we were in it. It was time to learn everything one step at a time. The summer flew by in a haze of sweat, blood, and tears.

Chapter 11

There were red flags with Jose before he even moved in, all of which I ignored to start my business. The first red flag I wasn't able to ignore happened as soon as he moved in. He told me, "I'm okay with you having a cat, but Gracie isn't allowed to sleep with us in our bedroom. I don't want a cat walking on my head while we are trying to sleep." Gracie was my number one, always, and there's no way that would change, and I let him know that.

As soon as our business took off, the second red flag I couldn't ignore popped up. He came home from work one afternoon, announcing his great news: he was no longer employed! He quit his job so that he could dedicate himself to our new business venture but didn't bother to talk with me about it first. It was uneasy, like he was up to something, and I definitely didn't trust his intentions. However, I brushed it to the side, telling myself to stop being so negative and start expecting the best.

We started our mowers at 6:30 a.m. and often finished with the help of my jeep headlights at 9 p.m. I found a personal joy and freedom from working outside all day, getting dirty and burned by the sun. It reminded me of the times I'd shared with Randy working in those apartments. I expected things to shift when school started again since I planned to attend school two nights a week and all day long on Saturdays. However, that's when I started to notice a big change with Jose.

When I got home from class, he smelled like perfume. He became very paranoid about protecting his phone and would disappear to go to the store for hours, never returning home with any bags. He always had a very clever way of explaining things, so much that I often questioned my sanity. Any time I questioned him, he insisted that my suspicions came from my own jealousy issues, that I was making up everything in my head.

I realized I hadn't seen my friends for months, and when I told him I was going to meet Lisa at a local pub for drinks, he became infuriated, telling me that we were Christians, and Christians don't drink or go to bars. I went anyway, which ended up with accusations from him that Lisa and I were romantically involved, and that if everything fell apart, it would be my fault for doing things I shouldn't be doing.

He was an exceptionally gifted gaslighting narcissist, and I began to believe that essentially, I was the one in the wrong and that maybe if I kept changing things about myself or my life, he would stop threatening to leave. I realized I was reliving what I had experienced in my home growing up, the dozens upon dozens of times that my dad would come home smelling like perfume or get caught with women's clothing in his car. He always had a mastermind approach to convincing my mom that she was certifiably crazy and these things all existed in her head.

I couldn't imagine running this new business by myself. Despite my constant requests that he show me how to use all the equipment, he always told me that I was doing a great job at what I was doing and that he could handle everything else. I didn't need to know everything. Then, I realized he didn't want me to know, because he didn't want me to have power. He wanted me to depend on him.

The next weekend when some of his church friends came over to grill out on Sunday after church, as they were laughing about all their children climbing around my big backyard like monkeys, the conversation suddenly got directed to me. "And when will you have yours?" All eyes were on me.

I thought they were joking, so I played along and laughed. They were dead serious.

"Oh, I don't want to have children." The women gasped. This was an abomination to Latino culture. "After I graduate in May with my associate degree, I want to work on a business degree and eventually get into real estate."

When the party left, Jose wanted to have a serious talk about how I embarrassed him in front of his friends.

"Nico and I can run the business so that you can stay home with our baby. We have the perfect setup to start a family," he reasoned. "A woman's body isn't built for doing heavy work. It's built for childbearing. You need to nurture your femininity and align yourself with God's plan for your life." He followed with justifications about why after graduating with my associate degree, I really had no need to keep going to school because we had our own business.

I realized I had made a huge mistake by being involved with him, but now everything was meshed together in a very complicated way. I had to be quiet until lawn season was over, and I started stashing cash to make sure I could cover my mortgage and bills when lawn season ended.

I overheard him on the phone laughing with a buddy from church. He had not heard me come in. He was telling his friend he was going to mess with my birth control pills so that I would get pregnant. From that point, I stopped having sex with him completely. I could not risk getting pregnant. Besides, I hated to fuck him anyway.

Every time we had sex, he begged me for anal. Even though I said no, often he would try anyway, which ended up in an ugly fight. One day, I came up with a crafty plan. After making him go without sex, I went to Christie's Toy Box and bought a massive strap-on dildo. I sent him a sexy text message in my lingerie, saying I was ready for the hottest anal I had ever had in my life. I failed to include in the picture that I was wearing a huge strapon, ready to take his sweet, churchboy ass. He raced home, and when he scrambled into the bedroom already stripped down to his underwear to make his appearance with his hard dick, I was hiding behind the door waiting for him to walk in, and I shut it behind him. I will never forget the look on his face when he saw me stroking this huge black dick strapped on me.

"What the fuck is this?" he sputtered in a shaky voice. "I thought we were going to do anal tonight." I was trying to keep a straight face, but his quivering lip was making it way too hard. I was going to use every single line with him that he used with me.

"We are! I'll be gentle, I promise."

"But I don't want a dick in my ass!" he said.

"But if you loved me, you would submit your body to me. Do it to bring honor to God!"

"But that's not what I like. It will hurt," he protetsted.

"But I have anal fantasies I need to fulfill, and if you can't give them to me, I will have no choice but to cheat on you, and it will be your choice to destroy everything we're building together since you won't give them to me." He used that one often.

It was genius. "Oh, come on, just let me put the tip in!" I pleaded. "You'll never know you like it if you don't try it. Isn't that what you always tell me?" I grabbed his arm and attempted to pull him to me so that I could rub that hard dildo against him. He took off, and I started chasing him around the room begging and pleading, using all his bullshit lines until he escaped the room. I yelled out the door, "But if you loved me, you'd give it to me!" He grabbed his pile of clothes and sprinted out the door. He left crying and stayed out all night. It was common for him to stay out all night mysteriously, but this time, I didn't care.

Right after that, I got a phone call from one of our mutual friends asking me if I was aware of what was going on with Jose. He had been stalking her. He found out where she worked, would send her flowers and chocolate, and would drive by and leave notes on her car. He would send her creepy messages about her outfits that he would see her wearing whenever she stepped outside to smoke. Of course, I had no idea that any of this was going on.

"I feel so bad," she said. "I have told him that I have a boyfriend, that I am not interested in him whatsoever, and I want him to stop. I told him that you were my friend and that he was being disrespectful to you, too. He told me that you told him to write me, since you are a bisexual, because you want to have a threesome."

I told her I had no idea this was going on, and it was definitely not something instigated by me. He was doing it behind my back to cheat. I told her that we needed to be smart about it. I needed to get through finals in a couple of weeks and get as much lawn work done as possible. I told her that I wasn't going to say anything yet. In the meantime, any messages he sent her, I requested that she send them to me for evidence.

I kept up the charade for a week. While we were together doing jobs, texts would come to my phone from her, messages that he was sending to her in that very moment that we were working together. He even drove by her work while I was next to him in the car. This went on for days until one night, I hit my limit. I was in the back room studying for finals, and he was sitting in the living room in my house, on my couch, watching my big screen TV, and he was texting her all kinds of crazy stuff. She was immediately forwarding the texts right to me. I walked through the living room pretending to go find some water, and he nervously dropped his phone.

"Hi baby," he said. "Can I help you with anything? You know you are the smartest woman I have ever met, and I am here to help where I can." He was literally two completely different people. The whole experience with him since day one had been a charade. I used the rest of the night to gather all the evidence I needed to confront him.

The next morning, I made us breakfast while he loaded up the lawn trailer. When he sat down to eat, he took one bite of his food and shoved it away. "I can't eat this shit. It's cold." I felt a flame of rage spark through me so strong, my face turned purple. That acid feeling kicked off in my stomach, and I felt it course through my blood and go through my whole body. I imagined grabbing that baseball bat from behind the couch, giving him one good solid blow right in the middle of his head, and burying him in the backyard. It was time for a confrontation.

"I want the truth. I think you're seeing someone else." I curtly stated.

He scoffed. "That's absurd. You're the love of my life. I am happy with you. You need to go see a doctor about that imagination you have."

"I am giving you one more chance to tell me the truth," I warned. "It will be easier for you that way. I already have the truth, and I am giving you the opportunity to tell it to me yourself." He continued to insist that everything was in my head. I brought out all the truth for him. I showed him the phone records and all the texts that Stephanie had sent me over the past few days. He started sobbing. "But she's not special to me," he cried. I pulled up the text message that she had forwarded me literally the night before and read it to him. "Girl, I want to be with you. You are so special for me," it read.

"Get the fuck out," were my final words. I texted a friend to please come with new locks, and as I waited for his arrival, Jose followed me around the house begging and pleading while I gathered all his things. I shoved him and his stuff out the door. A friend of his came to pick him and his things up at the same moment my friend showed up to help me change the locks.

The next day, I found out that Jose and his friends had gotten pulled over for running a red light, and every single one of them got deported. Karma is a bitch, one that I always want to be in my favor. After that phone call, I realized the secret hidey hole where I had been stashing cash wasn't so secret, after all. He had taken it all, every bill as well as the gallon jar where I had been saving loose change for over a year. I couldn't even report him.

But I didn't have time to cope with any of my new wounds. I had $6.71 in my bank account with a mortgage payment due, a stack of credit card bills piling up from my new business debt, and lawn season was officially over. I had to look for work, once again full-functioning in survivor mode.

I did, however, make note that instead of carrying a weapon for protection in the future, it may be a more effective strategy to pull out a dildo instead of a knife because that would possibly be more threatening than a gun or a knife.

Chapter 12

Thank you, ma'am, may I have another?

After Jose left, my life was hell, but I found another layer of what I was made of. I found a job at Golden Corral working dinner shifts and also a job at Home Depot working from 4 a.m. 'til 10 a.m., stocking shelves. My first lawn season was completely finished, and I had confided to my customers with whom I'd gotten close to tell them about my situation. Many of them helped me find odd jobs to increase my cash flow during the winter. Most of my customers were females who either chose to support female-owned business or simply didn't trust men being on their property.

For many, my lawn visits were the highlight of their day. They would make snacks or have cold beer for me, then we'd sit on the porch to visit for a while. I delighted in the freedom that I had to give customer service at the level these women deserved for MY business and my customers instead of working under a manager who didn't care about customer service at all.

As my customers turned into friends, I was often invited to meet their family and friends to share special occasions like birthdays, weddings, and funerals. They impacted my life just as much as I did theirs. I was surrounded by angels, really, even though things sucked a lot. I was better for it.

My first lawn season was over, and the time had come for me to learn how to run the business all by myself. To think about taking all of that on alone seemed insurmountable. I didn't even know how to put a trim line in my weed eater or sharpen a blade on my mower. I had no idea what I would do if anything broke down while I was out mowing. Hell, I couldn't even change a flat tire. Those machines were so heavy, and I would be lifting them all alone, one job after another, all day every day. How would I do bigger cleanup jobs? How would I use the chainsaw to do bigger trimming jobs? It was time to grow and expand. If some dude could figure out how to do all those things, I damn sure could, too. So, I did. I got to the point where I could do eight lawns in one day all by myself. Luckily for me, that year we had a drought, so I wasn't overwhelmed with work on a regular basis.

Then, in May, I finally graduated with my associate degree from the community college. I had worked so hard and finally gotten to the top. I wasn't the least bit embarrassed that a two-year degree had taken me four, when statistically, I should have been dead more than once throughout those years. Only I knew what I had sacrificed to get that diploma. Only I knew how many extra hours I had picked up, what I had given up to get there, or the time that I had put in to make it happen no matter what war was waging in my life. But, I had always felt like I owed it to school to be faithful to it because during those dark times, it was the only thing that kept me alive. Well, that and my Gracie.

My mom threw a beautiful graduation party with delicious snacks to enjoy with friends who had shared moments along the way. I invited friends I had made over the years as well as my lawn customers who had also been a pivotal part of my path getting there. I was so proud of graduating with my associate degree in May that I celebrated by enrolling in classes in a four-year university to continue toward my bachelor's degree beginning the following fall.

***

After all the brutal wounds I had received from the men in my life, I honestly believed my "picker" was inherently broken. I believed I was powerless and would never have any kind of a relationship with a man who would not harm me in some way. I had a long repetitive history of brief relationships with men that all ended very similarly. Something inside of me was done with being open to any new man in my life.

I had always been attracted to women for as long as I could remember, but I was never brave enough to explore that part of me, mostly from the guilt and shame that ensued daydreaming of it, imparted by years of programming by the church. It was yet another thing I buried deeply inside of me to be addressed later. Then, after so many terrible experiences with men, I thought, "I am obviously cursed with men. Maybe it's because I should never be with one. Maybe it's because I am gay!" The bad taste left in my mouth from Jose's abusive narcissistic behavior was enough to kick the door wide open into exploring it.

One night, I was outside working on one of my machines when one of my lawn customers called to invite me to meet her and a friend for dinner. I was so happy to have the invitation! I had just finished a long, hot week working outside, and it happened to be a Friday night. Eagerly accepting, I washed the grease off my hands, changed my clothes, threw some mascara on and some hoop earrings in, and out the door I went. I had no idea I was about to meet the woman with whom I would share my first romance.

I was intrigued by Kasey the moment we met, and the interest was obviously mutual as dinner progressed. For me, she was the most perfect combination of masculine and feminine with her short blonde hair, the feminine curves of her body layered with stout muscles from years of weightlifting. The men's v-neck shirt she wore fit perfectly across her strong shoulders, just barely accenting the veins popping out of her biceps. I couldn't stop looking at her all through dinner, intrigued by her as well as what was being set aflame inside my being.

After dinner, we went back to Kasey's house to have drinks and hang out. I found it so fascinating that she owned her own semi and pulled loads to Colorado and New Mexico for Walmart. I found it fascinating that in her free time she was a powerlifter with national records. Weightlifting was one of the many passions we shared. As beers continued to flow on her outside patio, eventually the friend who had invited me to dinner challenged Kasey and I to an arm-wrestling competition, which neither of us would ever turn down. We squared up and started our match, a match that I ended up winning. Kasey said that was the moment she really fell in love with me because it was the first time anyone had ever beat her in arm wrestling.

The next day she had to pull a load that would keep her on the road for a few days, but we exchanged numbers with the intention to hang out when she got back. Our first hangout session, we made a date to go to the gym together and get lunch afterward, and I knew when she pulled up in her loud-ass Harley Davidson that I was about to get on a motorcycle ride I would never forget.

From that point forward, we spent hours on the bike having adventures, lifting weights together all the time, had romantic date nights, and I learned how to two-step for the first time. We traveled to New Mexico for the hot air balloon festival, and I got to see everything from the view of her big semi. After the festival, we rolled into the mountains of Colorado to get potatoes from a farm for her to haul back to Oklahoma City. Seeing the world through the eyes of a truck driver impacted me significantly.

As all my other relationships had, this one moved way too fast. Just a couple months after dating, she moved in (all the jokes about lesbians and U-hauls are true!), and shortly after that, the fairytale was over. We both drank a lot, and there was something about the wounds we both had buried deep inside that brought out the worst in each other whenever we coated them with booze. Both of us were a mess of infected, internal wounds from trauma buried deep, years before we met, and all it took was one drink for both of us to open a door into heavy binge-drinking, which led to nasty fights. The honeymoon was over just about as quickly as it had started. It ended with a screaming match and her moving her stuff right back out, right in the middle of my first fall semester in my new degree program. Once again, school and work became my refuge.

My southside neighborhood was going downhill and houses were going up for sale all over. A slumlord bought several of those houses and rented them out cheap, which brought a new wave of insecurity to my street. There were gunshots fired, cars vandalized or stolen, houses looted, people fighting, and constant drug traffic. The guy who lived in the house catty-corner to my driveway was a 19-year-old meth addict on house arrest who lived with his mom. Day and night, he was taking apart machines and computers and putting them back together, pacing in endless circles around his house.

Drug dealers moved in across the street from me, and there was drug-related traffic at all hours. Another neighbor kept their pitbull on a short, heavy chain, barely alive enough to stand on wobbly legs before collapsing in his own excrement. The owners were also meth addicts who took the same level of care of their children as they did their dog, and no matter how often I called CPS and animal welfare, nobody ever came. This was no longer a safe neighborhood for me or my lawn business.

There I was, yet again, with the heaviness of a full semester, the heaviness of running a business myself, the heaviness of financial lack (the drought had made it less difficult to run things by myself but impossible to save for the winter), and yet another fucking heartbreak. One of the pieces of mail I received that rainy morning was a notice that my mortgage rate was going up *again* because of my homeowner's insurance, thanks to the worsening condition of the neighborhood. This was the third time my monthly payment had increased. This reality seemed like a far stretch from the good ol' American Dream. This did not feel like a dream. It seemed like no matter how hard I worked, I never got ahead. I coasted by to finish finals, and I remember the meltdown I had the day after I turned in my final projects. I just felt done.

Nothing had gone as I had intended with my house or my financial plan to move forward. This was not moving me toward the feeling I had while I was in Cozumel. I felt so trapped. I had so much pain inside of me. Kasey had given me a Walther PK-380 as an early gift for my birthday before our relationship blew to smithereens. The day after finals, I woke to a cold, rainy day and a mailbox full of bills from so much debt, which reminded me that my birthday was a couple days away. My birthday had always been a source of pain for me. Pain from everything had become surreal.

    I took my gun and its box of bullets and went for a long drive. I drove back to the field where I was raped, only to discover that it was now a housing sub-division, so I drove further into another small town, where I parked in another vacant field out in the country. I sat for a long time looking at the trees and crying, with the gun resting next to the box of bullets in my front seat, facing me, looking right at me. I had no idea how to load it, and I had never shot one. We just stared at each other for a long time while I cried. I had already attempted suicide twice before; this would be my third attempt. *I couldn't even kill myself right. I couldn't do anything right.*

    I made a deal with myself that I would give life a chance for one more day because I thought about Gracie, and I thought about the promise I had made to myself about riding motorcycles in more foreign countries. I couldn't quit before making it there again. I had experienced true joy. I knew it existed. That part of me had died, the ember that had always been slowly burning, the one that ignited when I took that rogue trip at 19 years old.

    At one point, I got a message from Jose saying that I was the love of his life, and that he would do anything to make things right with me, and was there any way that I could help him get back across the border into the United States? I told him to fuck himself. A week after that incident, sugar mysteriously made its way into the gas tank of my expensive zero-turn mower, which I discovered when the engine quit in the middle of mowing a five-acre lot on a hot day. I assumed it had to be him somehow, all the way from Mexico making a phone call to someone in the city who could keep an eye on my daily routine. It made me wonder what my rapist would do when he got out of prison one day.

Chapter 13

Sharianne Carson

Right before lawn season ended, I was mowing in a neighborhood in Yukon when a lady came out of the rental property where I was working. I had no idea who the owner of the place was because I was hired by another regular customer to go mow it once a week and send him an invoice for it. She informed me that she was the owner of that property and several others, and that she was also the owner of a bar named Edna's that her mother had started decades ago. I had never heard of it.

"Have you ever bartended?" she asked me.

"Not officially, but I have always mixed drinks at parties, and I've been told that my drinks are the best," I said.

"It's easy to learn, and I'm happy to teach you everything you need to know. A liquor license is cheap and easy to get. I am looking for a daytime bartender on Saturdays and Sundays. Would you be interested?" This literally landed in my lap in perfect timing. I had just enough time to train before the service industry got busy for the holidays.

This ended up fitting like a glove. I loved bartending, was good at it, and the money was great. The regulars who came in there had been regulars for years, and they were very generous with how they tipped me. They sometimes brought me food. The woman who had come out of the rental property that day to ask me about my interest in bartending was Edna's daughter, Tammy. Edna wasn't able to run the business anymore because of Alzheimer's, but I had the pleasure of meeting Edna and hearing a bit about her story.

She started Edna's in 1989 with her mother, and when they first opened their doors, Edna's brother came from Texas to hang a dollar on the wall to wish her the best of luck for her new business. From that point on, a trend began for customers to hang dollars to commemorate special moments. After nearly 30 years of that, every space of the walls and ceiling were completely covered with dollar bills that had special notes, names, or pictures sketched on them by customers who wanted to leave a piece of them with Edna's forever. When I met Edna, I knew she wasn't herself because of how her mind disease had begun to take over, but her real essence still shone through.

One day, she and Tammy came in to bring some kitchen supplies, and I asked Edna if there was a motto or a favorite quote that denoted her values that she ran her business by. She said, "Girl, my bar has always been a place where everyone gets treated equally. It doesn't matter where people come from. When they walk in, they are home, and they are treated equally in my bar."

The owner's nephew was supposed to work with me as security, kitchen help, etc., but if he ever showed up, he showed up stoned and was usually useless on the job. When it was busy, it got crazy being the only person there to make drinks, wash dishes, and also make food. Sometimes, I would have my bar top full, patio full, and a group of ten people would walk in for a wedding party or something, and every single person wanted food. With one hand, I made hamburgers, chicken wings, fried pickles, nachos, and with the other, I poured drinks and ran the register. At the end of my shifts I was spent, but I had a fat wad of cash in my pocket and drinks waiting for me on the other side of the bar. I became close friends with everyone working there, and we were all like a family. Plus, it was so much fun. I ended up working more day shifts, and it pulled me through my off-season perfectly.

In my off-season, my lawn customers also had odd jobs for me: house sitting and pet sitting for holiday vacations, deep cleaning for holiday parties, hanging Christmas lights, helping organize spare rooms and garages, translating documents or websites into Spanish for their businesses, trimming trees, or painting their spare bedrooms.

Then, on one boring Saturday that seemed the same as all the rest, I was lighting my first cigarette after opening the bar for another day, when I heard the front door open and someone sit down at my bar top. An unfamiliar voice ordered a Coors light, and when I turned around to see what face went with it, I met Sharianne Carson.

I was frozen. She was the most beautiful lesbian I had ever seen. The gay community in OKC was small, and I had definitely never seen her out anywhere in Gaytown. I also discovered that I was very shy with women, and I hadn't fully explored that part of me since I'd only had a relationship with one woman thus far. I pretended like everything was normal and avoided eye contact while serving her beer to avoid any awkward attempts of extra communication.

She started coming in regularly, and I found out she was a friend in the group of my regular customers. I followed this routine of ignoring her presence until one day when my shift was ending. All of her friends tabbed out and left, but she stayed. I had my back facing the bar while I counted down my drawer, but in the mirror above the register, I could see Shari with her chin resting on her hand, propped up by her elbow, watching me do my shift-closing duties.

Fuck, she's totally going to try to talk to me.

Then I heard it. "Do you have anything going on when you get off?" My palms started to sweat, and my throat closed up. I pretended like I was so surprised, like it was the first time I'd ever had any engagement with her, caught off guard and clueless about why she was asking.

"I've had several invites to go do stuff, but I still haven't decided which one I will be a part of," I informed her. I never was good at game-playing. What were the rules? Was I supposed to play hard to get?

"Why do you ask?"

"Well, I was going to see if after your shift you'd like to sit on this side of the bar and let me buy you a drink."

Inside of me I felt party balloons and confetti go berserk. My legs were shaking.

"Sure, a pre-gamer sounds cool," I nonchalantly said, but when I turned back around to finish counting my drawer, nobody could see me grinning from ear to ear.

During the first round of drinks at Edna's we agreed that we were hungry, so she took me to her favorite food place called Cousin's, another classic Oklahoma City place that was well known for its fantastic food and bar service. We discovered how many things we had in common. The coolest connection was that she went to Cozumel every year to go diving, and Cozumel was the island where I had lived at 19 years old. Our conversation never broke stride until the bartender called out for the last call, and we realized we had been there in that conversation for six straight hours. She took me back to my car, we had a steamy goodnight kiss, and the rest is history. I had no idea when I went to work that day at the bar that I would meet the person I would spend nearly five years in a relationship with, and that this person would so immensely impact and empower my life in such a positive way that it would change my destiny forever.

Randy drifted back into my life, and we agreed to be roommates in my house since we already knew each other. He was a huge help running my business. We worked out a deal with his pay from working and the rent at the house. I was there at my house working with him Monday through Thursday, and then each Thursday night I would pack a bag to go stay with Shari through the weekend. Gracie was miserable with this arrangement because she hated to share a space with all of Randy's cats. On top of my lawn business and working weekends, I still juggled classes. After a few months of this dance, Shari suggested that Gracie and I move in with her.

"If you totally rent out your house and have Randy run the business from that property, you will free yourself of so much burden, then you can focus on finishing school and moving forward with your goals and dreams." She was right. My house and my business weighed me down a lot, like I was treading mud for so long. I was so tired. I had been tired for so long, but I was never still long enough to let myself acknowledge it. I trusted Randy to run my business. All my customers knew him and loved his quality of work; he knew my lawn routes, and he was trustworthy. We talked out details, and everyone agreed that it seemed like a perfect fit for him to take the house furnished and me to transition a few of my basic belongings and Gracie to Shari's cozy little house.

Randy was happy to live alone, and we agreed that I would work with him only one or two days a week on the heaviest days while I took a full-time semester at UCO so that I could be on track to graduate the following spring, finally. My job at Edna's came to a screeching halt when the owner made big changes that forced my regulars to go elsewhere. That cut my income down to about one fourth of what it had been. I chose to let go of my job and just focus on school and working part time for my business, focusing mainly on the administrative part of it.

It was a great setup at least to finish out that lawn season, and then we could recalibrate over the holidays to figure out what needed to be adjusted for the following spring. It seemed to work really well until suddenly it didn't. When I was halfway through a crazy full semester with five classes on my shoulders, Randy's train went off the tracks. He was angry all the time, which was his normal way of being, but this time was different. He stopped answering my calls and texts. I let it coast for a couple of weeks because I knew him well enough to know that sometimes he would be totally reclusive and incapable of connecting with the outside world. I understood him because I was often the same way. Then, I started getting calls from customers. Randy had stopped mowing.

I thought he had died. I immediately drove over to the house one day to find out what was going on, expecting to find a murder scene upon entering my house. I hadn't been over there in a long time. When we worked together, he had just picked me up from Shari's. When I walked through the front door, this awful, rotten stench just about knocked me off my feet. I carried on, gagging, stuffing my mouth full of the tail of my shirt, to find Randy alive but extremely sick buried under blankets on my living room floor.

There were dozens upon dozens of cats in my house. I recognized his kitties from when I met him in the apartment complex. He had those cats for years and had moved them with him from California to Oklahoma when he took the job as manager at the apartment complex where we had met. But he started to hoard cats, strays from outside, strays that he found while working in other parts of town. They were inbreeding, and many were sick. They were on top of furniture, hiding in corners, hiding under furniture and in kitchen cabinets. There was urine, feces, and vomit everywhere matted in the carpet, and they had urinated into the air registers on the floor, so those were now full of cat urine. Every time the system kicked on for either heat or air conditioner, the poisonous toxins would get blown out of the vents and fill the house. That's what had made Randy sick.

The cats also sprayed everything. Every piece of furniture was saturated with cat spray. In my master bedroom, I had a queen-sized bed with a beautiful comforter and pillows, a matching curtain that covered the door leading to the patio outside my room, and everything else in the room matched. All of it was completely ruined. All the furniture in my guest room was completely ruined. In the closets where I stored spare clothes for different seasons: winter clothes with heavy coats and sweaters, an assortment of dress clothes for interviews and presentations with different colored heels and my box of jewelry that mix-and-matched with each dressy outfit was all ruined. All my clothes either had a yellow hue to them from the toxins in the air, or had been directly sprayed on.

All my boxes of books from years of university coursework, my extra towels and bedding and boxes of other things in the spare closets, my kitchen cabinets and everything in them. . . were ruined. The cats had wandered in and out of all the cabinets high and low, and urinated or pooped on everything. There were even dead cats inside of my couch, and I discovered that when some of his favorite cats died of a lung infection, he put them in the freezer because he couldn't let them go.

Randy was sick. Completely incapable of functioning. He had stopped going to work. My lawn schedule was now more than two weeks behind, and there was no way I could drop everything I was doing to catch up, not with my class load in the middle of midterm exams and presentations. I couldn't. I simply couldn't.

The iron statue finally broke. My lawn books were a mess. My finances were a mess. My house was ruined. My cup was empty. I was done. My house was going to cost several thousands of dollars to fix, money that I obviously didn't have. There was no point in suing Randy; he was broke and mentally ill on top of it. I didn't want to live in that house again and would have to spend thousands to make it rentable. I wanted out. I was so tired. With the only money I had left in my hand, I could either pay one more mortgage payment and then figure out how to keep chasing money during the winter, or invest it in a bankruptcy and wash my hands of it all. I chose the latter.

I walked out of my bankruptcy hearing with my Jeep Liberty and the few belongings I already had at Shari's, including Gracie. I lost *everything* else. My truck, my lawn equipment, my house, everything I had nearly sold my soul for over five years of sweating and bleeding to dig myself out of holes. All the overtime I had worked at so many different jobs to chase payments for these things was money that I could have just put into a shredder.

This was all a new rock bottom for me, and I sunk into a suicidal low where I would teeter for months. I relived the powerlessness from my rape like it had happened just the day before. After those traumas when I was 20 and my collapse into drugs afterward, the way that I had pushed forward with work, school, home, and my business was symbolic to me of the power I was trying to get back. I had been building a castle, but I had built it on a cracked foundation by not doing the inner work to heal wounds and reconcile the broken pieces inside of me. I just kept stacking more and more shit on top of it until one day the Jenga tower had to tumble.

I also realized that I had made those outer accomplishments as a major part of my identity, so when I lost them, I had no idea who I really was. Living with Shari was a choice while I rented out my house, but it became the only place I had to go after my bankruptcy, and once again, I felt I was on the verge of homelessness. I felt terribly vulnerable. It meant trusting her to provide for me during an incredibly difficult time. Any time I let anyone try to do that, they hurt me somehow. A rug would get pulled out from under my feet.

Shari and I had met in the bar scene, and that's where we made our home. After my bankruptcy was finalized, I delved more deeply into a world of booze than I ever thought possible. I was convinced that as long as I never blacked out, got abusive, or got a DUI, that I didn't have a problem and that it didn't cause problems with anyone else, either. I never wanted to be present. I couldn't face anything that was going on outside and especially not inside of me.

I was hellishly destructive with everyone and everything around me. Shari had gotten me a connection for a job at a ritzy restaurant in OKC via her friendship with the general manager of one of the locations, and the night before I was supposed to officially finish my orientation, Shari and I were wasted at a house party. Two guys at the house pulled me into the bathroom where they had lines of coke. I had never officially done coke before. Shari walked into the bathroom right as we were finishing our lines, and shit hit the fan, giving way to a screaming match as I drove us home drunk.

I was up all night long, enjoying the little bit of coke those guys had sent home with me. When Shari got up, saw the baggy, and discovered that I had blown off my last day of orientation, we got into another huge fight. This is when intervention came for me at this new rock bottom.

"I am willing to empower you in any way I can so that you can make it to the other side of this, but I will not enable you to destroy your life. If you don't make a change, then you will have to find somewhere else to go."

It was this same weekend that I went to my friend Brittany's house to tell her about my crazy fuck ups. She always listened and never ever judged. We had met in a management class in our final stretch of undergraduate coursework and were always hanging at her house doing homework together and drinking vodka or whiskey on her balcony. We were on her patio drinking, and while I was swirling my ice cubes around in my Crown Royal, she said, "Your 28th birthday is coming up. What do you think our 30s will be like? What do you want to be different then?"

Jeezus, her question made me look, truly look at my life, and be honest about how it felt to be alive both in the past and in that moment. It terrified me. Tears started to fall, and then they started to flood. I'd kept myself busy for so long, I never had time to look inward. Or feel.

"It hurts too much to think about living until my 30th birthday," I confessed. That truth spoken out loud scared us both.

After I'd given my all to build a home on the outside and everything had crumbled, I realized nothing would change in my life until I began to look inward to rebuild the home on the inside. The foundation of building something magical both on the outside and the inside was me, my belief systems about myself. As long as my foundation was cracked, anything I tried to build on it would fall. This was my lightbulb moment; on the balcony, over that glass of crown royal. I finally admitted that no matter who came into my life to break pieces, it was ultimately my responsibility to put them back together. Until I started doing so, nothing about my life would ever change.

Chapter 14

My lightbulb moment

A few days later I was scared to death walking into the first session with my new therapist. Why was I so scared? It was time to start looking at the foundation of what I had inside. I had no idea where to start. I knew that starting this path of healing was going to hurt. It was going to require opening up some chambers that had been closed for years, some that had been closed nearly my whole life.

When I looked inside, it was like a labyrinthian mansion that belonged to a hoarder, and there was stuff packed in every room from the floor to the ceiling. It went so far back that I couldn't even see the depth of it. All I could do was start with what was right in front of me, one thing at a time.

The trauma bombs that had been set off at different times of my life had left a colossal mess, and leaving it all there as it was had caused massive infections inside of me. These infections manifested in cycles of codependency, self-destructive binges of alcohol and food, unhealthy friendships, horrible sleep habits, and making poor life decisions that kept me unstable financially, emotionally, and physically.

Living in a state of dysfunction, pain, chaos, and anger had become my "normal," and to create a new "normal" meant facing monsters and reopening wounds so that I could clean them out and let them heal properly. My belief systems would change, my reality on the outside of me would change, my relationships would shift, therefore shifting my sense of belonging within certain communities.

I was scared because even though my way wasn't working, it was comfortable. I knew the scenery of the path I had been on for such a long time, and even though chaos and pain were a miserable way to live, I at least knew what to expect from them. What was on the other side of a path of healing was completely foreign to me. But I was ready to go into the unknown. I was desperate for the change. My life had become unbearable.

I felt like I had nothing in common with anyone, that I was the only one who had gone through my traumas, and I was terrified about opening up about anything inside because surely if my therapist knew how broken and damaged I really was, then she would leave me, too. The betrayal of my mom having an affair with my boyfriend and then being kidnapped and raped was my introduction into adulthood with no foundation or knowledge of what being a happy, healthy adult really looked like, and then I had to find my own way through all the rubble in what seemed like a cold and cruel place.

***

Once I was able to start opening up to my therapist, emotions started to come up like a tidal wave. It was common for me to go on drinking binges after therapy sessions because of the feelings that surfaced. It's easier to stay numb. When I came into her office with big open wounds on my elbows and knees, she took one look at me as I sat on her couch, and started chuckling from a place of compassion.

"Those nasty wounds wouldn't have anything to do with a bottle of vodka that you may have found after our last intensive session, would it?"

Yep, I had buried myself in a fifth as soon as I got home and had fallen outside in the driveway, tripping over my own feet when I'd tried to go talk to a neighbor's kitty.

It seemed like every time I got one chamber emptied out, it cleared the view to three more rooms stuffed full of more feelings to sort through. I felt hopeless at times, and I wanted to walk out and quit many times, but I was already too far in to quit.

We built trust to the point that it was time to dig into the kidnapping and the rape. We had two-hour sessions at this point because an hour wasn't enough to get into the chamber and then get back out. She went with me back to that Saturday morning and re-lived every detail. I let her see and feel with me, and then one day she invited me to take part in a Monday night group therapy session with other women who had been through similar traumas. This was a game changer for me.

This was the first time that I formed solidarity with other women who wanted to heal and thrive and then find their new life path. I learned that I was not the only one who had my fears and insecurities. I was sitting in a group of women who understood every step, but who also had their own story to tell and honored and validated the uniqueness of mine.

I learned in group therapy that I was not the only person who had experienced these things throughout life. Talking openly about such intimate things absolutely set off PTSD triggers, commencing night terrors, flashbacks, panic attacks, triggering food, drug, and alcohol binges. But I shared those, too. By learning from members of the group, I started finding ways to change those patterns a little bit at a time, and we found ways to help each other.

I still had my private session once a week, but attended this Monday night group session for a few weeks. During our final session, we talked about fear, how our traumas changed our view of life by the fears that were instilled because of it, and how those fears held us back. We each took turns expressing our fears to the group and were able to see how one's fear held that person back from living a truly fulfilled life, which in turn made me see how much *my* fears held *my* life back. My fears included: fear of never feeling safe and secure, fear of coming out fully with my story and still not being enough, fear of never having consistent income, fear of being raped or assaulted again, fear of being hurt again in relationships, fear of getting to the other side of healing but nothing better being there for me, fear that I would be stuck in Oklahoma forever with dead-end, boring job opportunities, fear that I wouldn't be loved or accepted unconditionally by anyone ever, and fear that I would never have a chance to change my ending.

At the end of our session, the therapist gave each of us a framed quote that said, "Everything you want is on the other side of fear. – George Addair."

When I got home, I hung that frame by my light switch in my room so that I would see it every morning, every night, and dozens of times in between. It challenged me to connect with my intentions for everything I did. It challenged me to keep venturing into unknowns, even if that meant making one small change at a time, like taking a new path when going for a walk, having the courage to talk to someone new, or releasing control. Gosh, if a ship at sea changes its compass the tiniest degree, its destination is entirely different.

The more I was growing and healing, the less I was okay with my current life and the contents of it. Shari and I started growing apart. Her lifestyle was one embedded in the bar, and that was starting to fall out of alignment with the direction I was going. To do so much work in therapy and then drink was as effective as doing an intense workout at the gym and then hitting the drive-thru for fast food. I also felt like I had less and less in common with friendships that revolved around the bar. I wanted to have real conversations about real shit, and that rarely happened in my friendships that were embedded in the bar scene.

I graduated from UCO with my business degree in June of 2014, and Shari and her friends threw me an unforgettable graduation party. I wasn't ashamed that a four-year degree had taken me ten years because I knew how many times, statistically, I should have been dead along the way.

I spent the summer looking for jobs that required undergraduate degrees, thinking that some magic door for a better opportunity would open, but it didn't. The job interviews I got were for minimum wage-paying entry-level positions doing basic tasks, work I would have been excruciatingly bored with. After having run my own operation for nearly five years, I had no motivation at all to say yes to a job like that, where I would make in one week what I could have made in one day running my business. To go from the freedom of self-employment to an office prison where I would be told when to take a piss break, I just couldn't do it.

I was venting about all of it to my friend Katie who lived in Connecticut, and she said, "Why don't you come here for a while? Stay on my couch. If you like it, you can stay, and we can figure out other housing arrangements. If you don't, you can leave, and you can say you tried, but at least you'll have a new experience. No bad could come out of it."

She was right. I needed a break from everything, from my relationship with Shari, from Oklahoma, from the bar scene and so much alcohol, and from my therapy. It was a huge step of courage to break out and make such a drastic change, but the framed quote next to my bed reminded me that it was okay to push myself outside of my comfort zone. *Everything you want is on the other side of fear.*

I told Shari that night that I was leaving for Connecticut. The next day, after shoving a couple of boxes and a suitcase in the backseat of my jeep, I pulled out to start my 27-hour drive to Connecticut.

It was nearly mid-October when I arrived there, and the scenery of the changing trees was stunning. The colors were so vibrant that I swore they had to be a painting or a calendar. Everything about Connecticut was beautiful. The way they spoke English, the architecture of the homes, the structure of neighborhoods and small towns, the narrow two-lane highways that wound through the hills and were covered with color-changing leaves.

Katie's best friend Erin lived close by, and she got me an entry-level position at the assembly plant where she was a floor manager, and that was the job that taught me how to build electronics. I'd never done anything like it, but I discovered I loved it and was really good at it. It didn't pay very much, but it paid enough for me to be responsible for my part of things and have adventures, and it gave me challenges that were fulfilling.

I experienced winter in the northeast, and the first snowfall of the season was tall enough to bury my whole vehicle. I learned things didn't close down for snow days like Oklahoma did. Katie brought me some of her military gear to bundle up in so that we could dig my jeep out. Luckily for us, my jeep was a four-wheel drive, so I could get us both around in snowy weather.

A couple months into my time there, Katie, her boyfriend, and I took a day trip to New York City, where we rode a train for the first time ever. I saw Times Square and Central Park, and then we went to eat pizza in Brooklyn.

Then, I took a road trip to Rhode Island. I remember driving down a long, long stretch of highway that was surrounded by stark blue ocean water as far as I could see on both sides. I've always been scared of the ocean, and driving across that vast body of water paralyzed me with fear. I had that steering wheel gripped with my sweaty hands, and I kept thinking about turning back, but I had nowhere to pull around. I had no choice but to feel all the feels until I made it to where I was going. It was the first time I ever saw a snowy beach, and the ocean around Rhode Island was the most stark blue of any water I had ever seen.

It was time to go back to Oklahoma. I'd been gone four months, and my time away had brought me so much insight about my life. I felt ready to go back to therapy, go back to Shari and our relationship to see if the time apart could help us restore something now, and I wanted to be with Gracie. My trip alone just driving 27 hours to get there had given me back some power. If I could face those long stretches of highway over the ocean, ride trains, be independent again, dig my jeep out of snow, and face life a different way all on my own, I could keep facing it in Oklahoma. I was ready to step into a new chapter with new power and go to my next step of healing in my therapy sessions. I had only just begun, and as hard as it was to do the work, it felt amazing. The more work I did, the better I felt. Had I never just started somewhere desperate for a change, nothing would have ever changed and I would have missed out on all of that.

Chapter 15

Keep Rising

"There's nowhere you can be that isn't where you're meant to be…"

– John Lennon

When I got back from Connecticut that February, I picked up my therapy sessions again and felt hopeful about seeing what the job market looked like. I got part-time gigs through a temp agency that gave me a chance to see what was out there until a friend that I went to UCO with called to tell me that her husband's bank had a full-time position open that paid a bonus for people who were bilingual and an extra bonus for working the 2nd shift, which I discovered was my favorite shift from when I'd worked at OnCue.

I knew that the job was going to be in a call center, which was a first for me, and I was excited about trying something new. I did not, however, know that the job in the call center included taking calls from people who were behind on mortgage payments. I did not know that when they got me out on the floor, they were going to put me on the outbound dialer to make phone calls to Spanish-speaking customers who were behind on house payments. I had gone through a bankruptcy myself, and I knew how stressful it was to live every day behind financially, and I hated my job every day. That was one of the worst jobs I ever had, but it served a huge purpose in forever changing my path.

One day in the break room I met a girl named Tiara who told me about the master's degree she was working on at OU. Even though my undergraduate degree had taken me so long, I loved the journey, and although I had enjoyed celebrating my graduation, I missed school. If she could do it, why couldn't I?

As soon as I got off work that day, I went home to check out the program. We were just starting summer break, and I was sliding in last minute to see if I could start the following fall. The program had three tracks: human relations, which focused on social justice and social work; human resources; and one in which extra hours could be taken to go the psychology route to become a licensed counselor at a master's level. I applied and in the meantime, I kept going to the terrible job I despised.

It hadn't taken me long to shift right back into the drinking cycle once I got back to Oklahoma City. I felt powerless to control it as long as Shari and I were together. I was right back next to her at the bar with all our mutual friends, and right back into the chamber of alcohol. I went to work hungover every day and counted down the minutes 'til I clocked out on Friday, then drove straight to the bar after work to start my weekend of checking out. The drinking made me feel miserable, and so did my job, but doing something I hated just made me want to check out that much more. It was a terrible cycle.

One day I came home for lunch to find my acceptance letter from OU in the mailbox! I danced around the kitchen with Gracie. I wanted something new so bad. I was going to celebrate my 30th birthday in a few months, and this was definitely one way to commemorate a huge positive shift in my life to welcome a new decade. I couldn't make myself go back to work that day, so I didn't. In fact, I never went back at all.

When Shari got home from work, I met her at the bar and shared my news. I was nervous about what she would say about me quitting my job because she had carried me financially for so long. I wanted to start doing my part, but I just couldn't do something that I hated. No paycheck would ever be enough to make up for how poisonous it felt inside to spend my life doing something empty and meaningless. Not only was she immensely supportive of my decision to go back for my master's, she also told me not to worry about income. She wanted me to just focus on my therapy, keep healing and growing, and allow myself to have the full, happy, college experience that I deserved. I looked forward to figuring out what my life path would be, being mentored by my professors, having the full classroom experience with peers, and building healthy friendships with other adults in the master's program.

I had definitely never had that. When I'd lived in the apartments by UCO right after my rape, I would walk through campus and watch all the students partake in game days, scavenger hunts, parties, movie nights, and other fun social engagements, and it made me feel so bitter and angry that I couldn't experience that. Shari's empowerment gave me a chance to recreate that experience for myself, so I did.

I committed to 30 days of being sober so that I could think about what I wanted for my life. I was tired of feeling like shit all the time. I saved some of my checks from the short period I worked at that awful call center. I have always been intrigued by women's bodybuilding, so I got a membership at a gym and hired a trainer. I wanted to eat clean, feel better about myself, and channel the things going on inside toward something empowering like heavy weightlifting. So I did, and I felt so great after 30 days away from alcohol that I decided to do another 30, which is when my semester started. I was still going to therapy sessions, but I didn't need to go once a week as often. I rarely had flashbacks or nightmares or night terrors, although my anxiety was still bad.

I'll always remember my walk through the Physical Science building to the first night of my first class and how scared I was to do something so new and big. I didn't feel like I was smart enough or ready enough or well-written enough to do higher education.

If you try it and it's not for you, at least you'll know. You can say you tried and learned something new about yourself.

My professor was a high-strung Palestinian woman who would be another person to cross my path and change my course forever. She taught me how to think. It was as if that woman flipped on every switch in my brain and ran all through me with her torch to set something on fire. She was so difficult, intimidating, tough, and mean, and I fell in love with the process of learning to a deeper level than I had before. I couldn't wait to come back for more every week. I was terrified of doing my first paper because I was self-conscious of my writing and was sure that my grade would reflect it.

I put my whole heart and soul into that paper, more than any paper in my previous 10 years of classes. A few days after I turned it in, I was in the library studying when Dr. H walked up to my table. My legs started shaking. Shit, she was so scary. She asked if I had time to meet with her privately in her office. When I went, it turns out she was extremely impressed with my paper, and she asked if I would be interested in helping her do research for a book project. I told her I had no idea how to do research, but she was willing to teach me everything I needed to know.

I knew it wasn't going to be paid, but I wanted to do it for the learning experience. By learning how to do research, I found out that I loved it. I loved it more than anything I had ever done, and through the things I did for her, I got really, really good at it. When the semester was over, I was offered a job as a research assistant for my department starting spring semester.

As soon as I finished finals for that semester, I celebrated my 30th birthday, and I took time to really celebrate how far I had come since my rock bottom point just two years before when my 28th was looming and I felt so hopeless about life in general. I stayed sober my entire semester, right through my 30th birthday. I wanted to welcome a new decade by feeling great. Everything that I had lived through in my 20s is more than what most people experience in their whole lives. I could see just how far I had come since the rape, my time in rehab, my bankruptcy, even my adventure in Connecticut.

When the new semester started, I was assigned to a different professor, which was divine placement from the universe. I fell into the hands of Dr. D, another angel who would impact my life forever. He had his doctorate in psychology and had run his own practice for a long time. He was published many times over, and not only would I help him do research for the publications he was working on, but I would also help him organize the notes he wrote on napkins, which mapped out the chapters for his next book. I couldn't read any of his writing, but he would read his notes out loud while I transcribed.

Dr. D was an angel on earth and highly revered, not for being a jackass like other tenured professors, but because he had earned it by being an authentically kind and empathic person. Being exposed to so much material in his field also had a huge part to play in my transformation because I was introduced to the work of Carl Rogers, who was the father of person-centered therapy.

Reading hundreds of pages of Carl Rogers' work was just what my soul needed. Working under Dr. D was impactful for me; not only was I getting paid to do something that I loved to do by researching, but I was growing through my classwork and his mentorship. After Shari, he was the second person I had ever met who actually listened to me, and he was the first man who I felt safe with.

After seven months of being broken up with alcohol, I got sucked back into a hurricane of alcohol in the bar scene with Shari, and figured out quickly that my commitment to my coursework did not leave room for binge drinking and hangovers. I'd felt more amazing than I ever thought possible throughout my sober months. I was so mad at myself for taking steps backward, but it showed me for sure that whenever I was with Shari and in her house, I could not stay away from alcohol. I started to become conscious enough to recognize that alcohol killed everything inside of me and around me. Why couldn't I just quit?

I called my mom to vent one morning after a weekend of heavy drinking, and she offered to pick me up so we could go to Lake Overholser. On our way there, we saw a sign in a front yard of a cozy house advertising a garage apartment for rent. My mom stopped and called the number immediately. This lady was home and invited us in on the spot to check it out. It was a little freestanding garage apartment in her backyard. The cost for the rent and utilities together was only a third of my simple monthly salary from the university.

"But I need to furnish it." I vocalized to mom my readiness to be on my own, so this was the perfect opportunity. She reminded me that she had recently gotten married and had many extra things that could be used for my place. I was scared to leave Shari's house where I'd hidden from the world for a long time, but I also knew that my cycles of alcoholism held me back from other things I wanted to do with my life.

Everything you want is on the other side of fear.

I was ready for the leap. It was time to keep pushing. My mom pulled out her checkbook and took care of the deposit and first month of rent right then. From there, we went to a big garage sale where we found a perfect kitchen table and chairs and other things I needed. We found a bed on clearance at the furniture store of a distant relative who let me buy it on credit and pay for it with my first two paychecks. We went to my mom's house for kitchen stuff, sheets, blankets, and pillows, and in just a couple days I had my new place all set up. I was on my own again in my own space for the first time in years. It felt like bliss!

We were just starting spring semester and then my job assisting Dr. D would end, so I would only have paychecks until mid-May. I was scared about what I would do over the summer to pay my rent, but at the last minute it all worked out! As we approached finals week, Dr. D told me that he had pulled some strings for me to get paid for work in a different department. That department needed a website translated from Spanish to English so that they could collaborate on a project with a university in Peru. I would not have a lapse in my university employment since I would do the translation over my summer break.

Absolutely everything worked out, and it didn't start moving until I said I was ready for a change. That was one moment in my life that showed me that I shouldn't wait for things around me to start changing in order for me to start moving. It's the other way around.

That summer is when my rapist got out of prison on parole. I loved that my new little home was hidden. Nobody could find me there, and my mail still went to

Shari's. I could never have my name affiliated with an address.

I got to the point in my healing that I thought I wanted to go into psychology. I felt I had something to give back to someone else because of where I was in my journey. By exposing myself to so much material in the field of psychology and by working with Dr. D on his research projects, I decided that maybe my career field would be psychology. So, that summer I did the translation work, read lots of psychology books, took my summer classes for psychology electives, and I still went to my therapy sessions every two weeks.

I poured myself into the field of psychology, doing research in the area of what happens in the brain when someone goes through a significant trauma. I connected with another professor in my department who had dedicated herself to working with women in prison, and I fell in love with the books she gave me of women's stories about serving time and the path in life that led them there. I thought many times that could have been me, but I just never got caught. I wished I could be on the inside with them to see what life looked like through their eyes. I learned so much from their stories.

The more I read, studied, grew, and healed, the more I aligned with what felt good inside of me. I wasn't sure that a path in psychology was meant for me. Dr. D and his other colleagues were eager to write letters of recommendation for me to get into a doctoral program. Dr. D said I could run my own practice one day, that I had everything it took to get there, and that he could show me how to do it from the business side. Sure, it was exciting to think about making several hundred dollars an hour, but that wasn't for me. The people who need help the most, those whose stories are unheard, are people who already have so many barriers to resources. Those were the people I wanted to work with. They were the ones I could relate to. I wanted to give my story to others who could be inspired by it, but did I need to go through five more years of school, get my PhD, and have my own office to do so? I loved school and loved learning, but I felt like it also restricted me from fully creating what I wanted. As long as I tried to create something via the university, I would be told how to do everything and in what format to do it, and that is a demotivator for me.

I took a heavy load the following fall along with my research assistantship, and about ten weeks into my semester I knew clearly that I didn't want to pursue a degree in psychology. I felt that it would restrict me from doing things my heart led me to. I was in Dr. D's office having a meltdown that day, and he just empathically listened to me, as always. He never interrupted, never judged, never tried to fix it. He felt what I felt and gave me wisdom if I asked for it. I told him I wanted to drop everything and go sell ice cream on a beach. He thought that was funny, but he said, "It's okay to have a bad day. You've got a heavy load. I will give you the rest of the week off from your office hours so that you can fill your cup, and you can turn in your assignments next week. But I won't let you drop your semester and throw what you've done in the trash. Let's meet next week to see if we can co-strategize some solutions."

When I went to my office hours next week, he presented a question to me, that—again--changed the course of my life. Looking back on previous life experiences, he asked, what had I done that made me the absolute happiest? I was quiet for awhile before answering.

"When I was 19 years old, I bought a one-way ticket to Cozumel, Mexico," I shared. "I had no plan, just showed up hoping to work and have a life like the locals. I rode motorcycles, lived with a local family, and learned how to live like them. I spoke Spanish all day and night and was completely immersed in a different culture. I promised myself I would find any way possible to travel again and finish what I started, but after I came back to the USA to start working and save some money, the trauma with my mom happened, and then six days after that, I was raped. I've been trying to put my life back together ever since. If I could find a way to make a living doing something I love while traveling, I would do it with my whole heart until I take my last breath."

His eyes sparkled when I said that. He was silent and thoughtful for a moment, and then he said, "How would you feel about taking a semester to study abroad? We can work out a way for you to fulfill your coursework projects remotely so that you can do it while you live somewhere else. Joanne in the study abroad office is from Bogotá and might have a connection for you in Colombia. Does this interest you at all?"

YES! To travel to a new country, engage in Spanish all day and night, and continue to do research--which I loved--and still be able to work on my degree? Absolutely. Fireworks went off like crazy inside my soul! I went to find Joanne immediately. She said she knew a lady who lived in a village called Jardín, about three hours south of Medellín. The woman was the director of a special science project for a rural school. It was possible I could do an internship there and then do writing projects to document my experience. All of it could be applied to my degree so that I could finish my Master of Human Relations.

I met with Joanne, who connected me to a guy named Hernan, who was from Jardín but currently living in Medellín. He and I kept in touch while I worked on my class material. The following spring semester, I was taking research classes, and the university really wanted to iron out details about my roundtrip flight, my internship details, and my housing arrangements.

I felt like all those details were trying to trap me in some way, like, how was I supposed to know how long to stay? What if I got there and didn't like it? Maybe I wouldn't want to do an internship there? I wouldn't know anything until I showed up. One of my research advisors wanted me to do some academic investigation about Colombia so that I could write a literature review about it before I went. I didn't feel right about that; I didn't want academic books to tell me what to think about Colombia before I even got there. I wanted to go there with a blank slate, without bias, without preconceived notions, and I wanted Colombian people in my everyday experiences to tell me about their Colombia.

I met Shari out at our local pub that night to catch up, as we were still living apart but remained close friends. As I sat there with her, I looked all around at the people sitting at the bar. They were the same people who had been sitting in the same seats every day, getting off work from the same job, taking the same routes to get there, drinking the same drinks, paying the same bar tabs, complaining about their same problems, and telling the same stories. As I looked at all these people, flashbacks of four years of bar scenes started whizzing by in my mind.

Jeezus, would that be me at 40? 50? With the same stories, the same heartaches I was trying to figure out the root of? *No fucking way.* All the regulars were at the bar top with their drinks, watching the news on TV. I wondered how much I was influenced by being born into systems? What would I think about life in general if I didn't have the family wounds? What would I think about life if I were born into a different political system? How would life look different if I were born into a different class system? What would life look like if we all just existed in spiritual form where nobody saw skin color or gender? What would the world be like if religion didn't exist, and people couldn't use "holy doctrine" to justify their hate toward other groups of people? To what degree was I programmed about all these things? Who would I be if I removed myself from the proximity of all of them and transplanted myself in a place where everything was radically different so that I could truly look at myself without the programming of those things hovering all around?

Buy a one-way ticket, I heard a faint whisper inside of myself. *You don't have to decide how long you want to be gone. You don't have to commit to anything with the university yet. Just go. You don't have to stay. You don't have to ever come back if you don't want to. You can do anything you want.*

So, I did as soon as I got home. I found a one-way ticket for Medellín, Colombia for $250.00 leaving on June 11th, 2017. I had a couple of months to finish my semester strong and prepare for a huge life change. I then re-learned a fact of humanity that I'd experienced at times before: people project their fears onto you and try to talk you out of doing things your heart desires.

"But what if…..it's dangerous? But what if…..you get kidnapped? But what if….you don't like it?" What if, what if, what if? Why do we always expect the worst things to happen when we go out of our comfort zone? What if the most magnificent thing thus far in our lives is waiting in the unknown?

The day before I was supposed to leave I was in my little cabin, packing. How should I pack for a one-way ticket? I had no idea what clothes to bring. I knew nothing about the climate where I was going. I had no idea if I would be there for a week and come back to Oklahoma or be there for a week and go somewhere else. I felt like I was falling backward, trusting that something or someone would catch me. What if nobody did?

Then, as I finished packing and was taking the smaller things off my walls so that I could leave the place clean, I saw the framed quote still hanging above the light switch by my door.

Everything you want is on the other side of fear.

I sat on my bed and held it in my hands for a long time. I went back in time to the Jenni who hit her rock bottom right before her 28th birthday, who was in so much pain, she couldn't imagine even being alive to celebrate her 30th birthday. I remembered how I'd walked through life in fear for years, scared of monsters that were under my bed, outside of my room, outside of my home, inside of me hiding in all those chambers. I recalled the Jenni who was scared to speak or make any new friends, talk in groups, try new things, or dream about anything bigger, and how this quote came at the perfect time in my counseling process. It had been the catalyst for me to push a little further every day and see what was beyond one more veil, and then one more.

When I went through my bankruptcy, it'd seemed like the most terrible thing that I could ever go through, but in that moment on my bed, holding that frame, reading that quote, I acknowledged out loud that it was the best thing that could have ever happened to me. I'd already had a house and filled it with stuff. If I still had all that, I wouldn't have the freedom to do what I was about to do. I was so grateful that I cut the cord to let that heavy load go, grateful for everything it taught me, for showing me what I don't want to experience again. I could drift with one simple bag on my back wherever my spirit called me to go.

Everything you want is on the other side of fear.

That implies that I must feel my fear, then. Being brave doesn't mean that one is fearless. It means you acknowledge fear and still go anyway. Courage can't exist in the absence of fear. I wished I could take that frame with me, but I knew I would now have to be wise about what I carried with me in my suitcase since my whole life would be on my back.

Oh, but I could still take that quote with me everywhere! I immediately went to 23rd Street to get it tattooed on my right forearm. I wanted to see it every single day to remind myself to keep pushing, keep growing, keep doing the work, and to not let anything ever get in my way. Before, fear paralyzed me and kept me on strings like a puppet. Because of my path of healing, growing, and expanding, I had begun to see fear as an "x" on a map that was a guide to buried treasure.

The next day, with my new tattoo throbbing on my right arm, I boarded my one-way flight to Medellín to see what was behind the "x" on my map.

Chapter 16

Touchdown in Colombia

After landing in Medellín, I got through immigration and stepped outside of the airport to breathe in my first taste of the air in Colombia. I gave the taxi driver the address of the hostel that Hernan had suggested, and off we went. My head hung out the window, and my jaw hung open wide as we wound our way down to Medellín from the airport, which was a 45-minute drive. When foliage and buildings ceased, I caught glimpses of the whole view of Medellín. I had the driver stop so that I could get a picture–my very first picture in Colombia of me with the city in the background and a mirage of the mountains in places where the air pollution let them peek through.

Suddenly, he stopped in front of the address I'd given him. I paid him, and stood there with my suitcases, looking at the crowd of people drinking beer and playing cards at a big table on the front patio. I had never been to a hostel. Actually, the only concept of a hostel I had was from horror movies, so I was afraid to try one, but I had promised myself I would try new things.

My Spanish was rusty, and I was not familiar with this Colombian dialect at all, so it was hard to communicate with the girl at the reception desk. I had imagined that I wouldn't have a linguistic barrier, but I did! That was one more thing that was way out of my comfort zone. After I got checked in, the receptionist led me down the hallway to my room where there were five twin beds in the same room. My bed was the one in the back corner. All the other beds were occupied by a group of girls who spoke a language I had never heard, and their stuff was strewn out everywhere. I stepped over their things and stacked my stuff at the foot of my mattress. My twin bed was rock hard, a slab of wood with a thin mattress and a worn out sheet, adorned with a paper-thin pillow leaning up against the wall in the corner. I sat there dazed and terrified, looking at these girls who hadn't even acknowledged my entrance, who were still speaking a language I didn't understand.

Just like that, I had transplanted myself into a new life. What now? I had no idea. Before leaving, I had changed my phone plan to an international plan so that I could have unlimited communication with anyone in the states. I pulled my phone out to let Shari and my mom know that I had made it, only to realize that my international plan was not working. I couldn't use my phone. I had never shared a space with so many people, let alone people I didn't know.

I had to pee. The receptionist showed me the bathrooms, and that's when I learned that the entire floor shared the three small bathrooms in the hallway. Each was a private bathroom with a toilet, sink, and a single shower stall with a curtain to block the water from getting the toilet wet.

I wandered down the street to go eat, and discovered that my bank card wouldn't work since the transaction was in a foreign country, which had triggered account fraud. Thankfully, I had just enough cash on me to pay for my meal, but that was all the cash I had left. I also found out that the taxi driver had charged me three times the legal rate for my cab ride, counting on my unfamiliarity with the local laws to allow him to scam me. At this point I was so overwhelmed, all I could do was walk back to my hostel. I had no working phone, no bank card, no cash, no friends.

That feeling was so awful, a level of utter terror that was foreign. Every fucking thing was foreign. Never in my life had I ever been so radically outside my comfort zone.

I wanted to hide. I needed to hide like an animal perceiving danger, burrowing deep inside of a hole. Walking back into the hostel, I heard someone at the front desk charge a bottle of liquor to their bed reservation. I stopped and noticed a cabinet behind the receptionist. It was full of bottles of Colombian rum, Ron Medellín.

"Excuse me, miss? If I want that fifth of rum must I pay cash, or may I charge it to my bed and pay for everything all together when I check out from this hostel?"

"You can charge it to your bed and pay later!" She informed me.

I went to my bunk with that bottle and crawled inside. I didn't have a cup or anything, just drank right from the bottle while I cried and cried in my bed.

"What the fuck have I done?" I questioned. I had a comfy bed in my cabin where I was living by myself for nearly a year. Why did I do this? What was I going to do about money? Dr. D told me I would still have my research job through the department, but that wouldn't start 'til August! I only had a few hundred bucks to last 'til then, and I didn't even know what I would be doing or where I would go. I wanted Gracie. I wanted my comfort zone back, all of it! I sat there in my bunk, swigging rum and crying. That was my comfort zone, the burn of that liquor in the back of my throat offering a refuge from my feelings and from a frightening, uncomfortable reality.

"Next time I'll be braver. I'll be my own savior when the thunder calls for me. Next time I'll be braver. I'll be my own savior, standing on my own two feet..."

I heard a beautiful voice from the lobby area, belting the lyrics from one of my favorite Adele songs, and those words that I had sung so many times couldn't have fit more perfectly for that very moment as I sat alone in my bed getting drunk. I found the liquid courage to creep outside of my room and go see where that voice was coming from. There sat one of the girls from my room, strumming a guitar and singing these lyrics, and around her sat people from her group and others from the hostel. I had met nobody. I sat down in awe of her courage to sing in front of so many strangers, and I thought, "Maybe one day I will be brave enough to face the fear of singing in front of people."

A bearded guy wandered up to our table with a fat blunt in his hand. "Anyone want to smoke? Get high?"

Why the fuck not? I followed their group outside. He smiled at me.

"Hi, I am Moshe, and singer girl named Or. You smoke," he said as he passed me the joint first. I was a lightweight smoker, always have been. I took one big hit and just about died coughing, and everyone around me just about died laughing about it, as usual.

I offered up my bottle of rum to get passed around one way as their blunt got passed around the other way. We were all sharing. As we all smoked, I listened to their stories. They were all from Israel, had met while traveling, and decided to travel together for a little while. The language they were speaking was Hebrew! I finally found my legs and then found my bed, and cried myself to sleep as I finished my first official day with my feet on foreign soil.

The next morning, I woke up to new challenges. One way that trauma had manifested its damage in my life was my need to control everything. I had become extremely OCD in my personal space, obsessively cleaning and organizing, doing things in a very specific way, and then often repeating those behaviors in a cycle. It helped me feel safe for a long time. It was such a colossal challenge and shock to have to get my shower stuff ready, out of my normal routine, to share a bathroom, to dress and undress in front of other people. That alone felt like learning to walk again, and to do it with so many radically new factors that were already so far away from anything I knew was amazingly difficult. I had control over nothing and nobody. Except me. I still wasn't sure what to think about me. But that was another reason why I had wanted to make this radical change.

After my shower, the girl who had been singing the night before approached my bunk. She plopped down next to me on my bed.

"I heard you telling the receptionist yesterday that you had a problem with your bank card and your phone. Can I help you figure it out?" I was so touched by her kindness. I hadn't eaten since lunch the day before, and my stomach pangs begged to let someone help. Yes, yes, I needed help. I just needed a little boost.

"Actually, would you like to go get coffee with me? My treat. I feel like I need to talk to you." I wondered what this stranger wanted to talk to me about. I wanted to go out and explore. I needed to find my legs. I knew I would find my wings, but first I needed to walk.

"Yes, I would love that," I responded.

We ventured out of the hostel and she began to show me the neighborhood. Everything was so drastically different than anything I had seen in the states. They had been there for a few days already and knew the area somewhat well. We followed the broken sidewalks through the twists and turns of the Poblado neighborhood until we found the Juan Valdez coffee joint, which I had no idea would become one of my favorite places. Eventually, I would visit dozens of them in many different places in different countries, writing bits and pieces of this book in some of them. My very first of many Juan Valdez coffees to come was right there on a table outside on the street on a Monday morning, my first morning to wake up in Colombia.

"You just started traveling. I can tell that you are new. Are you alone?" She studied me.

I nodded and sipped my coffee. She continued.

"I know exactly what you are feeling. You feel terrified. I had never been away from my home before I served in the Israeli army. While I served my time, I saved all my salary so that I could travel when I finished. The army changed me, and it prepared me to go travel alone wherever my heart led me." I was taking in all her feminine beauty, looking at her long hair cascading down over her petite, olive-colored skin. She was so beautiful. I couldn't imagine her dressed up in combat gear, fighting in a war. "When I faced my fears, their power started to go away, as will yours. Its moments like this that will change you. Let yourself feel all of it."

Her story made me think of Mukarram, a Muslim girl from Palestine who was in my degree program at OU and had become my friend. As a little girl, it was normal for her to have bombs go off in her city or have neighbors attacked by Israeli military. She was born into war trauma because of the conflict between Israel and Palestine, and here I was all the way on a different continent having coffee with a woman who served in the army that terrorized Mukarram and her family. How the world looked so radically different from the eyes of these two women.

I felt something move deeply inside of me. She had no idea that in the back of my mind, I was telling myself that it wasn't too late to turn back around and go back to what I knew.

She continued, "This isn't the first tough time you will have. You will have so many hard moments while you travel, but they are what transform you. Be more curious about what is behind your fears, and you will find out what you have inside that still needs to be opened. Do you want to go to Salento with us tomorrow?"

I had no idea what Salento was. "What is Salento?" The thought of going somewhere new again seemed so overwhelming. I wanted to hide in my bunk.

"Salento is a town about six hours south of Medellín. It is small and in the mountains. The pictures we saw looked beautiful. We want to do some hiking there."

I hadn't even seen Medellín yet. I had never been on a bus ride in a foreign country, either. I told her no.

"No? What else are you going to do? You came to hide in your bunk? When we leave, you will have five new people in your room. All you have in life now is a suitcase and an open road. You should start saying yes to every opportunity and see what paths open and unfold for you."

The new tattoo on my right arm caught her eye. She held up my forearm to read it. "Everything you want is on the other side of fear. See? You already know. You have a story, I feel. You aren't ready to tell it. You will know when it's time. Your life is a canvas, and it is time to paint whatever you want." She held up her coffee for us to toast.

"Let's figure out your phone and bank problem, then let's explore Medellín and get ready to leave for Salento in the morning. Yes?" I grinned. I felt butterflies go all through my tummy, and then I released them outward and watched them scatter symbolically into the air around the strangers milling about. Yes, I would go.

The next morning, we all crammed ourselves into a taxi and made it to the bus terminal. I sat with my face pressed up against the window, taking in all the city scenery as we got out of Medellín. About two hours outside of Medellín, the city scenery changed as we transitioned to winding roads that twisted and turned through the mountains of Colombia. The moment I first saw the mountains of Colombia, I knew I had gone through a portal and would never go back. It was the most magnificent thing I had ever seen. It was majesty that literally took my breath away, and all I could do was hold it, and then cry. I cried, feeling like the richest woman on the planet, seeing something so—there's not really even an appropriate word in a human language to describe what I felt. The terror and anxiety I'd felt dissipated to sheer joy, knowing I was barreling into the unknown. What if every single new place was this amazing? I couldn't imagine ever going back, not for one day, not for one house payment, one day clocking into an office, no more time in that dimly lit bar to hear the same stories over and over again. How could anyone miss out on this?

About halfway through our bus ride, we ran into a mudslide. Traffic from both directions was at a dead standstill so that a Bobcat could clear the road. There were trucks, motorcycles, buses, and cars backed up on both sides. When the bus driver turned the engine off, we knew we were going to be there awhile, so we got off. I saw a farmer herding goats down the road. There were pigs in the back of the truck in front of us, cattle trailers, truck beds full of bananas and kilos of coffee beans, and so many motorcycles.

Or brought out her guitar and began to sing her heart out right there on the side of that road. Banana trees decorated the landscape all around us as far back into the mountains as eyes could see. Or, Moshe, and I spent a couple of hours right there singing and making the detour an unforgettable moment, when suddenly, the Bobcat finished and everyone turned on their engines again to continue their path. We got to Salento very late at night and wandered the streets together in the dark trying to find our hostel on foot. Or had been kind enough to reserve a bed for me, too.

This hostel presented a new adventure since I was in a room that had six bunk beds, all full and all sharing the same bathroom inside the room. It was my first time to navigate my bathroom routine around eleven other people doing the same. In the morning, I was the first one in my room awake and I slipped out to the patio with my journal to enjoy my morning solitude while watching the sun come up over the mountains.

One of the hostel employees joined me shortly to start setting up the area for breakfast, which I found out was included in the price of my bunk bed. While I was eating breakfast, a lady from a different room came to join me and I found out that her name was Mariana. She was from Córdoba, Argentina, and she had taken a month off from work to explore different places in Colombia. She invited me to go hiking with her that day. She led me on a rigorous six-hour hike through Cocora Valley, which I learned people came from all over the world to experience. The end of the hike offered a view over the whole valley, gleaming with sunshine and palm trees, surrounded by mountain paradise.

The next day, I bid my farewells to Or and Moshe, promising them that one day I would go to Israel to see their culture, and then Mariana and I traveled back to Medellín together. When we got there, I went with Mariana to a hostel she found online, and I had a new adventure once again when I was put in a room that I shared with a random girl who I am guessing was a prostitute, although I never found out for sure. She didn't seem to speak English or Spanish, and I am guessing she was from Haiti since she was black and had very loud phone conversations in French.

She would sleep until late afternoon, would get dressed up like Julia Roberts did in the movie Pretty Woman, and then would sit on her bed and stare at me. She'd leave, come back an hour later, pull out a wet wipe to clean her private parts, change her underwear, do a bump of coke, sit down to stare at me for long periods of time, spray a ton of perfume all over herself, then she would leave again. She would do this over and over until the sun came up. We were there for three nights. I didn't sleep much. I tried to talk to her while she was staring at me, but she never responded, so I just stared back. I made a mental note that it was imperative that I learn French.

Mariana and I had a blast exploring around Medellín together, and I even had an opportunity to go to a live soccer game at the stadium in Medellín to watch their Nacional team play. The soccer game at the stadium was unforgettable and crazy.

Then, I got a message from Hernan asking if we could meet at the southern bus terminal on Monday morning so that we could travel together.

It was time to discover Jardín.

Chapter 17

Jardín

The farther we ventured into our four-hour bus ride, the farther along we got on the twisty, turny two-lane highway that took me into what I deemed as paradise. The coffee plants and banana trees that encompassed this path were so close that I could nearly reach out from my bus window to grab them. The weather was a perfect 70 degrees, and the windows were open with a fresh breeze blowing through my hair. The sky's blue was divinely complemented by the lush green of the rolling mountainous landscapes, which I got an impeccable view of when our bus would round a sharp corner. Through breaks in the foliage I saw the steep roadside drop-off where rocks from the road bounced off and tumbled to their death in the gorge below.

About halfway to Jardín, among the surrounding Andes Mountains stood one peak more prominent than them all. It had a perfect triangle top. "That is Cerro Tusa," Hernan informed me. "It has a legend and a hidden magic." Something told me that later on in my journey I would find that mountain and try to scale it.

The moment we arrived in Jardín, I was in love. I couldn't believe I'd be spending extended time in a place so magical. Everything about it seemed uncannily familiar to me, as if I'd been there my whole life and in other past lifetimes. Hernan took one of my bags and we hiked up a long hill to his friend's house where I would stay for a few days while further arrangements were made. She was out of town, and I would have the house to myself until

Hernan and I found myself an apartment to get settled into.

The first thing we did was go eat. He took me to a place called Margarita's, where I had my first ever bowl of plantain soup and my first conversation with a young man named Sebas, who would become my best friend there. Sebas and I connected immediately and exchanged contact info. Sebas wasn't even supposed to be working that day, and he wasn't assigned to our table. He had simply stopped to clear dirty dishes from our table and chose to strike up a conversation with me. It was a divine appointment that we ate there on the day Sebas randomly got called in to help with extra chores, and that we crossed paths. I had no idea that he would play a huge role in saving my life further into my adventure.

Hernan found an apartment for me to rent on the outskirts of town in Jardin. It was a two-bedroom, one-bathroom place with a portable gas burner where I could cook basic things. There was a "lavadero" next to the sink where my clothes could be washed by hand, and on the opposite side of that room was an open patio with no cover over it, where I weaved a thin rope back and forth twice up high so that I could hang my clothes to dry.

One of the women directors of the school where I would volunteer insisted that she pay for a maid to come twice a week to wash my clothes and clean my apartment, and she generously offered many things from her house to help me furnish my apartment. I was all set up to be comfortable there until December-ish, although I had no idea what my exact plans would be, which was the enthralling nature of a one-way ticket. It was a 45-minute walk into the mountains to get to the rural school where I would volunteer, and a 45-minute walk back to my apartment in town.

Sebas and I met in the park two to three times per week to study basic English and just share about life in general. We had so much to learn from each other, coming from two completely different countries and cultures. We agreed that we wanted to plan a trip to the coast together before my busy semester and internship start. He came over to my apartment to make us a delicious homemade breakfast once a week. He took me on hikes to nearby must-sees, like the big Jesus statue called *Cristo Rey* and a famous waterfall that most tourists pay to ride on horses to get to. We always walked.

Hernan took me to the rural sector of the schoolhouse where I would do my internship. He introduced me to a group of my high school students who would come by my apartment often to take me on long walks and hikes to show me new things around Jardín. They took me on "La Garrucha", cable cars that lifted us up to a rural sector embedded in the side of the mountain where there was a place to eat fresh empanadas at a table overlooking the village. They took me on a long walk to a trout farm and on hidden paths that only farmers used to get from their farms to town to sell their products, which could include coffee, fruit, vegetables from their farms, or handmade baskets and furniture. The student I connected with the most significantly and very quickly was Juancho, who was 16. I would spend a lot of time with him and his family.

One day, Joanne messaged me that she was coming to Colombia to visit her family in Bogotá and also take part in a tour through Huila (a different department in Colombia) with a group of University professors who rented a private bus. She said my spot on the tour bus would be paid for and that she could cover my hotel room. I would only pay for my flight there and my expense for food or drinks. Of course, I could not miss out on seeing new parts of Colombia, so I said yes! Sebas and I would schedule our trip to the coast for the week after that trip, and I would just stay in Medellín 'til he could meet me there.

I packed a bag of only my essentials and began my adventure for the first time by myself, navigating transport in Colombia! I intentionally arrived in Neiva, Huila a couple of days before Joanne planned to so that I could have my own adventure. My journey began with a bus ride back to Medellín, where I would take a taxi toward downtown, catch the bus that went the 45-minute route to the airport, and navigate domestic flights for the first time all by myself. I couldn't believe that a flight from Medellín to Neiva, the capital of Huila, was only 30 bucks! Being in a country so much cheaper than the United States opened up a whole new quality of life for me.

As soon as I got to Neiva, I found a room that would give me shelter for a couple of nights, then I hit the streets! Huila was a drastic hot and dry change from the "Eternal Spring" of Medellín. The first thing I always do in a new place is drop my things on my bed wherever I'm staying and go find a place where I can sit down and try a regional dish.

I walked a few blocks from my hotel and found a pathway that led to a little hidden park. Had I not walked down the path, I wouldn't have seen this park—it isn't visible from the main road. There were people selling arts and crafts, and in the back sat a woman at her food cart with no customers. She was the one! I sat with her for an hour, eating homemade soup and fresh Lulu juice that she made with her own precious hands as we began to chat. She told me the next day her 15-year-old daughter would be free all day to hang out, if I was interested in having a tour guide.

Her daughter came by for me at my hotel the next morning, and we began an outstanding day of exploring. She took me to a park next to the Magdalena River where there was a large Monument with winding stairs built up the center. We climbed to the top for a view of the River. Once we got up there, I saw that a long ways down the river there was a speedboat taking people across the river to a place where I could see people lived.

"What are they doing?" I asked her.

"The boat works as a taxi, taking people across to where they live on the other side. Those people across the river live in their own community."

I had never taken a boat taxi before. I'd taken a ferry to get from Cozumel to the mainland years ago, but never an actual speed boat taxi.

"Can we go over there if I pay for our taxi fares?" I asked her. She eagerly nodded her head, equally excited about our random adventure as I was.

We climbed back down to wander down the riverbank 'til we found the guy with the boat taxi. It was just a buck apiece to get there and back. He kicked his speedboat into full throttle, throwing us back into startled laughter. We gleefully laughed so hard at the freedom of the land blowing by us and hot desert air whipping through our hair and clothes.

"I will be back here to pick you up in exactly one hour," the taxi driver informed us. "Do not miss your ride."

We were off. We hopped onto a narrow dirt path that led us into a whole colony of people who lived by the river. The foliage started to resemble more jungle and banana trees encompassing our dirt path. There were areas on either side of the dirt path where the river ran through but was just standing water, and there were huts constructed on stilts where people lived over the water.

I saw a man with a backpack step out of his hut and climb down into a kayak. He pulled out oars and began to maneuver his way between the river plants and wooden stilts of other houses to get to the main river where he could row to land. I wondered if he did this every single day just to go to work. By another house on stilts, we saw a little pen on stable land that had chickens, and there was a boy fishing. We ran into a farmer who was picking bananas off a tree and he sold me enough bananas to fill my little backpack for a dollar.

We took selfies and pictures of exotic flowers, ate bananas until we were stuffed, then ate more while we sat on the Riverbank waiting for our boat to pick us back up. Once we got back to the mainland, she took me to the market. There were dozens upon dozens of vendors lining the streets, selling fresh produce from their farms, handmade clothing, baskets, blankets, shoes, and lots of street food. She took me to the main plaza so that I could take pictures of the famous Church. Finally, it was time to take her home, where her mom invited me in for dinner with the family. I slept so well that night and had great pictures of an unforgettable day to explain why.

The next morning, Joanne messaged me that she had arrived at our hotel and arranged for a taxi to come pick me up. I couldn't believe my eyes when we pulled up to the hotel where she was waiting. It was a glamorous, five-star place. I would learn that this was how Joanne traveled and had very kindly offered to pay for a room with two beds so I could join her. We gave each other a hearty hello hug, as she had literally just arrived from the states. She brought me a gift - a small, lightweight, black Columbia brand backpack with thin waterproof fabric that was a perfect size for hiking or bringing back goods from the store.

We met with her colleagues from the University of Neiva and began our trip the next day. I wasn't even sure exactly what we would be doing, but I was just excited to be with a new group of Colombians on our private tour bus seeing new places. First, we went to the Tatacoa Desert, the second largest desert in Colombia (with the Guajira being the biggest) in the northeast corner of the country along the border of Venezuela. I didn't even know we were going to a desert until we got there, and I was just in awe of the unique arid beauty: the stone monuments and vibrant flowers blooming out of cacti. There were huge cacti towering over me.

We got out to explore. I discovered to my delight that there were two sections of desert: the one we first arrived at was brown, and the one we went to next, on the other side, was all gray. The experience was intoxicating. Three days ago, I woke up in my apartment, smelling my neighbors' cooking breakfast, then sat to drink my coffee and behold the beauty of the Andes Mountains from my kitchen window. Now, I was exploring a desert. I had to do this forever, crossing borders one after another!

The next day, we started our longer road trip to the city of San Augustín in southern Huila, where we went to the archaeological Park to see historical sculptures. On our way back from San Augustín, we stopped at a lookout point at the side of a steep canyon that gave us a view of the Magdalena river and the whole valley below. Our bus driver made lots of stops in small towns and villages so we could see famous old churches, legendary artwork, and try street food. Before we left this place to start our adventure in Bogotá, my new friends from the University gifted me a long-sleeve soccer jersey from Neiva's soccer stadium, a jersey specifically representing Huila's soccer team. It was a lasting, tangible souvenir from that remarkable trip with remarkable people who I will carry in my heart forever.

Next came my first experience in Bogotá! This presented a new climate surprise, sitting at 2,644 meters above sea level, making it one of the highest altitude cities in all South America. It was cold and rainy, with the sun making an occasional appearance. It felt like a shock from the dry, desert climate I just left in Huila.

I had no idea that Joanne was from an extremely affluent family. Her father was one of the most prestigious architects in Colombian history. His name and work I won't share out of respect for the family's privacy. A private car picked us up from the airport, driven by the family's chauffeur. We drove nearly an hour to the fanciest area of Bogotá. The chauffeur unlocked the gate for us to go through, giving us access to a mini complex of five elegant houses built up with state-of-the-art architecture, adorned with pristine landscaping. Joanne's family owned all these houses; the complex was all theirs.

I had all next day to myself to go explore. Joanne said she would have the driver drop me off in an area of Bogotá named La Candelaria, which was where Bogotá started long ago. I woke up that morning with an insatiable desire to get a tattoo, and I wanted "Love Conquers All" translated into Arabic along the length of my left forearm. I messaged my Palestinian friend Mukarram from OU for the Arabic translation.

In the car on the way to La Candelaria, Joanne told me the history about a lot of things along the way. Arriving at my stop, she handed me a list of museums that she suggested I check out while I was out exploring.

"Thank you so much," my lips said to her, while "*Boresviiiiille*" rang out in my mind. I would stick that list in my bra in case I needed it for toilet paper later, but I was going to have a wide-open day full of exciting adventures, one of which would include a tattoo and none of which included a library or museum.

As soon as I was by myself with wide open roads for me to wander, fireworks started going off in my soul spaces. BOOM BOOM BOOM. There was so much character in the cobblestone streets, the narrow sidewalks, and hand-painted artwork on the buildings. *First, I want a piece of chocolate cake and a cup of Colombian coffee,* I thought. I noticed a sign ahead for a coffee shop. As soon as I ordered and sat down, the barista started to play Adele's album 19, and the song Daydreamer began to chime in the background. I couldn't believe it. Adele was my favorite artist. I knew every song by heart, and this tiny coffee shop in Bogotá was playing her entire first album, and not even a song that was a big hit on mainstream music channels. It was like the universe did that just for me in that exact moment in that exact location.

I literally sat there and cried. I was so happy, singing along spitting chocolate crumbs everywhere. Gosh, maybe one day I would write books about my life and my travels and they would be just as famous, read in places across the world. Just like Adele's music is scattered across the world. Or even better, maybe somehow Adele would read my books and visit me in whatever foreign place I happen to be visiting!

"Is there a tattoo shop around here?" I asked the barista, who was so smitten about our mutual love for Adele. He had told me that it was by means of her music that he taught himself so much English.

"I have no idea! Let me check." He gave me some suggestions, but I decided to just walk until I stumbled across one.

I did, an hour later, after many rights and lefts. I saw a sign on a window and walked in to discover that one side of the room was a tattoo shop, and the other side of the room was a barber shop.

The Other Side of Fear

"Are you taking clients?" I ask the tattoo artist. I showed him the Arabic translation I had. I sent it to his email so that he could use his computer to enlarge it to the size I wanted.

"We don't have running water right now," he said. "Will that be a problem for you?"

"Not as long as you use new needles and can still give me a beautiful tattoo just the way I wish," I told him, and we were off. While I got tattooed, I chitchatted with the two barbers when they had a break between customers. When I finished with my tattoo, everyone asked me if I would like to stay to eat lunch with them.

"Only if we do shots of tequila!" I counter offered.

Nobody had ever shot tequila before. I was honored to give them their first experience. Everyone chipped in on a bottle, and on our way back from the liquor store, we got some salt and limes from a guy selling mangoes. My God, the rest of the day we had so much fun, playing board games and doing tequila shots. They still stopped to attend to customers, tattooing and cutting hair between shots. Finally, I bid them a heartfelt farewell and connected with all of them on social media before using the last hour of daylight to continue exploring.

As I searched out stunning street art to photograph, I found a cozy pub that had plantain soup available as a dinner feature. The chilly Bogotá climate made it difficult to say no, especially since that soup was my new favorite, so I sat at the bar top to eat my soup and enjoy frothy, locally-brewed tap beer. I struck up a conversation with the guy sitting next to me, who shared that his wife was an attorney who works with victims of the political conflict. He personally was working on a documentary about the peace agreement in Colombia's turbulent history with military violence. He asked if I would like to meet his wife. He, his wife, their German Shepherd, and I watched the sun set over the city from the rooftop at their high-rise apartment building, which is a very rare thing to see because of rain and air pollution in Bogotá. Again, it was a moment from the universe only for me.

When I got back to Joanne's, I can only imagine how shocked they were. They expected a quiet conversation over dinner about museums and newly-acquired information about Colombian history, and instead I stumbled into the house reeking of tequila, with my left arm wrapped in plastic to protect my new tattoo.

"I can't take my eyes off you for one moment," she told me. "You are quite the basket of surprises." The rest of her family chewed their food in silence, exchanging uncomfortable glances as I animatedly shared my stories about board games, tequila shots with strangers, tattoos, and sharing a sunset on a rooftop with more strangers. They were a tough crowd. I confirmed my suspicions about not having much in common with them and excused myself from the table after I shared all my stories and finished eating all their expensive cheese.

It was time to pack! I was heading back to Medellín the next day for a new round of adventures.

Chapter 18

Up in Flames

"I destroyed myself as often as possible, just to see what else I could become."

– Mira Hadlow

I arrived back in Medellín the first Friday in August, which also marked the last weekend of the famous Flower Festival that took place every year. I wasn't too crazy about pushing and shoving my way through nearly 30,000 people filling the streets, but I also knew that if I didn't go, I may never have the chance again. My God, I am so glad I went. It was a life-changing experience. Hernan and I had four marvelous days of fun.

He took me to the Flower Festival, on a long hike to a lookout tower that showed a 360-degree view of Medellín and then to a bookstore where we talked for hours about our favorite literary works and shared our life's dreams and passions while we stuffed ourselves on homemade desserts and coffee. My last night there, he surprised me with a candlelit dinner on the rooftop of his apartment building. What made it so special was that his love was pure. He never tried to touch me, kiss me, or flirt with me. He shared genuine, pure love and generosity. I remember that night like it was yesterday, how the moon and stars adorned the night-light-speckled city of my queen Medellín.

Then, it was time for me to meet Sebas at a restaurant by a busy subway station so that we could have lunch and then drop our things off at our hotel. Not every place has a contract to accept foreigners, but after asking around, we finally found a place that would be fine to stay for one night.

Sebas kept talking about how excited he was to go partying that night at a bar where a friend was bartending in Medellín's gay district. I was exhausted and not remotely in the mood for any such fuckery, but all his sashaying around the hotel room, waving his ass around to Beyoncé finally convinced me to make a compromise. It wasn't safe for him to go alone, so I offered to go for a couple of hours with him ONLY if he promised to leave whenever I was ready.

In Colombia, it is rare to find a place that sells single drinks unless it is a kiosk with a vendor selling drinks in the street (it's legal to drink everywhere in public at any hour). Bars and clubs sell what's called "bottle service," where you choose the size of the bottle, and a server brings the bottle, the mixer of your choice, a bucket of ice, and however many glasses your table needs. We got there so early that by 8 p.m., we were set up with a bottle service on our table, surveying the night scene. I was slumped over on the table, watching men from the ages of 15 or older interact. I couldn't connect to the music. I didn't feel like I had anything in common with anyone around me. My whole body felt like a lead weight. I was so tired. A Red Bull was not going to help me.

Sebas was engaged in a conversation next to me, and I was gazing into space in the direction of the bar, when it caught my eye that the bartender tossed a small bag of something on the bar top for a customer. The customer opened the baggy, did a bump of the white powder, gave a nod to the bartender, and then took off with a friend and the baggy to the bathroom.

Did they just do cocaine? I had flashbacks of the episode many years ago at an after-party, the one time I had ever done it. Sebas's buddy got up to get a drink, and I turned to him. "Did they just do coke?" He laughed and said yes.

"I want to try it." Oh, my censors went off inside. *You're playing with fire.* Then came the lies where the fuckery always began. *You're in a different mental state now. It will be different. Do anything you want, you badass.*

He did a double take and studied my eyes, very surprised at my proposition. He had never been acquainted with this side of me, the side of me that had the power to build a village with one hand and then burn it down with the other.

He looked at me square in the eyes and said, "Jenni, I will not judge you. We are on vacation. Do it if you wish, but with the condition that you promise me that it will only be a vacation thing. We are away from 'home,' so there are no judgments, no responsibilities, no talk of work. Nothing is off limits on vacation, but you must leave it behind when we are done with Santa Marta. When our vacation ends, you are done. Promise me."

I let him look into my eyes, and our eyes were locked for what seemed like a while. He was serious. I knew I was opening a chamber of darkness. I knew I was playing with fire. I pretended like I didn't know anything about the world of drugs and addiction. What I really learned about myself in that moment is that it didn't matter how many borders I crossed, there was still an ember alive in me whose glow beckoned self-destruction. It always burned, and just a blow of oxygen on it ignited it into fire, burning down myself and everything around me. I felt powerless to choose anything different. That had been my home for years.

"Okay, I promise," I said. He nodded and got up to go to the bar.

Sebas whispered something in the bartender's ear and came back to drop a gram of coke in front of me on the table. I couldn't believe that I just ordered a gram of coke from a bar like it was nothing. I asked Sebas how much it cost. Ten thousand Colombian pesos, which was three dollars in United States currency. I could order a gram of coke for three bucks from a bartender. I was fucked.

I looked at the white powder in the bag laying on the table in front of me. I remembered bits and pieces of the night years ago after my bankruptcy, and thought about Alex in the bathroom the night he shot heroin. I wanted an adventure, some excitement. I felt invincible. Maybe it would have a different ending. Maybe it wouldn't end in destruction. I wouldn't know unless I tried it, just like I'd always learned to swim by diving into things head-first.

"Let's do shots!" Sebastian poured two shots of aguardiente. "And put that away. I don't want to be associated with that shit." I stuck it in my bra.

We started drinking, people-watching, and lip-syncing the music. The alcohol made me even more tired, and being so tired escalated the effect of the alcohol. I felt buzzed and sloppy, like having a conversation was such an effort, and in my effort, I sounded like a drunk slob. I hated it when I got drunk too fast. It was not a combination for a promising evening until I remembered the magic baggy in my bra. I decided I was tipsy enough to take a trip to the bathroom.

I was about to do real cocaine in the bathroom of a bar in Colombia.

I didn't have a straw on me. I would have to do a line with a rolled-up bill, just like I saw people do hundreds of times in my earlier addiction years. *I could pretend like it was a hundred-dollar bill like rich people do in Vegas.* I cut two fat lines on the back of the toilet, but first, I looked in the mirror at myself. *You know you may not ever come back out of this, right?* Was the truth I was staring at right in the mirror. *What good would it ever do you to be successful in your life if it always ends on a path of self-destruction, anyway?* It always had, no matter how hard I tried to do anything else. *May as well go out of this world feeling numb, then. You're a survivor, and you will survive this, too.* I rolled that bill as tightly as I could, and then made those lines disappear like a pro, like I had done it every day for my whole life. I obviously was a pro at anything that set myself on fire.

I tilted my head back to make sure it had all gone in, just like the guy at the party had shown me. Then, I wiped my nose with some toilet paper. I looked in the mirror on the way out of the bathroom.

By the time I got back to my table, the whole right side of my head was numb from my forehead all the way down my neck. I felt completely sobered up from alcohol, my heart was pounding, and I felt an orgasmic euphoria in my brain. This coke was way different than the coke before. This coke was fucking incredible.

I didn't feel sloppy anymore. Actually, I felt like I could do anything. It was like I had a whole new window to the world, and I couldn't wait to explore all of it. It was a feeling like nothing else I had ever experienced. I wanted more. Feeling the coke directly was too much, but to tame its effect with alcohol was the perfect sensation ever. Too much alcohol was unpleasant, but to tame its effect with coke was fantastic. It was a match made in hell.

For the rest of the evening, I went back and forth between the two. We ended up getting a new bottle, and when I felt too tipsy, all I had to do was take a trip to the bathroom and do a bump or two. I had no concept of what time it was. I just knew I was having amazing conversations with so many new people, and the alcohol didn't take me out like it usually did. Suddenly, Sebas told me that we needed to finish the rest of our bottle and tab out since the bar was about to close at 4 a.m. How could it be 4 a.m. already? I finished my gram about an hour before that. I wanted more. I was about to start four stressful months of internship work and university responsibilities, and I wanted to check out as much as possible before that began.

I didn't tell Sebas I was going to get more. I went back up to the bartender, Alexander, and asked him for two more grams of the best coke he had. He told me that a gram of something better would be six dollars instead of three. I couldn't believe something so amazing was so cheap. Maybe there would be no coke wherever I was going. I couldn't risk being on vacation for a week without it. I had no idea that Santa Marta was a major port for coke exportation all around the world and that I would be surrounded with the purest coke that Colombia had to offer. I didn't need to know that yet.

We got back to our hotel room, and I was finally able to doze off, just to take restless naps off and on until about noon the next day. I woke up fully expecting to feel the scratchy-eyed shakiness that would usually follow a night of drinking, but I didn't feel hungover at all! How could we have drunk that much and not been hungover? I realized then that coke was not only a buffer for being too drunk, but also for alcohol-induced hangovers. The coke I did before was such terrible quality that I didn't know. Wow, I hit the jackpot. I never had to face drunkenness or hangovers again. I had a new friend for the rest of my life!

We had to shower off the club from the night before, gather our things, and head to the airport to catch our flight to Santa Marta. I took my shower first so that I could have privacy gathering my things while Sebas took his.

When I was making sure that my passport and wallet were in my satchel, I saw those baggies of white powder in the bottom. *Jesus, I almost forgot I had them.* What if I would have forgotten they were there and gone through airport security with them just hanging out in the bottom of my purse? *Dumbass,* I told myself. *Get your head on straight.* That was the first of many months to come where my head would be sideways.

Then, the thought of having coke in an airport sent adrenaline surging through my whole body. It was far too fantastic to leave behind. I couldn't wait to see what a whole week of this euphoria would feel like. Other people pay hundreds and hundreds of dollars for something like this, and for me, it was like hitting the dollar menu. I heard the shower shut off. I stuffed the two grams inside my shoe.

Surely, it would be fine. Who would know? I couldn't wait to do my first line as soon as I got to our hotel room by the beach. I felt my panties get wet just thinking about it. Sebas stepped out of the bathroom finally and peeked out to see what I was doing.

"Ready?" I felt the corner of one of the baggies poking me in my right foot like a dirty little secret.

"Yep. I can't wait."

We got to the airport and printed off our boarding passes at the electronic ticket booths. We followed the signs pointing the way for domestic flights. We got to the door where we were required to show our boarding passes and passports, got through that checkpoint, and then I was staring straight at the TSA agent station where we were required to go through the metal detectors. I felt my stomach drop to the floor. What if they required us to take off our shoes? Jesus, I didn't think to put that coke inside of my sock! How could I get that coke inside of my sock without anyone noticing?

Shit, this might get bad. What if I get caught? Once you are through that door, it's too late to go back.

My palms started sweating profusely.

Chill. Maybe they're not making people take off their shoes. You just took a domestic flight last week and didn't have to take off your shoes. What are the people ahead of you doing?

I felt the butterflies in my tummy flee as I took a deep breath and casually looked at the people ahead of me. Wheeewww, nobody was taking off their shoes. Oh my God, I got a green light. I got through security. As soon as I got to the area where there were terminals, I felt this orgasmic adrenaline rush surge through my body. I had to celebrate. We still had an hour to kill before we boarded, and both agreed that a piece of chocolate cake and a coffee from Juan Valdez sounded superb. We got situated there, and then I told Sebas I was going to the bathroom.

As soon as I got to the private family bathroom and locked the door, I took off my shoe and sat on the toilet, looking at that coke in my hand. How amazing would it be to do a line of coke in the airport bathroom? My dirty little secret, like a hidden lover I wasn't allowed to show the world. I stood up and looked in the mirror, got out my key, and did two bumps off my key while looking at my nose in the mirror. I made sure to get all the residue off so that nobody from the outside world would know what I just did. I wondered if that's how every office secretary felt after getting loaded with afternoon dick behind closed doors, straightening hair and wiping off mascara that had run underneath eyes. This time, I put the coke inside of my sock, and then put my shoes back on. I was ready to have a crazy week on the beach.

I went back to where Sebas was and let him have my portion of the cake and coffee. That was another thing that coke depleted–my appetite. I sure didn't need any coffee. If I were too jumpy, it would be obvious to the others around me that I just had a rendezvous with drugs in the bathroom. My heart was racing, and I secretly enjoyed the euphoria in my head. It felt even more erotic knowing I did it in public and nobody knew. I wanted more. I decided to wear my sunglasses so that nobody could see my eyes.

Finally, it was time to board our flight, so we got up and stood in line. I was standing behind Sebas, enjoying my high and studying people around me who couldn't see me checking them out behind my shades. Suddenly, out of my right eye, I saw two police officers and a drug dog nonchalantly strolling along, headed toward us.

Holy. Shit.

During the domestic flights I had just taken while traveling in Huila and Bogotá, I hadn't seen dogs. Not for domestic flights. For an international flight, understandable. I felt my stomach drop again, and my palms started dripping from sweat. If they didn't smell the coke in my shoes while they walked by, the dog would definitely smell my nervous system putting off crazy toxins. They were still about 30 feet away. It was too late to go hide anywhere. Our flight was about to board.

Panicked thoughts were racing through my mind. I was fucked. There's no way I was getting past this one. It was only a couple grams, but would that be enough to be arrested? The police were always looking for a reason to fuck with foreigners because of corruption. They were always looking for ways to make people pay money. I recalled the episodes of "Locked Up Abroad" that I used to watch. We would miss our flight. I would be the reason our trip was ruined.

Sebas felt my energy shift and turned his head to glance back at me. He needed to know.

"Sebas, I have coke in my shoe," I whispered forcefully under my breath just loud enough for him to barely hear me. "Last night, I bought two more grams and put them in my shoe before we left our room."

He hissed back at me from the corner of his mouth, "Are you fucking insane? Through an airport?"

I responded, "If anything happens, you don't know me. Get on your flight; don't wait for me," and then nodded in the direction of the approaching dogs. He turned to look at them and then felt all the terror that I felt. About ten feet before us, one of the officers got a call and stopped to talk.

Jesus fuck, start boarding the plane. Board, board.

Our line started to move.

Go, go, go.

Both officers were engaged in a conversation on their cell with another officer who was dealing with a conflict at the airport entrance on the first floor. They were trying to figure out if they were needed there. *Yes! Go, go the other direction.*

Our line moved past them, and then they ended the call and continued to stroll along. Someone ahead of us in our line had lost their ID at some point between security checks and our boarding. Our line stopped. I felt my intestines literally drop to the floor, and between the coke I had just done and my adrenaline surging through my body, I thought my heart was going to blow out of my chest. They already moved past us for a few seconds when suddenly the dog started barking. My eyes got wide behind my sunglasses.

I was fucked. They got me. The dog smelled me. I closed my eyes and waited for the dog to grab my ankle any second. I waited for what seemed like an eternity. What would I say to them? They were going to arrest me in front of all these people.

The dog was still barking but never came. Our line was still stopped. I stood there waiting for a dog to grab my leg, and time seemed to be frozen. Sebas turned his head to see what was going on, and he whispered to me, "They got someone else."

Huh? I casually looked back to see what was going on. The officers had subdued a couple of European guys who were in a line to board a flight to San Andres, a famous island destination off the coast of Colombia. The guys were sitting on the ground with their hands behind their back, and the cops were going through all their belongings in their open suitcase. The dog sniffed out an eight ball from each of their bags. Holy shit, that was almost me! How in the world did I escape that?

Our line started to move again. Now, I only had to get through the jet bridge and onto the plane. We boarded our plane. I just got through an airport with two grams of coke in my shoe. I was sitting in my seat looking at the window, and my adrenaline level was so extreme that I was certain I was going to have a blowout orgasm right there in front of God and everyone. If it were that erotic of an experience to get through with just a couple grams, how much more intense would it be to get through a port of entry with a large shipment and make tens of thousands of dollars?

As soon as we got back from stocking our room with goodies, I had to celebrate by bustin' out one of those grams and doing a fat line. We brought a fifth of aguardiente to our room to commence a week of fucking off on the beach. We did shots and hit the streets to start exploring the beach and the neighborhoods. That night, we found the local hotspot, a club called "La Puerta," where they played African music, salsa, merengue, and reggaeton music. We were there dancing for hours while I took breaks to go do bumps of coke in the bathroom.

Our first full day there, we met the guy downstairs, Carlos, who sold tours. We instantly connected and agreed later we must have known each other in a previous lifetime, or some similar connection. We knew we would be life-long friends; we didn't know he would be a lifeline to save my ass later.

I did this all week long: sleep during the day, venture out to explore in the late morning or early afternoon, end up having day drinks, start the coke whenever I got tipsy, and be up almost all night with drinks and coke. Sebas would go to bed between midnight and 2 a.m. after we got back from La Puerta. I would stay up by myself and snort lines off the bathroom counter, taking breaks to take shots, smoke cigarettes out the window, write, and listen to music in my earbuds.

By the time the week was over, I couldn't imagine leaving coke behind until my next vacation. It felt so normal now, as normal as having my best friend over for dinner, her letting herself in my house any time she wanted, taking what she wanted from the fridge, and staying for however long she liked. Did I love how it made me feel, or did I love how it prevented me from feeling? Which was it? It didn't matter. It was a part of me now. I could keep it as my dirty little secret.

Chapter 19

Giovani

When I got back on a Saturday afternoon from those crazy few weeks of traveling, I had until Monday to get ready for my routine to begin because my semester was kicking off. That semester, I had an online class, my volunteer work which counted as another full-time graduate class, and my research assistantship helping Dr. D for 20 hours each week so that I could get paid by my department.

Sebas came over for movie night when our schedules allowed. One night, we made a nest in my bed and watched Forrest Gump in Spanish on my laptop. After that, he always referred to me as his carrot, or even better, his "yucca"–a root vegetable used as a stable in many Colombian dishes. I was his yucca, and he was my chicharron, two things that were often paired together in traditional, Colombian dishes.

I remember one night, the electricity and internet service went out for the whole village, so I was literally cut off from the world. I lit a candle on my kitchen table and hung out my window that overlooked the Andes mountains and rooftops between us. That night in particular there was a thunderstorm moving in. I could see the lightning show to one side of my view of the mountains, while on the other side the full moon and stars illuminated the breathtaking Andean landscape.

I don't think anyone in the states has experienced a moment of beauty like this one right here. No phone service, no TV, no internet, no light. I felt like I hit the jackpot. The irony of simplicity being the jackpot. Who knew?

My first month proved to be a very challenging experience with my new internship. I had never taught before. I was really supposed to serve as ESL support for the teachers, but the professors of the young kids would leave me alone with their room full of them. They stood outside laughing at me through the window, witnessing my mental breakdown as the kids ran around like crazy, yelling, climbing, and then dispersing outside into nature like the seeds off a dandelion.

It was definitely frustrating at times, but it was worth it for everything that they taught me. Some of my kids walked over an hour to get to that little schoolhouse. I had the honor of getting to know them and their families as time went by. I learned more from them than they learned from me.

The life I had lived for a week with Sebas in Santa Marta was 100% different than my life in Jardín. It took me a few days to recover psychologically from bending my mind so hard on my vacation coke binge. It was like a switch was flipped from 'on' to 'off'. What made me want to twist off like that? I felt powerless to change the cycle for years because I knew things would only be great for so long before I would drop a bomb and blow it up. I felt in danger about when it would happen again, and it would. I had been a danger to myself for years.

My students knew where I lived and came over to have movie day on Saturdays. I would lay out blankets on the floor where they could watch science documentaries in English, and we would enjoy snacks. One of my university friends from OU told me about an international program that I should help Juancho get into. If Juancho got admitted into the program through UWC (United World Colleges), he would have the honor of finishing high school abroad with a high chance of gaining a scholarship to a four-year degree program, also abroad. While the other kids watched their Netflix movies, Juancho and I used his computer to work on his application.

Everything went smoothly for the first few weeks. Then one Friday, I got a wild hair to go to the park and drink some beers. I was so exhausted from all the hours working with the kids, doing my coursework, having really early mornings, and making long walks back and forth every day. I was sitting alone at a table outside, looking at the stars over the mountains, when the server who was taking care of my table asked if he could sit down. His other patrons had left, and he wanted to have a conversation with me. He shared with me about his family, his life, and Colombia. I shared about mine, where I was from, and why I was in Jardín. His name was Giovani, and he said, "It was a pleasure to welcome you to Jardín."

I had that shitty, scratchy feeling behind my eyes that told me I'd over-drank, and I knew I would be hungover the next day. I was starting to slur and feel sloppy, and I hated that feeling. He brought me a couple free shots of aguardiente to say welcome to Jardín. When he offered to bring out a third, I politely declined, telling him I didn't want to be any more hungover the next day than I already would be.

"I never get hangovers," he said under his breath and glanced down. My eyes followed suit, only to see him flashing the corner of a gram of coke from his apron pocket.

Shit, shit, shit, not right in front of my face. I can't unsee it now.

My heart immediately started to race. Sitting there drunk and mildly bored with my adult routine, I knew I didn't stand a chance against this power. I looked back up at him and gave him a nod. He tossed the baggy to me.

"Take that girl to the bathroom and see if you like what she does," he joked, although he was very serious. There was nobody else around at the moment.

But remember what you promised to Sebas. I heard the desperate voice in my head starting to speak sense. I sat there looking at the gram in my hand, feeling my palm sweat underneath it.

Just this one time, just because I got too drunk. After tonight, I will be on my best behavior. Besides, I deserve to fuck off for a night after working so hard.

I knew those were all lies, and I knew I was playing with fire. I was just starting my semester. Nobody could know or I would jeopardize my relationship with the kids and my degree program at OU. The tingle in my gut told me I was putting myself in grave danger. I snuffed it out, and off to the bathroom I went.

That one decision set everything into motion for my life to go up in flames, and rather quickly. My intentions of just doing a couple bumps that night to rid myself of intoxication shifted radically into killing several grams together with him while we sat there all night drinking and snorting. One part of me was watching in horror, looking down over the whole scenario, screaming "STOOOPPPPPP, what are you doing?" The other part of me was saying, "Calm the fuck down. It's just one night off. You can wash your guilt off in the shower tomorrow. Nobody except you two will know what happened, and you won't do it again."

At first, I had thought that coke was only in party places like the coast or big cities such as Medellín. But, after I opened the door to it there in Jardin, it was as though a veil was lifted and I could see how many people were involved with it in some way. It didn't take too long for people to figure out what I was meddling in, and I was surrounded by users, sellers, and town gossipers. I was bombarded by offers to partake every time I went out, even when my intentions were sincerely pure. It didn't take long for it to become a daily habit, and it was common to have some on me at all times. It was so easy. It was everywhere, and it was cheap. It took away my hunger, my sleep, my drunkenness, all my worries; a magic fix-all.

After crossing that threshold, it didn't take long to figure out which faculty members at the school were users and which of the users bought their coke from the high school students in their classes. Those of us who were users would use together at lunchtime to combat the midday comedowns. We were always tired. Using with other faculty members aided in numbing myself to the possibility of consequences. I had begun to feel invincible, and I was most certainly in denial.

My raging curiosity to test out the limits with my new lover was constantly throbbing in the back of my mind. I hadn't been on a total bender since I was 21 and landed myself in rehab. I started testing the limits on benders, alone in my apartment on the weekends. After a couple months of living like this I knew I was in over my head, but I couldn't stop. Things were starting to spin out of control like it had when I was 21. The small mistakes that began to happen quickly transformed into much bigger ones that couldn't be brushed off or explained away so easily. I fell obviously behind on my university-related responsibilities, and I avoided phone calls from loved ones.

I still got in my hours for OU, but I started to have conflicts, and not just because of my own personal hell; there was also conflict ensuing with the nonprofit part of my internship hours.

Before my addiction had totally taken over, I spent time at my students' houses on the weekends and after school, experiencing home-cooked food and documenting how people live their everyday lives. The nonprofit that I was working with to get hours toward my master's degree asked that since families trusted me enough to allow me into their homes and share their personal lives, that I make videos recording the things I experienced, with special attention to "poverty" so that they could use the videos for fundraising. The owner of the nonprofit said showing that kind of poverty up-close-and-personal could really move their donors to make significant contributions. However, they didn't want to use the donations for the families in the videos, but rather for other projects and other places in Colombia. I felt that was completely unethical and was unwilling to exploit the precious people who trusted me enough to come into their homes.

I already rocked the boat by telling the nonprofit organization I would not be affiliated with anything related to exploiting others for their fundraising; the only hours I would complete would be the ones I used to translate their webpage, and after that, we would go no further with our relationship.

Also, the activities that were supposed to be organized at the school were completely disorganized, through no fault of mine, but by the director's decisions. He frequently switched my class hours around last minute so I had different students in class each day. Not one of my students spent time in class on subsequent days, so it was impossible to plan daily lessons where they could actually learn something. Between all that frustration and my new romance with cocaine, I knew I was going to end up walking out. There's no way I could keep up with this dance through December.

***

My first near-death experience happened one Friday night after finishing my exhausting work week. Some "friends" were supposed to come over to party, so on my way home I got ten grams of coke and a half-gallon of aguardiente to kick off our weekend. Nobody ended up coming, so I partied by myself, putting back line and shot combos, singing karaoke by myself, writing about things that I had experienced both in the states and in Colombia thus far, and watching documentaries in a medley of other languages. I found the limit to my bender, and it wasn't as fun as I had anticipated.

My solo party became unforgettable when, 30 hours later, suddenly my eyes started twitching like crazy in their sockets. I began sweating profusely, yet I was so cold I thought I might be literally freezing to death. My heart was beating so hard, I swore it was going to fly right out of my chest. My skin was crawling, and I couldn't stop shaking.

The only person I thought to call was Shari since she'd worked in the medical field for 30 years. She was at work but answered immediately, and I told her what I was experiencing.

"Tell me what you did, Jenni," she demanded. Then came inventory: One, two, six, seven, EIGHT little bags.

"Eight grams of cocaine, nearly a half gallon of aguardiente and three packs of cigarettes."

"WITH WHO? Who did you party with? Did someone slip something in your drink? Are you alone? Are you safe?"

I was rocking back and forth with my eyes shut, trying to calm the twitching, and holding the phone to my ear with my shaking arms. Sia's song "Chandelier" chimed in the background from my laptop playlist. *Party girls, don't get hurt, can't feel anything, when will I learn? I push it down, I push it dow – ow – ooowwwn.*

"Nobody. Just me alone in my apartment."

She took a huge breath.

"You're probably overdosing. Your body cannot process everything you just did. Start drinking water to help flush your system and ride out the pain. Hopefully, I will see you on the other side."

I hung up.

I'm gonna live, like tomorrow doesn't exist, like it doesn't exiiiiii-iiiistt.

Reminiscing about how perfect everything was when I had arrived, I thought of all the wonderful families with whom I had communed, the places I hadn't yet seen. This perfect apartment and its simple beauty brought me peace and tranquility in the beginning. I sobbed in my bed, still sweating, thinking about my students; they taught me so much. I had to get through this because I had to see all the sunsets over the mountains that were waiting for me.

But I'm holdin' on for dear life. Won't look down won't open my eyes.

The pain was unbearable. The pain of my guilt and shame, the pain of this comedown spiraled me into a suicidal low so wicked that I would have stuck a pistol in my mouth and pulled the trigger to avoid feeling the depth of it. There was no sleeping it out, no waking up when the worst was over. There was only wide-eyed awakeness with the cold sweats all night long until I heard a knock at my door early the next morning.

"Jenni, it's Juan!" I heard someone yell through my front door.

Fuck. I had forgotten that I'd made a commitment with my star student Juan to come over Sunday morning and finish his application to do the study-abroad program we had discussed. We already tried to meet twice, but I had cancelled because of my addiction getting in the way of things. His deadline to submit his things was later that night, so there was no rescheduling. I had to push through. I had been awake for nearly 40 hours, was sick, still high on coke, and unsure about whether I was going to finally overdose or live through it. I had to put on my best game face and let him in. I ran to the bathroom, splashed my face, and I was sure I looked something like death. I didn't actually look in the mirror, but that had become a common thing.

"I'll be right there," I yelled. I ran around the kitchen picking up all the party trash I had strewn about, paranoid that I would overlook an empty baggy or a line left on the glare of the glass table. I hid the liquor, wiped everything down, and dumped my coffee mug full of cigarette butts in the kitchen trash. All the evidence was gone.

"Are you okay?" He asked when he walked in. "You look like you don't feel too good, Miss Jenni."

My sweet boy.

"I was up all night with a stomach virus, I think."

I made him breakfast while I set up his laptop and notebooks. I was hallucinating and shaking. We got his YouTube video and application completely done and submitted. He confessed to me that he was apprehensive about even applying.

"If I get accepted, I will have to do round two in Bogotá," he said. "There's no way my family can afford my flight, food, or lodging for me to go there for a week."

I told him that everything would work out in his favor if he chose to go through that door. The universe has a way of moving things when someone is ready to make a move. If you wait to make a move, things may never change, but when you step into the unknown, you create the movement, and then things conspire in your favor.

I knew I needed to make a move soon, too. I was officially behind in my online class. Dr. D sent me an email requesting that I help him find some TED Talks or YouTube videos to show in his drug addiction class. I couldn't get past the irony of that.

Who needed a pep talk from Susie Ph.D. about that topic? I could make a documentary about the crazy fuckery currently transpiring in my life.

I was getting random knocks on my door from people I didn't know at all hours of the day and night. I don't know how they knew me or what they wanted. I didn't foresee anything "going back to normal" because of the mess I created.

***

I contacted my soul brother, Carlos, in Santa Marta and filled him in on what my life had become. He told me immediately that I was welcome to come there to be close to him. He said that he and his life partner were moving into a new apartment in the next month or two, and I could stay with them once they got moved in. I noted it as the most favorable option, and then told myself I would get through another week or two at school while I decided what to do. I just wanted to disappear, honestly, from everything. I was surrounded by so much temptation, especially at the school.

My chance to disappear came soon, but not before one last love affair with my favorite mistress, as if my near overdose wasn't enough.

Chapter 20

Yucca & Chicharron

I made it without coke for a whole week.

The next Friday night rolled around, and in spite of what I just survived the weekend before, my body was still full on Friday night, triggered with a desire to party. "Just one beer," my body pleaded. I could no longer have a drink without using coke also; just smelling alcohol sent my body into a full-fledged response as if I had done coke. One beer kicked the coke door wide open.

I snuck down to the corner store for some snacks after firmly deciding that I would *only* get snacks--no beer, no shots, no cigarettes. I heard someone call out my name as I walked by, and when I backed up to see who it was, I found my neighbor and her friends all having a house party. They were watching a Colombian soccer game on TV and convinced me that since I was wearing my Colombian jersey it was meant to be that I stay to party with them. Of course, I found it impossible to say no.

"Just five minutes won't hurt," I coaxed myself through the front door. I didn't have a TV in my apartment and loved to watch soccer games with the locals.

Five minutes turned to 30, and nobody would take "no" for an answer. Drinks flowed in my direction from all sides, not that I was firm about sending them away.

"It's just one drink, it's fine," my lying to myself began. One shot turned into two, which led to four, and then a group of men showed up. It wasn't long before I found out they were off-duty policemen dressed in casual clothes. Also, they were there to bring the drugs, and they weren't only coming to party hard, but to have sexual hookups with the women who were waiting for their arrival.

As we all drank and snorted together, there was one guy who seemed to be infatuated with me. He told the other guys that I was off limits and tried to hold my attention the whole time. The harder he tried, the more annoyed I became.

"You're married," he accused. I denied it. "You must be married because otherwise, why wouldn't you give me a chance?"

I scoffed at the sexist nature of this comment. So basically, as a woman, my options are to belong to a husband or if I don't, to be up for grabs by any other man who lusts after me?!

After the group was several lines and shots into the party, the soccer game was replaced with sexy music. The men and women started to pair up and disappear into private rooms, and it was time for me to go. As I started for the door, the guy who had hit on me all night suddenly appeared from the shadows, where he had waited for my exit. He caught me by surprise, especially in my impaired state, and successfully pushed me down on a nearby bed and mounted me.

"You'll love it. I promise you will," he breathed his liquor breath all over my face, and I had flashbacks of how Oscar's liquor breath had smelled.

He had his dick out and thrust his hips, trying to find an opening around my shorts so that he could push himself into me. His arms and hands held mine down. I could tell that he was not stronger than me. I could overpower him, but I had to be strategic and intentional about it.

"Get the fuck off me or I will get you off, and you won't like it," I warned him. He did not take my warning seriously, and tried to push my legs apart with his knees. I silently counted down and when I got to number three, I channeled my energy and strength into bench pressing this guy off me. The momentum made him roll off the bed, hitting his head on the dresser. I ran home as fast as I could.

The next morning, I thought about whether I should report what happened. Not only had I consumed drugs with the men, but I knew nobody would believe me. In South America, rape is always a woman's fault. It would have been my fault for wearing shorts, for being drunk, for making eye contact, for not being married, or for having participated in any dialogue with my would-be rapist.

I hadn't been in contact with Sebas. I'd avoided his calls and texts as much as everyone else's because of my shame at the second life I lived. I was ashamed that I broke my promise to him. I was ashamed that I made such a mess of things. I messaged him when I woke up and he asked if I wanted to go have breakfast with him. Tears immediately began to flood down my cheeks.

Yes, yes I did. A part of me longed to go back on vacation and restart everything so my memories wouldn't be stained with being coked out and drunk. I wished that Sebas had a magic wand to fix everything I had messed up. I was about to go face him, and I was so scared that he would see the truth, although I knew I had to be honest with him. I was so tired of living a huge lie. More than anything, I was scared that he would reject me, which would confirm the painful belief that had always haunted me: that I was unlovable and unworthy of being loved.

On my way to meet Sebas at our favorite breakfast place, I saw the neon green fleece jackets on a group of officers gathered by the fountain in a park. I saw him, the officer who had tried to rape me the night before. There was no way in hell I was going to let him have the last word.

It seemed that the guy who assaulted me was a leader in the group of police officers. His uniform was a different color and he led the conversation. As I approached the group he refused to acknowledge me, but his officers redirected their attention from his speech to my presence. I stood right next to my assailant and looked at him square in the face. He had a cut on his left cheek, and the left side of his face was swollen underneath his eye. That must have been from hitting his head on the dresser the night before.

"Is there a gym here?" I asked him. The group of officers in front of him exchanged puzzled glances. One chimed in, "Yeah, there are two, one by –"

I cut him off.

"Not you. Him." I pointed at my assailant who was still insisting not to acknowledge me. "I'm asking him."

Passers-by started to stop and rubberneck. It broke cultural norms for a woman, particularly a foreigner, to approach a group of officers, and especially to address the one in charge.

He cleared his throat, still refusing to look at me in the eyes. He remained silent. I refused to break my stare at him, then I finally said, "Since there are two gyms, as your officer just stated, I suggest that you start working out; that way the next time that you try to rape a woman, she won't kick your ass."

His eyes flashed black, and his face turned red and purple. The silence among the officers could be cut with a machete. I raised my arms to show everyone my cuts and bruises. I looked like I had been in a boxing ring.

"You see? He did this, and may the record show that he didn't get what he wanted."

I made my statement, and I knew my danger in stating it. They could take my passport and make it disappear, deny having ever seen it. They could write fake reports with fake evidence saying I was involved in some criminal activity to detain me. I was willing to face my consequences. If they knew one officer could try it and get away with it, I could be an easy target for anyone.

Sebas took one look at me when I showed up for breakfast and his face told me he knew everything. Besides, it was a small village and I had not bothered to avoid shitting where I ate. Not only do people from small towns have nothing better to do than meddle in the lives of others, but as a foreigner, I stuck out like a sore thumb.

I told Sebas everything that I had been so badly messing up over the past few months. I did not tell him what happened the night before or about the confrontation that just occurred in the park. He told me that he had been worried about me but was waiting for me to figure some things out on my own. Apparently, my secret life was not so secret, after all. I was in a cycle of destruction that was not only destroying me but set everything around me on fire.

There was no school that week because of a local holiday and then a teachers' strike, so I had a few days off. I had to get caught up with my online classwork, write reports for my volunteer shift hours, and have a virtual meeting with Dr. D for his research so I could get in my graduate assistantship hours. I also knew it was time to face my consequences by telling the truth to my department because I knew I couldn't keep up with my hours at the school and my work hours for the nonprofit. I had to make a radical change to get out of the rut I was in, or I would push myself six feet under. I had no idea what was on the other side of that veil of speaking my truth.

One night, Sebas and I met, and while we were talking, he leaned forward and said, "There is a guy in the corner who has been recording you with his phone off and on for the past hour. DON'T look now. At first, I thought he was just playing with his phone, but now I know that he is filming you. Casually look over when you get up to go to the bathroom." I waited a couple minutes, and when I glanced over on my way to the bathroom, I saw that it was the officer who had tried to rape me a few nights before.

When I got back to the table, I confessed the whole story to Sebas and told him how I confronted the officer on my way to meet him for breakfast.

"Jenni, you can't talk to men like that here, especially not officers. They will not let you have the last word. From this point forward, it will not be safe to go hiking alone, and don't be alone outside at night, even when you can't sleep."

It was time to walk away from my internship and come out with the truth to one of my leaders. Sebas and I both agreed it was best to leave Jardín for a while until everything settled, and that leaving first thing in the morning before the sun came up was best, so that I could just disappear into thin air.

Sebas went to the bus station with my passport info to buy me a ticket out. My bus would leave at 4:30 a.m. the following day for Medellín. We spent the rest of the day together laughing, playing, and packing. Whatever I had accumulated over the past few months in Colombia that wouldn't fit in my suitcase, it was time to let go of. I left a pile of clothes and books for Sebas to give to whoever needed them. I left him cash to pay someone to return the furnishing that had been lent to me back to their owners. I communicated with Hernan that I needed to leave and told him a short version about why with a promise for more details later.

I had to let him know since my apartment was in his name. He didn't meet me with judgment at all, but instead with tender concern, empathy, compassion, and understanding. He was worried about me more than anything, and asked me why I hadn't reached out in the midst of going through so much darkness, especially as a foreigner alone in a new country in a dangerous situation. He asked me to please let him know when I was safe and to keep him in the loop about what was going on.

The next morning, Sebas and I walked together to the bus stop. There was a kiosk open for business for early morning travelers.

"When you get to Medellín, where will you go from there?" he asked.

"To Santa Marta. Carlos said that I can stay in a hotel until he and his spouse move into their apartment, and then I can stay with them."

He was so sad I was leaving, although I felt in my soul that I would be back to Jardín many times later in my journey. "Want to do a shot before you leave? To toast your new path? You can't forget about me and the happy memories we have made here."

"Silly. We have so many more memories to make. I will be back here many times, and you will travel with me away from here many more times."

We did our double shots and shivered them off as pros do, downing hard liquor before the sun had even greeted the new day.

"No matter how far away you are, always remember that you are my yucca, and I am your chicharron." His *Forrest Gump* analogy reminded me of the scene when Forrest was about to go to fight in the Vietnam War, and Jenny's parting words to him were, "Forrest, if you're ever in trouble, you don't have to be brave. You just run, you run far, far away, you promise? You just run."

The bus driver loaded my stuff in the luggage rack. I climbed on board to claim my window seat and waved goodbye to Sebas from my window as we pulled out.

Just like that, as a phantom does, I disappeared into the empty morning darkness to push beyond another veil into another unknown. Jenny and I, we sure knew how to run.

Chapter 21

The Rose that Grew from Concrete

Did you hear about the rose that grew from a crack in the concrete? Proving nature's law is wrong it learned to walk without having feet. Funny it seems, but by keeping its dreams, it learned to breathe fresh air. Long live the rose that grew from concrete when no one else ever cared.

By Tupac Shakur

After a 24-hour bus ride north through excruciatingly curvy mountains, I made it to Santa Marta. Once there, I got a room at the same place where Sebas and I stayed on our vacation. Carlos wasn't working there anymore, but I knew the staff and the neighborhood around it.

The first thing I did after checking in and getting my things settled was thoughtfully write out an email to Joanne. The bus ride provided me 24 long hours of self-reflection. I'd made some big mistakes along life's way, but I always owned them and the damage they caused. My blunt honesty has had a history of being off-putting for most people, and although it is a commendable quality, it doesn't work well if it is not administered with wisdom. Wisdom to know how to speak the truth, in what timing to speak it, and how much of it to share in what timing based on how the receiver of it is capable of processing it. For example, in my email to Joanne, I should have just politely informed her that because of personal reasons, I could not continue with my commitment for the internship, and left it at that.

In my email, I didn't share the full nature of what my living nightmare had become in Jardín: the near overdose, strangers knocking on my door day and night, a police officer attempting to rape me, how dangerous it was to walk by myself to the school, not only the new danger of being assaulted again but danger due to temptation to use cocaine with faculty and friends. I only shared that I was in a battle with cocaine addiction, that I had gotten myself into a difficult situation, that I had left Jardín to safeguard my life and focus on recovery. I fully acknowledged how my actions had negatively impacted those around me, and for that I was truly sorry. I found at least five more ways to express my understanding of what I had done and how many ways I was sorry. I signed very sincerely with cascades of guilt and shame, and sent.

Next, I communicated with Dr. D since he was essentially the main supervisor of all my internship credits. We had organized the internship through the nonprofit, but he was the only one who could sign off on all paperwork related to it, placing the final decisions ultimately in only his hands.

Carlos came to get me, and we went to have lunch at our favorite local place called The Office. They had the best authentic food and made our favorite passionfruit juice. We sat outside at a table, sweating and swatting flies off our food, and Carlos had some great questions for me. With or without the university, what did I want to do with my time abroad? When did my tourist stamp expire? I hadn't even thought that far ahead. I was in survival mode.

With or without the university, if I decided to stay in Colombia, what would I do for work? By teaching in Jardín, I learned about a thing called a TESOL or TEFL certificate, which most companies require in order to teach English. I found companies offering those certificates online for a very economical price. Carlos encouraged me to think ahead about those things because in reality, a finished master's degree would open a door for a job, but to teach English at a university or something like that, and I would still need that TEFL certificate.

He said his apartment would hopefully be ready in a month or less, and in the meantime, I would have to be comfortable in my hotel room.

That's okay, I thought. *I will hear back from Joanne, who will have just as much grace, kindness, and compassion as Hernan and Sebas had. I will figure out a different route for internship hours, I will focus on finishing my semester, everything will be fine. And in my spare time, I will enjoy new adventures here and be on my best behavior.*

Little did I know, little ole me from a whole continent away had created an entire shitstorm all the way in Oklahoma, and what would really happen was far from the story in my head.

Joanne received the email I sent and before she spoke personally with me, took the liberty to forward it to the dean who supervises the entire university's graduate college programs, who in turn called a meeting with the high-ranking faculty in my department. Joanne didn't stop there, but also shared it with the director of the school in Jardín, who in turn shared it with his faculty members.

I was bombarded with emails stating that I was in no way allowed anywhere near the school property, I was not to be in contact with students or be affiliated with any projects related to the school, and the owners of the nonprofit also sent me the same messages about the work

I did for them as a part of my internship. I got an email from Dr. D asking when we could schedule a video chat so that we could speak personally immediately.

Dr. D was a beacon of light during this dark time. I knew that I alone screwed everything up, and I had consequences to face. I understood that I made some big mistakes, and nobody was harder on me for it than *me*. I was the one suffering through addiction alone, in a foreign country, and buried in the mess of my own creation. Dr. D was the only one involved who engaged in a true, empathic conversation with me. The others heard me with their egos and responded as such, worried about their own reputations, worried that my mistakes would tarnish the reputation of the university. Dr. D heard me with his heart, and he responded as such, wanting to know how I was doing on the inside, what had led up to this mess, and what I wanted out of it all.

"The director of our department called a meeting to share your email to Joanne and discuss with other faculty members how to handle this. He suggests that you be removed completely from the program and not given the opportunity to finish your master's," Dr. D filled me in during our video chat.

Fuck. I was humiliated that all those people knew my personal business. I thought about all the years it had taken me to get where I was, all the sacrifices I made to get through my undergraduate degree, the student loans I acquired to get to that point in my studies, and how much self-work I'd done with a therapist to conquer enough fears to even have the confidence to join this master's program. All to not finish?

Dr. D continued, "However, since he and I have worked together for years, he respects my decisions and I have asked him to wait to enforce such harsh consequences until speaking personally with you. I have a suggestion about what you can do to still finish your degree. Are you wanting to stay abroad longer than December?"

Yes.

"Do you want to finish your degree by May? Are you safe now? Are you going to keep your nose clean and get your shit straight?"

Yes. I was 100 percent ready to say yes to all the questions he asked me.

"I am willing to stick out my neck for you this time, but if I pull strings to help make all this work out for you and you drop a bomb on it, the bridge will be burned and the consequences irreversible. Do you understand this?"

Yes. He planned to meet with the dean and the head of the department to see what he could do. In the meantime, I was instructed to keep up with my research work and finish out my semester of online coursework.

Carlos and I went to the immigration department and learned a few days after the New Year that I would have to leave Colombia for at least six months. Americans are only allowed to spend six months per year in Colombia, and my time was almost up. I had to cross a border, but which one? I looked at a map. I was at almost the northernmost point of Colombia. I could take a boat to Panama and backpack my way up through Central America, or catch a flight from Medellín to any other country around South America.

I was connected to the Jenni I'd been at 19, who fearlessly showed up in Cozumel on a one-way ticket. I felt again the internal anguish I'd had on my flight back to the states when I found out I couldn't stay. I didn't have to go back to the states this time, though. Looking at the map, all I saw were infinite possibilities. The world was mine, and the borders only existed for crossing and experiencing adventures.

Where next? I can get on a bus and go south until I feel like stopping.

After the New Year, I would take bus rides south, cross the border into Ecuador, and find adventure waiting for me there. I could get on a bus that would take me south, place by place, until eventually I would reach the border of a new country and just keep hopping borders. I had no idea what it would be like to cross a border by land, but the idea of it enthralled me. I wanted to just keep going on buses until the roads ran out or the buses stopped running.

***

Once plans were made, it helped me to know how to spend my time with Carlos. I stayed with him and his spouse in their apartment, where I had a cot on the floor, a desk, chair, and Wi-Fi so I could finish my semester. I spent time with Carlos' family, ate homemade food at his grandma's where we went to wash our clothes by hand. That was a long, 45-minute walk in the sweltering heat with our laundry bags hoisted up on our shoulders, soaked in sweat, all to wash it and haul it back wet, until we could hang it up in our apartment.

Carlos took me to places that only locals go and introduced me to his friends. Carlos is a professional dancer and is a highly-respected mentor in his community who spends his time giving dance classes. He took me to beaches where we watched countless sunsets. My favorite part of those beaches were the Afro-Colombian women who carried platters of coconut desserts called, "Cocadas" on their heads. I could buy a whole assorted bag of them for a couple bucks, and we would eat them until we were in a sugar coma with our feet in the sand watching people around us party. We talked for hours and hours, watching waves roll up onto the beach.

My time in Colombia was ending, but I had so much left to see in Colombia. I was crushed that I ruined such a beautiful experience with my cocaine divergence.

Colombia will always be here, and you can come back again and again. You made mistakes, but they don't have to be the ending of this story.

One morning I woke up with the vision of a vibrantly colored orchid. A memory came to mind of a woman I met while hiking, who had been outside watering her flowers as I hiked by. She had a little house tucked away in the side of the mountain, surrounded by coffee plants and banana trees, and her house was adorned with all kinds of gardens with a medley of different flowers planted in tiered beds. I stopped to compliment her on her beautiful flowers. She offered me some water and told me a piece of her story. I learned that her "husband" (who was also the town drunk) wouldn't "let" her walk into town to work anywhere, so she started her own flower business as a means of finding her independence. The people in town who had all those potted orchids hanging on their balconies bought their flowers from her. Her story inspired me. I wanted that flower to always remind me that no matter how hard things may seem, there is always an answer.

I already knew that I wanted to get a tattoo before I finished this part of my adventure, and now I knew it needed to be a vibrant orchid on the left side of my neck, placed so I could see its beautiful open blossom every day. I went to a tattoo shop to explain my design idea.

The next morning, he had the drawing ready, but I was shocked when I saw it. I imagined something small, maybe two inches in diameter. The orchid he designed was at least twice the size of what I had in mind, and it would take up a considerable space on my neck. I was on the verge of changing my mind when I heard a girl by the register up front say to her friend softly, "If she walks out without getting tatted right now, I am stealing that flower design for me. Those colors are so beautiful."

Oh, hell no! That was *my* flower. I earned it.

"Let's start right now," I told my artist.

The four hours of excruciating pain was worth it, and I love my beautiful flower more every day. People often ask me what it means. It has numerous meanings, and as I continue to travel, it grows to have more. At first, it represented Jardín. I found the start of a new life path in Jardín in spite of the darkness that ensued from my bad decisions. I began to open and bloom in a new way, and I want to see that flower every day to remind me to always keep blooming no matter what. The remaining meanings are only for me to know.

I spent my birthday and Christmas with Carlos and his family. It was the first Christmas I ever spent on a beach. However, I knew that the day after Christmas was the day I needed to go. On my way back south toward the border, I wanted to go back through Jardín one last time, sober, to pay my respects and show my face with my head held high. I always own my mistakes, and my journey started in this magical place. I wanted to say goodbye to Juancho and Sebas. I wanted to pay my respects to the place that had so immensely impacted my life for the better, and I wanted to apologize, even if just to myself. I wanted to close things on a positive note before I left the country. I had no idea when I would come back to Colombia, although my soul told me I would eventually make a lot more memories there. I wanted to close the old chapter so that I could make a new, better one next time.

Chapter 22

Bucaramanga

At the Santa Marta bus terminal, I had every intention of getting a ticket to head back to Medellín, but I heard a ticket vendor yelling another city's name. When I heard the name of the city, something inside me went *ping ping*.

"Bucaramangaaaaaaaaaa," this little guy in a pressed t-shirt and ball cap yelled down the corridor.

"Where is that?" I asked him.

"About 9 hours southeast of here. Getting closer to the border of Venezuela."

He showed me on a map. It wasn't that far away from Medellín and wouldn't take me too far off my path to get south to the border. After paying $20 for my bus ticket, I followed him around the kiosks to the boarding docks, stuffed my bag onto the back of the bus, and off I went.

It was only 9 a.m., so I would arrive in Bucaramanga early in the evening, although it would be dark. I hoped that the bus had Wi-Fi so that I could use my phone to look for a hostel and have a clue of where to go upon arriving.

I reflected on how nervous I had been when I first arrived in Medellín, how scared I was to go on that bus trip with the singing girl and her friends, and marveled at how far I had come, just letting things unfold and flow.

I secretly adore bus rides. They became part of the life I now lived, like the wind, free to blow anywhere I wanted, when I wanted. I had anywhere from 9 to 12 hours (or possibly longer in Colombian time) if there was a mudslide, motorcycle accident, or a police check that held us up. Sometimes, all these things could happen in one bus ride, but it never bothered me because it's all a part of the adventure.

I popped my earbuds in to drown out surrounding noises. My nerves were shattered. I was exhausted on a soul level. Several hours alone with my thoughts at home would have driven me crazy; several hours alone with my thoughts during a bus ride adventure was a welcome experience. I never took night buses, not only because they are more dangerous and I can't sleep on buses, but mostly because during the day I could see how nature scenery and architecture differ among places.

With my face pressed against the bus window, waves of nausea rolled through my body in sync with the tossing and turning of the bus driving around curves, then around traffic, before finding other curves. If I didn't fear for my life at least once on a bus ride in Colombia, I didn't feel like it was an authentic experience. I enjoyed the thrill of dangerous experiences, but as scenery rolled on by, I was left with the question in my mind, *But why do I choose self-destructive ones?*

Sometimes, drivers passed slow motorcycles, whipping around curves where they couldn't see anything that was coming around the corner, and I would see the drop off the side of the mountain through my window. I could see small rocks being thrown from the tires of the bus, bouncing to their new location in the valley below. Every time we stopped because of a landslide, I thought about how one could happen to our bus at any time, knocking us off that feeble path like a toy car, sending us tumbling down the mountain. It was scary, but mostly it sent adrenaline surging through my body.

I connected my phone to Wi-Fi so that I could check out hostels in Bucaramanga. There were several with beds available, but I was looking for a specific *ping ping* inside me before I made my choice. Finally, after scrolling through several pages of options, I found it. It was the last one, and it had no reviews since it was a new listing. Something about its name, Hostal Chitota, resonated with me. I only booked one night there since it had no reviews. I wouldn't know if I wanted to stay there longer until I gave it a chance. I found out when I got to Bucaramanga that the hostel was about 15 minutes away from town in the country. My cranky taxi driver wasn't too thrilled about having to find it at night. The entrance was not easy to see until you were right in front of it. The owner watched for me to arrive so that he could unlock the heavy, black iron gate.

As soon as the gate latched behind me, the sight in front of my eyes drew the air from my lungs, and I gasped. The path leading to the property was lined with tiki torches, which offered a comely glow. The light flirtatiously revealed a cobblestone path that was very obviously laid by hand with love. The fire revealed just enough of the foliage to know it was grown intentionally around the path.

I felt like the universe rolled out a red carpet intentionally for me in that very moment when I needed it the most. The owner, Don Enrique, graciously and kindly welcomed me and insisted on helping me carry in my pack. Inside his home, he showed me the bunk beds where I reserved a bed for seven bucks a night, and then he said, "This is what you reserved for the price you found online. However, we have no other guests. You have the whole place to yourself. We would like to offer you our honeymoon suite outside, where we believe you will be much more comfortable. My wife would like to include three meals a day, which you are welcome to eat with our family. The price for all of this included would be $20 a night. Would this interest you?"

I only had one check left from OU, and I hadn't imagined spending that much per night, but it was so cheap compared to what something like that in the U.S. would cost. I said yes. I trusted that money would come somehow, from somewhere.

As they showed me the rest of their property, I was awed by the magical haven they had created for guests. The honeymoon suite was a stand-alone cabin-like room, which included a soft, clean double bed with soft pillows and lace curtains that untied to flow around it. The walls around the cabin were a canvas tent stretched sturdily around a strong wooden frame. The door had zip-up openings, the inner one being see-through and the outer one being a solid canvas covering for when I wanted privacy.

This space was big enough for a waist-high suitcase rack, and there was also a card table with two chairs in the corner that had plug-ins for my electronics, laptop, and cell phone. There was full Wi-Fi coverage in the outside space as well, making it possible for me to sit in the privacy of my room to work on my laptop. The walk outside the suite was even more stunning. In between the private suite and the other vacant private suite outside was a covered area where there was a couch, a shelf with books in several different languages to accommodate travelers from all over the world, and a glass table-top spanning two tree trunks. Behind the reading area and sleeping suites was a simple stand-alone wood install built by hand with beautiful local wood where there was a toilet and a sink. On the backside of the structure was an outdoor shower with a curtain that I could pull around if I desired privacy.

This was absolute paradise. I could only be there a few nights since I planned to spend New Year's Eve in

Jardín, closing that chapter before heading to the border of Ecuador.

There I was, just me and my private honeymoon suite all to myself, the luxury of soft blankets on a big soft bed with puffy pillows, and the sound of the river rushing by. This was my definition of pure bliss.

The next morning, the owner's wife brought me fresh breakfast served on a platter. She made arepas that were from that specific part of Colombia, topped with fresh cheese, a side of fresh-cut fruit from one of her trees, and hot coffee. I ate my breakfast in blissful solitude, gazing at the river scenery. My spirit was begging to go explore this new city, but first I needed a quiet day to myself.

I explored the banks of the river and walking trails in the woods before coming back for a homemade lunch with Don Enrique's wife, Stella, over which we had a lovely conversation. It was her husband's dream for years to have a hostel like this, and after saving for most of their marriage, he finally created it.

The cool breeze of the natural air was enough to keep me comfortable that night while I cuddled, warm and cozy, under the soft blankets in the plush bed, nestled in my mountain of pillows. The days got warm enough to be hot, making the outside shower experience absolutely divine under the open sky, surrounded on all sides by stunning views of nature. The water was cool, but not unpleasantly cold, and since Stella and I were alone on the property during the day, I didn't bother to pull the curtain around me. I shivered and shook under the refreshing crystalline water that rippled over my voluptuous frame. I was in love with how my white skin looked in contrast to the vibrant green of the lush jungle foliage around me.

I woke up cozy in my bed the next morning to the peaceful sound of the Suratá river flowing nearby. After breakfast, Stella drove me to downtown Bucamaranga. I wanted to set out on foot to explore everywhere my strong legs could carry me. I wandered through markets, down alleyways, and dodged traffic while crossing busy intersections into crowded neighborhoods. I smiled at strangers and had traditional, local food from a hole-in-the-wall restaurant where I tried new food.

While traipsing around downtown people-watching, I saw a guy sitting on a curb tying his shoes who had two motorcycle helmets hanging on his left arm. Two helmets indicated to me that he was either a moto taxi driver, or he was holding his girlfriend's helmet who was somewhere shopping or using the bathroom.

"Hey!" I hollered, and he looked up at me as I approached.

"Do you have a moto taxi?" I asked him in Spanish.

"Yeah. Where do you want to go?"

"On a two or three-hour ride to see stuff around here before the sun goes down and then back to my hostel when we are finished."

He studied me, trying to figure out what he could get away with charging. "Thirty bucks," he said.

"Ha. Ten bucks," I low-balled him.

He scoffed. "25."

"$20. Final offer," I said. That was still good money for two to three hours of his time, and other moto taxi guys were starting to come up to me with better offers. He knew he was about to lose me.

"Deal," he said and handed me my helmet. From the back of the motorcycle, I was surrounded by a new world all around with no barrier in between us. Oh, the air! It smelled different everywhere I went, even towns three hours apart in the same region. I wanted to just be engulfed in that air. The air and I had so much in common. I wished I could be naked on that motorcycle so that I could intimately embody the whole physical experience.

Being on a motorcycle was as close as I could get to being on a magic carpet ride.

Colombian traffic is nuts, especially in big cities, on a motorcycle surrounded by countless other motorcycles and big work trucks, everyone fighting for the right of way. It was exhilarating every time, and I loved it. People around me were so close we could reach out to grab each other. We swooped between cars and wove in and out around trucks.

He took me to the famous Bicentennial Bridge of Bucaramanga that was in a movie. He took me to famous churches all around the hub of downtown. We motored through the outskirts of town where there were several huge shoe factories; he taught me that Bucaramanga is the capital of shoe production, not only for Colombia but also neighboring countries in South America. Shoe production is a staple of the economy, which explains why I saw so many shoe outlets lining the streets around downtown. From the outskirts of town, he drove me to a neighboring Village called Girón whose population was around 200,000 people. It was only about 15 minutes away, making it a popular place for locals to spend their days off when they wanted to escape the chaos in the big city. It's an enchanting village, and I wandered around for about 20 minutes soaking in the architecture of the colonial buildings and the beauty of the church in the main plaza.

We sat down in the shade, soaking in the scenery, when I saw a local farmer pushing a fruit cart piled high with fresh mango and papaya.

"Do you want some fruit?" I asked. "My treat."

He accepted, and the farmer cut open a papaya, filled two cups with slices, and then did the same with a ripe mango. We were enjoying our fruit when a little old lady walked by selling homemade coconut ice cream.

Oh my God, coconut is one of my favorites, and she made this homemade ice cream with real coconut and pure cream from her cow's milk. They were so good that I ate one scoop after another until my stomach couldn't fit any more.

From there, we made our way back to the city to a lookout point near the airport. I could see the entire scope of Bucamaranga and the shadows of small towns like Girón that neighbored the city. I watched the sun go down, and just like that I had seen a new city. My taxi driver dropped me off at my hostel just in time for a late dinner with Don Enrique and Stella, even though my tummy was still full of coconut ice cream.

When I got back to my room, I thought, *What a perfect ending to a perfect day.* I remembered what Or told me about saying yes to everything I possibly could as far as trying new things and going to as many places as possible. *This* is how I wanted to live my adventures. *This* is what I deserved.

But first, it was time to go back to Jardín with my head held high, face the mess I had abandoned, and close that chapter before carrying on south toward the border of Ecuador.

Chapter 23

Nevertheless, She Persisted

The next day, those wonderful hostel owners pulled me in for a heartfelt hug as they dropped me off at the bus terminal. I faced a long ride back to Medellín, where I would stay the night at Hernan's before heading back to Jardín the next morning. I would arrive just in time to bring in the New Year in my beloved village.

My body was begging for coke, but I knew my decision to be sober was a choice between life and death. As we rolled through the mountains toward Jardín, the chemical smell of coke invaded my nose. We were going through an area where coke was being made deep in the mountains. My body went into a full-blown reaction as if I had just used. My heart pounded, and my palms were sweating profusely. My desire for coke felt like a monster inside me roaring to be released. I wondered if this is what Alex had felt about heroin, as I recalled the incident in that bathroom the night I disappeared from rehab.

I knew that I could never touch it again, not one bump, not one line, not even once. Just one bump meant a door would open for me to dive into a kilo, and if I did that, there was a high probability I would never make it back out again. I knew that for New Year's Eve I had to be completely sober. I knew what I was walking into by returning to Jardín--all the temptations and triggers, including the guilt and shame I carried on my back from the consequences of my poor decisions and the people I had hurt.

Smelling booze sent my body into a full-blown reaction because both habits were married as codependents, and I had to choke both of them at the same time, at least until my divorce with cocaine was finalized. Just one drink to bring in the New Year would open the door for that monster to barge through. If I chose coke, I would be choosing to die, and I wasn't ready to die. I had more adventures to discover on this incredible path I chose. I felt like I had more to give the world and more for the world to give to me.

I arrived in Jardín around noon and people whispered and stared. Faculty members who had been a part of the "crucifixion committee" glared down their noses, while other faculty members with whom I'd partied hung their heads and looked the other way, knowing they had let me take the hit for our group as a whole. I held my head high, sober, owning my mistakes, and also knowing that on my way down, I had not taken anyone else with me. Mostly, I think they were surprised that I came back to show my face after being humiliated, especially so soon.

I found a hotel room to drop my bag in and a private place to wish Sebas and other friends a happy New Year. Giovani saw me walk by and texted me. He wanted to know the full story about what happened.

"Come party for old time's sake! Epic New Year's party!"

I knew this temptation would be present, and I had prepared myself. There could be no "one last time." By the time 9 p.m. rolled around, the entire park was filled with people drinking and dancing, and this party would last at least 24 hours to bring in the New Year. I couldn't be around for that, and I wouldn't.

I retreated to the refuge of my quiet hotel room by the time the party really kicked off. Juancho texted me asking if I was back in Jardín, and then he came to see me.

The Other Side of Fear

While we sat on my balcony talking, he shared with me what he had heard. I told him the truth, all the truth, as he deserved nothing less. He was excited that he made it to the second round of his application process, and within a couple weeks I found donations from a sponsor that would cover all his expenses in Bogotá for his second round of tryouts.

Little did I know at that time that Juan would end up getting accepted into this program, would go to Armenia, Georgia to finish high school in Europe, and then would win a full scholarship for an anthropology degree at the University of Oklahoma. That was one of the great things that came from my time spent there, in spite of the mistakes I made. I stayed inside all night writing in my journal about all the things I needed to let go of to close my chapter in Jardín.

I woke up the next morning to the news that Giovani had been murdered in the night. Sometime around 3 a.m., he was stabbed 40 times and left to die in a pool of blood outside the bar where we always partied. Had I not safeguarded my life, I would have been there with him, as I had been so many times. I guess his big boss came to collect a debt, but he didn't have the money because he consumed the product he was supposed to sell. He left behind his wife and eight-year-old special-needs daughter. The news broke my heart, but it also reminded me of Alex and the fate he shared with me the day before I escaped rehab so many years ago. I had chosen life not a moment too soon.

***

I left on New Year's Day morning to begin making my trek south toward the border of Ecuador. I wanted to take time to see important places along the way, starting with Manizales in the main coffee region of Colombia, six hours south of Jardín. The first morning that I woke up there in my hostel I ventured to the town center where I found the famous cathedral in Plaza Simon Bolivar. I paid $3 for a tour that would take me up a winding staircase to the tallest point of the tower (it's the tallest cathedral in the country of Colombia), and from the top, I drank in the view of Manizales. I also saw Pereira, Armenia, and Buena Vista while I was in that region.

After exploring the Eje Cafetero, I made it to Popayán, "the white" city. I was sitting at a table outside of the Juan Valdez coffee shop, drinking my coffee, eating a piece of their famous chocolate cake and writing, when this guy and his daughter sat down at a table next to me to start a conversation. It turned out he was a famous singer in Colombia.

He had me pull up his YouTube videos and played songs for me on his guitar. Unfortunately, I don't remember what his name was, but it was definitely an unforgettable moment to take in the stark contrast of the striking blue sky above the whitewashed colonial buildings that lined the streets while this handsome Colombian man serenaded me with his beautiful music.

The next day, I studied a map, choosing my path from there to the border and making decisions about where I wanted to stop along the way. My original idea would have taken me through a bigger town called Cali, but my intuition told me that was a bad idea. Although it is the salsa-dancing capital of the world, rich with Colombian history, it is also the violent home of the Cali cartel. I knew I would be hit from all sides with teenagers competing with one another for my cocaine business, and I knew I was not strong enough to withstand such temptation. My life depended on my decision to not see Cali at that point in my journey. I paid for a $12 ticket straight from where I was in Popayán all the way to the border town of Ipiales, which would be my last stop in Colombia before crossing the border into Ecuador.

I was all geared up to have my border-crossing adventure. I planned on staying in Ipiales for a couple of nights. There was a sacred temple there that other travelers had mentioned, and while they shared their experience, something in me had gone *ping ping*.

A bus station vendor snagged me and stuck me on the last available seat inside of a microbus, in the front seat next to the driver, and he even had to clear his personal things to make room for me. I've always loved the front seat on bus rides, not only to mitigate motion sickness, but because of the front-row seat to the beautiful views.

I was busy taking pictures, rolling along, in love with the glorious mountain views and elated about the thought of exploring every square inch of the paradise Colombia had to offer. The bus driver tried to converse casually with me and offered me snacks and Coca Cola, which I politely declined, pretending I didn't speak Spanish.

About seven hours into our trip, the bus driver pulled into the bus terminal of a small town called Pasto, where several passengers got off. I heard the bus driver tell someone we would be there for at least 15 minutes, so I ran inside to go pee and get some plantain chips. I came back out and leisurely scrolled through the pictures on my phone of the scenery from my front-seat view. The driver finally climbed up into his seat and off we went, navigating tight turns of local traffic before finally coasting onto the highway, heading straight into the mountains.

"So, where do you want to go?" the bus driver suddenly asked me in Spanish.

I thought that maybe I had misunderstood, so I asked in Spanish, "Excuse me?"

"Where do you want to go?" He repeated.

My stomach started to turn itself inside out. Suddenly, I spoke perfect Spanish. "Um, well, I bought a ticket to Ipiales, so how about you take me there?"

He kind of chuckled. He looked over at me. "I'm not taking you to Ipiales."

All the hair on my arms stood up.

"Look in the back," he said. I did. Every other passenger on the bus had gotten off. I was all alone with this jackass, who was now threatening me and speeding down the highway.

"Let me out right now," I demanded. My voice was shaky, but I was trying to control it so he wouldn't see any emotion.

"I want to be alone with you. I promise I will leave you with a souvenir you will remember forever." He said just like the cop the night before I fled Jardín. This time, I was sober.

"Pull over and let me out right fucking now," I demanded in Spanish.

"I promise you will love it," he said. "Look at those mountains that are now so close. We can have the mountains all to ourselves, and nobody will hear us, señorita." *Yuck*, the cop promised I'd love it, too.

After the incident in Jardín with the officer who assaulted me, I had seen a shiny switchblade for sale in the window of a local shop and decided to always carry it in my bra. Oh, thank fuck I had my knife in my bra. I had to threaten him, and I had to threaten him so hard it scared the shit out of him.

I didn't know if this guy had a knife or a gun. Just against him, I knew I could win; I could even kill him if I had to, but if he took me some place where it was me against more than one man, I wouldn't stand a chance. It was my life or his. I chose mine, and I had to continue to do it in such a way that he needed to fear for his. So much adrenaline was plunging through my veins that I felt like I had the strength to lift a car.

As these thoughts flashed through my head, we rolled farther and farther from town. The scenery flashed by, along with flashbacks of the scenery that whizzed by the day that Oscar kidnapped me in his truck. I didn't have a knife then. I didn't have a fighting chance. This time I did, and I had a weapon. I remember how Oscar's sweat smelled when it dripped onto my face during the rape, and this time my story would have a different ending. I remembered the day that I'd looked over at Oscar while he ground his teeth and threatened to kill me. Back then, I'd thought that if I had a knife I could stick it in his neck. I couldn't do it then, but I could do it now.

I knew I had to be calculated and quick. He glanced to his left out the window, and in a split second, I snatched the knife from inside of my left bra cup. At that moment, an angel called his cell phone. Between his answered phone call and the low noise of the radio, he didn't hear me pop the blade out. This time I would have the last word. Nobody would ever take anything from me again. He ended the call, and I prepared myself to attack, knowing I had to measure my force so I wouldn't stick the knife all the way into his neck.

When he hung up his phone, I startled him with my threat, pulling my knife and holding it to his neck. "Pull over now or I will fucking kill you," I yelled in his ear.

I had no idea whether his reaction would be to take my threat seriously, try to take my weapon from me, or pull out one of his own, but based on his response, I was fully prepared to stick the whole knife in his neck in a split second if needed. Luckily, I scared the shit out of him. He swerved all over the highway and immediately pulled over.

"Tranquila, I was just messing with you!" He pleaded.

When he stopped the bus, he put his hands up. "Miss, I was just playing with you. I would never harm a woman." I knew I could not get out of the bus first because I risked him speeding off with the only few belongings I had.

"Your bags are right behind your seat, miss. I swear to God I wouldn't hurt a woman. I have daughters." As soon as he got out, I also got out, with the knife still in my hand.

I guess while we were stopped in Cali, he moved my bags from the very back of the bus where they usually get stuffed to the floor right behind my seat. He didn't want to have to take me all the way to the border since I was the only passenger. That was something he should have mentioned at the bus stop. He should have said, "Miss, you are my only passenger. Here's a refund for the rest of your ticket. Catch a different bus heading to Ipiales at a different time with more passengers."

But, he hadn't said that. Now, he pulled out my bags and dropped them to the ground. He apologized again for scaring me and asked if he could take me back into town. I told him I wanted a refund for the rest of my ticket, and that I wanted him to leave or I would kill him and drive myself to the border in his bus. He pulled a bill from his pocket, dropped it on my bags, and left, profusely apologizing the whole time.

There I was, alone on the side of the dusty road, about three miles from the town I had just passed through. *What if he comes back for me? What if he comes back with more men?* All I knew was I had to walk back into town with all my shit loaded on my back. The whole time, I kept looking back over my shoulder to see if anyone was trailing behind. *Hadn't I felt like this for years, though, feeling ghosts breathe down my neck and villains spy on me from around corners?* On my long walk back into town, I chuckled at the contemplation of whether that asshole would've been as scared if I had pulled out a dildo instead of a knife, and I vowed that one day I would carry a dildo in my shoulder satchel to try my theory.

An hour later, I found a shitty hotel on the outskirts of town. The only thing that mattered to me is that it had a deadbolt so I could feel safe that night. The little hotel was so gross that I was only charged $4 for a single room with no Wi-Fi, no hot water, and plenty of cockroaches to keep me company. I was fine to dump all my shit on the floor, sleep on top of the bed fully clothed in what I'd worn that day and head out the next morning to get to the border. I just wanted to feel safe for a few moments.

My nerves were smoked. My trauma trigger had been tripped and I had mentally prepared myself to kill that man. Adrenaline still surged rampantly in my body; I was desperate for a release. The first place my mind went was a double shot of liquor and a fat line of Colombian-grade cocaine, but I knew that under no circumstances could I alter my mind. I knew myself well enough to have the genuine understanding that if I introduced substances, there would be no limit. Instead, I had to protect myself, my life, and my mind. I had to start making different decisions. My life at that moment depended on my decision to stay sober, not only because of the risk of a bender, but I had to stay aware of my surroundings given what just happened.

I still needed a release. After I locked my room, I went outside to smoke a cigarette. I took a drag off my cheap menthol and was looking off into the distance when a broken sign a few blocks away caught my eye. Enough of the letters were lit up for me to read, "Tattoo." A tattoo! That would give me my release.

Even though I was trauma-triggered, I was proud of defending myself from that bus driver. I got a piece of my power back by recreating the ending to a former story. I was overwhelmingly grateful for the tragedy in my life at 20 because had Oscar not put me through that, I wouldn't have been prepared to defend myself in the situation I just survived.

I wanted a tattoo that denoted the symbolism of the story I recreated my ending to. I wanted a colorful butterfly with the Latin phrase around it, "Eat amen perseverabat," which means, "Nevertheless, she persisted." Yes, I did.

People following my journey on social media would often message me with their travel questions. Fear-based questions that I commonly heard were, "Aren't you scared of being kidnapped? What if there are bad guys in your path who target women traveling alone?" Kidnappings and assaults happen in parking lots a few blocks down the street from one's backyard in small towns like Yukon, Oklahoma. Bad things can happen anywhere, to anyone. Why not live my life regardless? What Oscar did to me didn't hold me back, and this guy's attempt to harm me damn sure wouldn't either.

Besides, now I knew that I could face anything and plow my way through it. So, I persisted. I persisted through four hours of tattooing done by the hand of a 17-year-old boy who was just starting his tattoo business. I didn't care that he was new. I showed him what I wanted and told him to let his creativity flow, just be sure he used clean needles. My tattoo came out crooked with uneven wings and ink that permanently ran into my white skin on the underside of my bicep, but since it was the flesh of my arm hidden by my armpit, I didn't even care. It is still stained there, and I still don't care. My wings aren't perfect, either, and the road to finding them has been rocky, but they are mine, and I know they are both beautiful and perfect enough.

The Other Side of Fear

    The tattoo gave me what I needed. Beyond the message of persistence, it helped me have an energy release. I could finally come down. I slept well that night with all my little cockroach friends. The next day, I awoke with a renewed view about life. It was time to go see the magical temple and then brave the border into Ecuador.

Chapter 24

The Sacred Temple

When I arrived at the bus terminal of Ipiales the next day, I immediately heard a driver calling out, "Temple! Taxi to the Las Lajas Temple! The universe provided guideposts every step of the way. They had a place where I could store my bags right there in the bus terminal for a dollar, and then a taxi would take me to the sacred sanctuary for another dollar. No time to lose!

Stuffed in a taxi bus with other travelers packed in like sardines, I sat gazing out the window, and the heat of the sun was making my new tattoos on my neck and arm tingle. The taxi parked at the opening of a paved road that disappeared around a bend. All I could see were people wandering around the bend in both directions. The excitement of the unknown pulled me onward, out of the taxi, and onto the path by myself.

Around the bend, the paved road continued into the distance, bursting with street vendors selling everything you can imagine: handbags, woven blankets and quilts, keychains, pottery, clothing, embroidered sandals, and a medley of street fruit. I spent time checking out every little thing, step-by-step, until the path curved to the right, and there it was.

I froze. My intuition had told me it would be magnificent, but this was even more astonishing than anything I could conjure with my human mind. It looked like a palace built for kings and queens right between mountain passes, bridging the canyon over the Guáritara River. The mystic power it held pulled me closer without my acknowledgment, leading my feet one in front of the other until I reached the bridge. According to Colombia's legends, the mystic power I felt also created miracles that occurred there dating back to the 1700's. Visiting the temple is viewed as a pilgrimage by those who believe in its magical power. I didn't know the details of the specific legends, nor did I feel a draw to dig into them. I knew it had its own kind of magic just for me.

I was rendered speechless by the power, yet my feet carried me across the bridge while the river roared below. Tears flooded my cheeks, and more than anything, I was thankful that I was so treasured and loved that life itself would give me the opportunity to see something so exquisite in person with my own eyes. I could hear the gasps of others around me having their own holy experience, the river, and spiritual songs sung in the different languages spoken around me.

I saw a glimpse at how big God really is, that it isn't about a religion, but a spiritual experience. This moment was a spiritual experience that didn't divide people by doctrine and details, but instead transcended every man-made boundary. It transcended language barriers, skin color, and religious beliefs. I felt the divine force of holy love that beckoned me forward with tenderness, open arms, and divine feminine grace. It wanted to show me and give me something.

After exploring both inside and outside the temple, I stood outside basking in the glory of how the turrets of this Neo-Gothic architecture elegantly contrasted the green foliage of the Colombian mountains. *I want to be closer to the river.* I immediately saw the opening to a path leading me down to where I wanted to go. The river rushed through the canyon about 150 feet below, and in that moment, I had never been so grateful for a strong, healthy body, which could take me anywhere I wanted to go.

I descended the steps, taking in the beauty around me from new angles. When I reached the bottom, I was rendered speechless again by the living beauty surrounding me and the roar of the rushing river. Hidden among the trees was a narrow dirt path that led into the woods. Dreamily walking along the path, I found an opening to the riverbank where I found a boulder and relaxed near the water.

The immense holy, pure love allowed me to access the truth held within my skin. I understood the toxicity of the adrenaline hangover left from the dangerous situation I had escaped the day before. The experience flooded me with rage, anxiety, powerlessness, victimization, shame, and awoke the maggot feeling I had felt on the inside at different times throughout my life.

The incessant vibration of love emanating from the sacred land around me did something that drastically impacted my life from that moment forward and into forever. I longed to feel the water of the river. As I knelt by it, I saw a little girl crouched down on a rock looking at me with a huge smile on her face. I blinked twice, thinking I was imagining things. I realized the only thing covering her skin was a handmade skirt and baubles adorning her wrists. Her hair was long and dark, cascading around her face, her skin a light brown color, like coffee with a splash of milk.

We remained still, looking at each other from afar. I called out to her, and she shook her head. She pointed to the water, and my instincts told me she wanted me to look there. I studied my reflection in the crystalline water. My short hair, barely long enough to clip back on the sides, guided my thoughts to the femininity I had hidden for years because it made me feel weak and vulnerable.

I let the feeling of pure love flow all over me and welcomed it to come inside. I closed my eyes and splashed my face and hair with the cold water from that river. "I want you to hate me forever" were Oscar's final words to me, and they had been in the soundtrack of my mind for more than ten years. My hate for him expired years ago, but converted into hate for myself. I carried the hate and disgust for so long it seemed normal. The previous day's incident conjured flashbacks from the rape when I was 20. I let them come forward, and I intentionally thought of them as I cleansed my head with that river water.

When I looked up, the girl was gone. After that day, I never felt maggots on the inside of me ever again. The path had led me right to that perfect symbolic ending to a chapter and to a cycle of destruction in my life.

***

From the Ipiales bus terminal, a taxi shepherded passengers to the border for a couple bucks. The border was a madhouse with a long line for the exit stamp to leave Colombia, and another long line for entry into Ecuador. *Welcome to Ecuador* read an imposing blue sign hoisted above several lanes of car traffic, waiting for inspection by immigration officials. Again, I felt fireworks exploding within me. When I first arrived in Colombia back in June, I had no idea I would cross the border into Ecuador. What other borders would I cross?

Rugged backpackers who wandered alone on their journeys stood beside me in line with their worn, dirty packs on their backs. The man who happened to be standing in line in front of me was another angel in my path. He was not only a veteran of crossing borders by land, but as a team, we watched over each other's things during runs to public restrooms.

After five hours of waiting in lines I finally made it across the border, and I paid another dollar for a cab to take me to Tulcan, my first glimpse of a town in Ecuador. This was the closest border town with a bus station where I could get a ticket to Ecuador's capital, Quito. I hadn't given any thought to where in Ecuador I would go. I just showed up. I got there in the nick of time to catch the last seat on the last bus to Quito, where I arrived at 11 p.m. and found a room in a run-down hotel a few blocks from the bus terminal.

My final semester at OU started in a week, and I would have no more paychecks from the university. My next income bump would come with the arrival of my tax return sometime in February. For both of these reasons, I knew I needed to remain in one, economical place for the duration of my 90-day visa. After spending a couple days in Quito, I chose to visit the coast before making my decision about where to set down temporary roots.

During the last few months, I gained access to the web page workaway.com, where travelers can find opportunities to exchange volunteer hours for a place to stay. Once I decided to leave Quito, I logged on to the website and connected with a lady who needed help building her bamboo house. She was delighted to receive me, so off I went with my few possessions on my back, once again bus-hopping to join her. I took a five-hour bus from Quito to Esmeraldas, and from there caught a little microbus of ten people which carried me three hours north on a primitive, hidden path decked with jungle flora I had never seen before! For three sun-filled days, I stayed at her partially-constructed bamboo house. I learned how to build a roof with branches of trees and apply a special wood treatment to the bigger pieces of bamboo used for pillars. I met a Mexican girl named Rita while staying there. She was a professional surfer, fulfilling her life-long dream of traveling the coast of South America, surfing every tide in every country that she possibly could. At night, I slept in a hammock with a mosquito net around me because the jungle-esque coastline of Ecuador had the biggest mosquitos I had ever seen. There must have been a hole in my mosquito net somewhere because I was awake all night scratching, and the next day I had huge red welts all over my arms and legs.

I followed Rita as she headed out surfing with her buddies one day. The beaches were sparsely populated with people, which was a far cry from my experience on the coast of Colombia in Santa Marta. There were locals fishing, and the three of us looking for the right place for my two house-buddies to hop on some waves.

Before long, I met an Argentinian who owned a local surf shop. He invited me to go with him to Playa Negra (Black Beach) where the beaches were covered with dark gray sand and lined with coconut trees, rugged jungle plants, and a handful of local fishermen. The dark beach starkly contrasted clear blue-green ocean waves washing up on the shore. The locals explained to me that the sand was so dark because of its rich composition of metals: uranium, copper, and titanium.

At one point, the beach was getting torn up by miners looking for minerals, but the local people protested. In 2017, a petition with more than five thousand signatures demanded that the beach be left alone. There I was, standing on it with my bare feet. It was so beautiful, it looked like a picture off a calendar.

A group of strangers arrived on the beach, and while chatting, I learned they were on vacation from Uruguay. I played soccer barefoot on the beach for the first time in my life with their kids. Every second was an incredible experience, until the adults opened a cooler of cold beer and popped out an eight ball of coke to start the party.

I knew I was too fragile to stay, so I came up with a story to leave immediately. The realization that I couldn't ever hide completely from coke-- or any drug or alcohol-- struck me, but I still couldn't be around it.

I decided that Mompiche was not the right place to stay long term, so I took a couple of days to explore the area my own way, not knowing if I would ever see the coast of Ecuador again. I needed the stability of a bigger city like Quito while I focused on my academic endeavors.

Before leaving Quito the first time, I exchanged numbers with a new friend who worked the front desk of the hotel where I stayed. He told me that if I decided to come back to Quito he would find a better place for me to stay long-term. See, the universe had everything lined up for me, as always. By the time I got back, he had responded with an address to the new place and I was able to get a taxi directly there to meet the property manager who was expecting my visit.

The boarding house had rooms full of occupied bunk beds, but the room on the top floor was vacant. It was meant for two or three people, with two beds, a private bathroom, and a desk and chair in the corner. The whole floor shared a kitchen at the end of the hall. I was happy to pay the extra monthly expense to have the space to myself. I knew there was no way I could focus on my school stuff if I shared a space with a room full of people.

The building was beautiful and clean, and the owner and his mother were kind to me. At the end of the hallway hung a balcony with vibrant red and pink flowers growing up the wall and through the iron designs of the balcony architecture. I sat out there to drink black coffee, and their bulldog joined me every morning to hump my leg like clockwork.

I grew close with the Venezuelan people in my hostel who made traditional food to share with me. Their stories about what they suffered before fleeing their country in crisis and what they endured was humbling, and it continues to be among the most important knowledge I gained.

Some of my new friends took me to the "Middle of the World," the literal equator itself. There is a telescope you can use to see the volcanoes which surround the city. I made a friend named Jenny who reminded me of myself when I was younger. She was in her early 20s, already an entrepreneur running her very own restaurant selling artisanal hamburgers and thick milkshakes. She used her fluency in three languages to engage with customers in English, Spanish, and French. I cherished the time I spent sitting in her shop listening to stories and writing.

All day, every day, I worked on my final research projects for OU. I had my final comprehension project that every student was required to complete before graduating from the program. Additionally, I had the research project that Dr. D created as a means for making up the internship I'd screwed up.

Dr. D's project consisted of reading eight books of his choice and discussing the process of trauma recovery and resilience exhibited by the main characters, my own life trauma recovery, and the concept of resilience itself, all while adding the academic resources to support my discussions.

I pulled the trigger on finding an online TEFL certificate that I could work toward, hoping it would open doors for teaching jobs as I traveled. My job through the university was officially over, my next income bump was still a few weeks away, and it would have to last until I graduated in May, when I could find a job teaching English.

Twice a week I walked to the restaurant down the road where they sold homemade lunches for a dollar fifty.

Each lunch included soup of the day in an enormous bowl, plus the main plate with the meat of my choice, salad, and rice, topped off with a bottomless glass of fresh juice. Other times, I took my laptop and journal to the Juan Valdez a few blocks away in Plaza Foch, where I bought a large house coffee for less than a dollar. It included free refills served by the handsome clerk behind the counter who was tickled pink to practice English with me. I st there for hours reading, writing, and people-watching. I didn't know it then, but that's when I really started writing this book.

When I needed a break, I snagged a last-minute getaway to Baños, a small nature town located in a valley surrounded by mountains. It was only about four hours south of Quito by bus, and I'd heard great things about it. I wasn't sure how long I would be in Ecuador or if I would ever come back. I remember leaving behind my books, laptop, and everything I had been focused on, cutting loose and having fun for those four days. At my hostel, I met a French girl named Manon, who lived in Spain for years with her grandma and preferred not to be associated at all with her French culture. Manon, another lady from Italy who we'd befriended at our hostel named Fiamme, and I decided to go whitewater rafting together. Manon and I had similar spirits, traveling alone and free on an open road with no plans, but this was Fiamme's first trip alone. In fact, she hadn't traveled at all for years.

The next day, Fiamme and I caught a bus to a nature park right outside of town where she'd heard there was a waterfall worth seeing. While hiking through the forest to find the entrance to the waterfall, I ran into an American guy named Ezra who tagged along. I learned that he had been traveling alone for more than three years and experienced more than 60 countries. Hearing his story was a pivotal part of my journey at that point because it was the first time I had met someone doing that, and it was what I also wanted to do.

I couldn't have braved the waterfall path without both of them. There was a narrow tunnel we had to crawl through to get to the path up behind the waterfall. I suffered from claustrophobia for years after my kidnapping when I was 20, so wiggling my way through a rock tunnel on my stomach was something that took a tremendous amount of courage for me. Ezra and Fiamme talked me through it, especially the moments where I froze, convinced that I couldn't keep going. I am so glad I faced that fear, though, because once I got to the other side, I was able to stand behind the waterfall and look at the rainbow-laced view of the gorge that parted the mountains as far as my eyes could see.

Everything you want is on the other side of fear.

Chapter 25

A 5,000-kilometer Road Trip, Yeehaw

My intensely powerful experience at the temple opened my soul for the next step in my personal transformation, even though I didn't know it at the time. Dr. D's extra research project would provide one of my life's mile markers, which was the inspiration for this book. My takeaways from this time in my life were too impactful to keep to myself.

As I mentioned before, Dr. D's project entailed reading eight books that were memoirs written by people who suffered seemingly-insurmountable hardships, but survived. I analyzed their process of suffering and recovery, examined what resilience meant for them, and then detailed my own process of suffering and recovery. To conclude the project, I compared what I have in common with the books I read and added my own personal data.

Each of the books was so deeply impactful in its own way and imparted meaning that changed me, but one was specifically a catalyst for my spiritual awakening in Quito. It's a memoir called *The Night trilogy* by Elie Wiesel.

In the first part of the trilogy of his memoir *Night*, he spares no discretion sharing the trauma he suffered by surviving Auschwitz. The second part of his trilogy, *Dawn*, begins in France, where he sought political asylum, was recruited by a terrorist group, and was ordered by the leader of his group to execute a political official.

He transitioned from the role of victim--having suffered the cruelest of tragedies at the hands of men committing heinous acts of hate to thousands of people they knew nothing about--to the role of murderer, ordered to take the life of a man he didn't even know. It was his own anger and pain that drove him to want to murder, and he realized that now he had something in common with the men who terrorized him in Auschwitz. He had become like them. Hate and rage were a common cord binding him to those Nazis. They took the life of his father, and now he was doing the same thing to other people, who would look at him the same way that he once looked at the Nazis. The pain and cruelty that he once would wish on no other human life he was now enforcing.

The third part of the trilogy, *Day*, is about the vision he had on his deathbed about love. He was able to see that he hurt others because he was hurt, which helped him see that those who had wounded him were also wounded, and the only way to break that cycle of wounding is to love. He explained all the reasons why he felt unworthy to experience pure love, and I found myself relating to all his points so well. There is much more to be said of the story and all the powerful takeaways in it, and I encourage you to read it yourself if what I just shared resonates with you.

This book was very powerful to me because it allowed me to see myself and each chapter of my life through a new lens. I was able to look at people who hurt me and see them differently. How wounded did a man have to be to rape a woman? I felt that divine love that I had been shown at the temple flow through me toward such men. I had hurt others for years of my life because I was hurt first. Carrying so much anger, bitterness, and hate kept me bound to those who wounded me. I didn't want anything in common with my rapist anymore. This is how I forgave him, alone in my room, writing this paper for Dr

D. I imagined how different his life could be if he experienced the new love that I was experiencing, and I symbolically wished that love to envelope his life.

For years, I lived with the belief my rapist had taken something away from me I could never get back. It was a pillar of my feelings of powerlessness, and I discovered that it's not true. I reclaimed a huge piece of myself by taking my power back from him and then cutting cords to let him go. I took the piece of me back that he was still holding onto. Its edges were torn, but that didn't take away from its value. It was *my* piece, and every jagged edge made it more valuable and more precious. Those fractures and scars made me more beautiful, like exquisite, complex artwork.

I found myself resistant to this process, and I was able to ask myself why? Why does it feel good to feel *bad*? Why does it feel good to hang onto things that wound me? I was resistant to the concept of forgiveness for a number of reasons, one being I thought that it meant what the other person did was okay. Another reason is that I thought forgiving someone meant I was giving a green light for that person to be back in my life. A third reason is because I felt my resentment and anger had kept me safe for a long time, and by no longer cushioning myself with them, I would be weak and vulnerable. I discovered that none of those statements is true. Forgiveness has nothing to do with any of the people who hurt me and *everything* to do with me taking my power back, cutting ties with those who have harmed me and giving myself permission to feel as good as I can every day.

***

I was approaching spring break when a couple from Venezuela with whom I had become friends approached me with a proposition. Did I want to go to Santiago, Chile with them? They wanted to go by bus. We sat down and looked at the map together.

Jesus, the bus ride from Quito to Santiago would be over five thousand kilometers along the Pan-American Highway. It was nearly two-thirds the length of the whole continent from north to south. We would have to cross the border into Peru by land, ride the entire length of the country of Peru, cross the border into Chile, then make it all the way to Chile's capital, Santiago.

Chile, because of its strong economy and promise for better job opportunities, was considered the "United States" of South America and was fled to by many immigrants seeking better opportunities. I had every intention of making it there eventually. I hadn't considered going so soon, especially not in the middle of my last semester at OU while I finished time-sensitive projects. However, I was running low on funds. I had received my tax return, which hadn't been much, and I needed to find work somehow.

I had four days to think about it, but I decided it wouldn't make much of a difference whether I thought hard about it. I wanted to explore Peru after Ecuador but didn't have much money to do anything and had no idea how I was going to secure more yet. I decided to go. I said yes. I worked as much as I could on my school projects, taking breaks only to pack and say goodbyes to friends.

Two Venezuelan friends I'd met in Ecuador were struggling with how companies exploited them (and everyone from Venezuela), knowing they could do so without consequences. My friend Jose, who I met at my hostel, worked for a small hotel for nearly a month, every week hearing a promise of a weekly check being on the way. At the end of the month, the hotel owners let him go with no payment at all. He stayed on site and worked himself into exhaustion doing front-desk duties and housekeeping. He was out a month of his time and energy, had no money for rent or food, and no money to send back to his family in Venezuela who needed food and medicine. He was about to be homeless.

My other Venezuelan friend, Orlando, who was an engineer in Venezuela, had been looking for any kind of work in Ecuador for a year, work at McDonald's, work as a janitor, work doing literally anything. He was currently being offered a couch, a shower, and food in a house with a family also one small push away from being homeless, in exchange for maid services and help with their kids.

I was in my room packing, knowing only four days stood between me and embarking on my longest road trip ever, when it dawned on me to ask Jose and Orlando if they wanted to go to Santiago, Chile. They both said they would love to have the opportunity to thrive in a stronger economy, but if they didn't even have money for food or secure shelter over their head, how could they make 5,000 kilometers south to start over somewhere new?

I launched a campaign on GoFundMe to raise funds for their tickets in hopes for a bit extra to cover the cost of food or lodging. I pushed the campaign hard for three days, and thanks to the donations of my social media followers, a new opportunity for them was made available! Orlando said he had a place to go once we got to Santiago, but Jose didn't. I told him I had enough to cover our tickets there with two weeks of shelter once we arrived, but I couldn't do anything more. I only raised enough to cover tickets. – To cover shelter for two people for two weeks would put me in the negatives in my account, but it was too late to go back on my offer to help get them to Santiago. I knew something else would come through. It had to, and it always did.

On day number five, we boarded our night bus from Quito that would take us twelve hours south to Huaquillas, the last town before the border. Our bus ride was easy, and so was the border crossing from there into Peru. We got there as the sun was coming up, so there weren't many people there. Once we crossed the border, we all crammed into little tuk-tuk taxis to get to Tumbes, the closest town with a bus terminal. Peru was so hot and sandy! Just crossing the border it felt like we had walked through a portal that took us to a far-away land with a totally different climate.

Jose disappeared to talk to a street vendor about how to find bus tickets to get to Lima. Suddenly, Jose and the vendor re-appeared and we were being loaded up into a minivan with all our luggage. It was allegedly going to take us to a bus terminal that ran hauls to Lima. We were getting nervous because the van took us to the middle of nowhere with only sand as far as we could see until we arrived at this little terminal, which looked like a hut in the middle of the desert. Underneath the tin roof was a small crowd of hot, sweaty people standing, sitting, and lying on the dirt floor, surrounded by their luggage stacked up, chicken cages, and children running amuck. There were three filthy showers that consisted of handmade partitions and curtain doors.

"We'd better shower while we have the chance," Orlando suggested. "Who knows when our next chance to shower will be."

He was right. Our bus from there to Lima would be twenty hours in our seats. In Lima, we would have to change bus terminals, and our bus from there to the Chilean border would be another 24 hours. We each braved a shower, and we could all agree afterward it was the dirtiest shower experience we ever had. All we could do about it was laugh. I chuckled at the memory of my very first shower at my very first hostel in Medellín when I met Or in my bunk room. I thought, "If you would have told me then that I would be doing what I am doing right now, there's no way I would believe you."

We sat in the sweltering heat, smelling the unforgettable marriage of smells that were wafting off the toilets with whatever hot lunches the lady was selling from her cart next to the dirty showers. Finally our bus came, and it was packed full. We loaded up and took off, with no AC, all of us hot and sweaty, screaming kids, and roosters crowing from the underneath storage. Our voyage through the first half of Peru was underway, chickens, children, and all.

I enjoyed not having Wi-Fi because I didn't miss a single moment of the scenery with my nose buried in my phone. I had never seen a desert like the one in Peru. Our bus twisted and turned along beige, sandy roads through mini desert mountains, revealing tiny shack-filled communities built into sand dunes. I wondered how people in those communities lived on a daily basis. Where did they get their water? How did they make money? Then, suddenly, the bus would take a sharp right or left, and we would be back in front of the ocean. All its shades of blue contrasted magnificently against all the shades of white and beige of this massive desert.

Buses that go long distances always have a bathroom on board, and it is made very clear that these bathrooms are for urine only. As the sun came up the next morning, we were all awakened by the smell of raw shit suffocating us. Someone apparently couldn't hold it any longer and took a big dump in the dirty little bus bathroom. We were still surrounded by desert, and the furious bus driver pulled over where we waited on the side of the desert road while his assistant cleaned all the poop out of the bathroom system. It didn't help the smell, though. It covered us like a blanket until we got to Lima.

We hadn't eaten a meal since we'd left Quito 36 hours prior. Our funds were super tight, and we couldn't afford for us to all to have a meal more than once, so we staved off hunger with pieces of bread or crackers washed down with a little cup of water that we shared from a gallon jug tucked under a seat. Plus, it was never wise to take a chance on a heavy meal while traveling long distances since we didn't have a place to poop.

The first thing we did when we got to Lima was find a hole-in-the-wall restaurant that sold local Peruvian dishes where we could stack all our stuff in a corner and *eat*. We were so hungry, sandy, sweaty, and tired. After lunch, we loaded our stuff on our backs and walked what seemed like a long time, following Jose and Edson as they navigated through people-filled sidewalks to find our next bus terminal. When we found it, we were so grateful we had chosen to bathe at the last terminal, because this one had no showers. We boarded another bus, and off we went with more children and chickens to begin another 24-hour trip with no AC through the second half of the desert.

After 24 hours on board, our magic carpet ride finally stopped in Tacna, the last town in Peru before the border of Chile. We were able to take turns showering there, finally, after nearly 48 hours of sweat and sand. I felt like I had a bus-full of people's sweat and sand stuck to me, too, including that one guy's poop. Everything had gone smoothly thus far, but a curveball would be waiting for us at border crossing number three.

Chapter 26

Santiago, Chile

"The Chilean border patrol officers are assholes," our cab driver told us. "They hate Venezuelans, and they hate Americans. They will demand that each person has $500 USD in hand before they let you in, *if* they let you in."

We all sat in silence, looking back and forth at each other with fear in our eyes. We didn't have that. Hell, I hadn't even raised enough to totally help these two guys the way that I intended. I intended on having enough to cover two weeks of shelter for both Jose and I once we got there, but I hadn't raised that much. I could not abandon Jose once we got there. I was already going to have to overdraw my account to cover the expense for a shelter somewhere for us both. That didn't even include food. The Chilean border patrol were only enforcing this rule to discriminate against poor Venezuelans seeking asylum.

When we were getting close to the border, the driver made eye contact with me in his mirror and said, "And you. I wouldn't tell them you are traveling with them since they are Venezuelans. Tell them you are traveling by yourself."

"Let's pull together what funds everyone has to see if we have $500 total," Yasmin said. "If we go one at a time, we can show the $500 and then pass it back to the person behind us." She had a great idea. All our money pulled together was just a hair more than $500. We had to see if this would work, and we worried what our consequences would be if it did not.

"If they don't let one of you through this time, try again after they switch guards on shift change," was the last piece of parting advice from the driver before he sped away.

Orlando and Edson decided the order of our group. Orlando first, then Edson, Jasmine, me, and Jose would be last. We lined up in order and stood there quietly observing what was going on through the immigration windows. They were turning away people left and right, and there were a lot of people ahead of us waiting their turn. Besides the immigration officials who were working the windows, there were also officers with dogs watching everyone who was waiting in line. It reminded me of the time in the Colombian airport when I smuggled cocaine in my shoe. I shook my head at the crazy decisions I had made and was grateful I was alive after making so many of them. My life was already so different than the one I left behind when I crossed the border to leave Colombia.

We were all nervous, and then it was our turn. Orlando went first. They asked him tons of questions, and then he showed the money. Finally, after a few more minutes of interrogation, they gave him the green light and called for the next person. Orlando slid over to the left and pretended to be organizing his documents, and as soon as Edson stepped up to the counter, Orlando passed the wad of money into Edson's hand. It all worked like a charm until it was Yasmin's turn.

Orlando and Edson got through, but they did not give the green light to Yasmin. Edson and Yasmin stood there looking at each other wide-eyed. They had never been separated like this before, and here they were about to part ways with a border between them. Yasmin slid to the right and pretended to organize her things, slipping the money into my hand as I stepped up to the counter. The wad fell from my nervous fingers and bills scattered all over the pavement in front of my feet. I handed the lady behind the window my passport and stooped down to scoop it all up with shaky hands. My heart was pounding.

The lady officer behind the counter was very rude and asked me all kinds of questions. Why was I traveling? Why was I traveling alone? What did I do for income that allowed me to travel for so long outside of my country? What was my reason to come to Chile? Did I know anyone in Chile that could validate my stay there? What was the financial condition of my bank account? She informed me that it was very expensive to live in Chile and asked how I intended on supporting myself financially if my intention was to backpack for three months and not work?

It was the first time I had heard Chilean Spanish, and it was hard to understand her. She was asking me questions I didn't understand because of her accent, and when I asked her to please repeat one of her questions, she said to me, "I see on your passport you have been traveling for months in South America, six months in Colombia, and three months in Ecuador. You should speak Spanish. There is no reason for you to not understand what I'm saying."

I felt a rush of rage burst into my bloodstream, and I'm sure it was written all over my face. I thought of the 20 years of fluency I had acquired in the Spanish language, all the professional interpreting and translating I had done, most times out of sheer kindness of my heart without getting paid for it. I knew I was probably more educated about her language than she was, and it took all I had in me not to lose my temper, but I succeeded. I knew that if I had to have the last word, she may not let me cross to the other side.

"You Americans. Entitled to everything, you think. I will give you only 30 days, and then you leave. Do not work. It is illegal. Enjoy my country. Next!"

She let me through!

"Thank you so much, ma'am," I said with a huge grin on my face. I slid to the left to pretend to organize my bag and slipped Jose the wad of money under the counter before joining Edson and Orlando, who were watching anxiously from a few feet away.

She did not let Jose go through. He and Yasmin stood there with their belongings looking at us, the immigration window and about ten feet separating us. We couldn't talk to make a plan. Immigration officials approached us almost immediately to tell us we couldn't stay there. The three of us were ushered to the end of a runway about a hundred meters away where we found taxis that would take us to the next nearest town with a bus terminal, which was Arica. Yasmin and Jose were ushered off in the opposite direction where we had just come from, and *they disappeared into the night with the money!*

Edson had just enough change on him to pay for a cab to get to the bus terminal in Arica. "We will figure it out once we get there," Edson and Orlando stated. I couldn't imagine how scary all this would be if I did it alone.

Since Jose and Yasmin had all the money, we had nothing to get a loaf of bread or bottled water to quench our parched throats. We had no way to change SIM cards to use our phones to text or call, and nowhere to connect to Wi-Fi. We had no way to do anything. All we could do was lay together with our luggage on that littered ground and wait.

Eight hours later, a cab pulled up, and out of it popped Yasmin and Jose. We all jumped up to hug each other. They had followed the cab driver's advice to wait until shift change, and the new guards, who arrived in a great mood to start their day's work, let them go by with minimal questioning. There was one seat left on the next bus to Santiago, and the next bus after that would leave in a couple of hours. I chose to take the single seat alone so that I could find a place for us to stay upon arriving.

I had one more big stretch. The bus trip from Arica to Santiago was 30 hours long. The thought of that made me cringe, but one more push and the marathon would be finished. I got the window seat on the right side in the very first row of the bus, and I sat next to a little, older lady who was so excited to show me all the pictures of her grandkids. I saw the coastline again, but this one was radically different than the one I just saw in Peru. The shores were rocky, and the water was dark and rough. I fell asleep watching the sunset over the Chilean tide. In the past four days, I had seen nearly 5,000 kilometers of the coast through three countries along the continent – and the sunset over the shores of each country's tide.

The last bus ride was the most pleasant of them all, with a clean bathroom on board, a meal I didn't know was included in the ticket price, and Wi-Fi. My seatmate didn't want her meal, so I was lucky enough to have two meals to spread over my 30-hour trip. I used the Wi-Fi to look for a place when I got to Santiago, and the best place I decided on was called The Red House Hostel.

When our bus pulled into the terminal in Santiago the next day, I don't think I had ever been so happy to get somewhere. I stood outside with my bag on my back, bamboozled, stretching my legs from nearly five days of being crammed on buses. Had I really been across three borders and five thousand kilometers in so few days? I was in Santiago, Chile!

As soon as I got there and worked out a two-week stay for two people, I dropped my things on my bunk. Jose and I would share a bunk bed in a room with eight other people. I went to explore the hostel a bit and was so impressed by everything that was there. Up a set of rickety wooden stairs were several rooms with bunk beds and a big bathroom. On the first floor, where my room was, I found an outside patio with four tables and chairs, a movie room with a pool table, and a huge kitchen equipped with anything someone would need to cook. There were three more rooms full of bunk beds and two big bathrooms that we all shared, one for men and one for women. I followed the hallway through a doorway, which took me outside, where I found a swimming pool with a bar right next to it. The bar top was big enough for six stools, and behind it was a patio shaded with beautiful landscaping of trees, vibrant flowers, and trimmed hedges with a ping pong table in the corner.

This place was absolute paradise. I got a text from Jose saying that their bus had broken down, which held them back for six hours. I gave him the address for the hostel so that he would know how to find me once he finally made it. Jose got there late at night, and he was as ecstatic as I was about our new digs. We went to explore outside of our hostel a bit, and while we were eating hot dogs from a food cart, we had a serious talk. He told me that Orlando had been picked up by his friend, and that Yasmin and Edson made it to Conception, a coastal town where they would join their family who were already settled there. We all made it safely.

Then, reality hit. I still had six weeks to finish Dr. D's projects, but I only had five days to finish my comprehensive exam for my department. I was very clear with Jose that for the next five days, I would be working on my final paper all day, every day while he looked for work. I could only use my time for this final paper because it determined whether I graduated with my master's at the end of the semester.

So, that was our first few days in Chile. I got up at 6 a.m. and had the whole hostel to myself every morning. Most of the people who were there were travelers, so they were usually up really late partying and woke up late. I took my things to an outside patio table to breathe in fresh, early morning air while I wrote for my final. While I was working on my paper, the hostel kitty Pantera always hopped up into my laptop to purr, coaxing me through the pain of academic anguish.

While I worked on my paper, Jose shared information about a job opportunity he'd seen for me. One opportunity was with a company looking for an ESL teacher, which required the applicant to be a native speaker of English. I decided to use 30 minutes to update my resume and apply for the job during one of my breaks from my paper. I found out from the police there that the cranky immigration officer was wrong. In spite of her announcement that I was only given a 30-day allowance, the paper that she printed out and stuck in my passport gave 90 days on my tourist visa.

I got called for an interview at the job teaching English, and the owner of the company said that even though a TEFL certificate and experience teaching were required, he thought I would be a good fit. He asked me to start immediately with the stipulation that I would have my certificate finished within a couple weeks. I was relieved that I had followed my intuition about starting my TEFL certificate previously.

I got my first official paid job teaching English, and I started the day after I turned in my final paper. Not only did this come in perfect timing financially, but it would expose me to a whole new world. The company was on the 7th floor of a fancy high-rise building with wide windows overlooking downtown Santiago. There were desks partitioned in rows of cubicles, each space with its own computer and headset. All I had to do was show up to work at my scheduled time and teach the classes I was assigned that day. All the teaching was done online, mostly in group situations with anywhere from four to seven students attending, and the lesson plans were provided. My students were from countries all over the world ranging from beginners' level to advanced level and proficiency level.

Teaching was exhausting, especially on days I was scheduled 8 to 10 hours of classes, but I adjusted. At the end of my first week, I overheard the lady next to me talking to a student during a private lesson, and as she finished her class, I said, "That sounds like American English!"

She lit up and said, "Yeah baby! Midland Texas! I left there a year ago, and I will never look back!" We were friends immediately. We saw each other every day and often had a two-hour break between shifts during which we walked around together outside. We quickly discovered that we had a lot in common.

The weather was getting colder, as we were on the verge of transitioning to winter, and all I had was an oversized, thin long-sleeved shirt that Hernan gifted me the last time I saw him in Medellín. I was always freezing. One day, Lisa asked me if that's all I had to keep warm. The next day, she brought me a maroon hoodie that said "Harvard" across the front of it.

"I have a friend who teaches there," she said. "I have several warm coats, and he can send me another one." The universe provided exactly what I needed in the moment I needed it.

After a couple weeks, I finished my TEFL certificate, which released me from my probation period and opened my schedule for students to book private lessons with me. My schedule was booked to the gills and I rarely worked less than fifty hours a week. Every day, I was up at dawn for work and got home really late. It was getting hard to juggle my crazy schedule while living at the hostel and sharing a room with so many people. They often scheduled me for four hours early in the morning, then a four-hour break, and then booked again for six-eight classes in a row until 11 p.m. Navigating the subway system was already a huge stretch out of my comfort zone, but to do it during morning rush hour with crowds of people pushing and shoving for their spot, and then doing it again so late at night made my routine even more difficult.

My first paycheck would only be a partial one, and it was time to figure out more rent at the hostel. Jose knew he would be on his own, and luckily, the owners of the hostel let him volunteer at the reception desk in exchange for rent.

I brainstormed where to go because I didn't have money yet and didn't want to keep staying at that hostel. In our office at work, there was a spare room tucked down the hall around a corner, and I'd heard the owner talk to his staff members about how frustrated he was that a paint crew was going to take a month to finish their work in there. I had the crazy idea that I could sneak in there after my late class, hide until everyone left the office, and sleep there until I got my paycheck the following week.

I'm already here early in the morning and late at night. Nobody will even know.

I noticed a big gym that was two blocks away from my office building, so I went in there one day acting interested in a membership. The owner gave me a free one-week pass, which I fully intended to use so that I could lock my bag up in a locker and shower every day between work shifts. The next day, I found myself on the subway with all my gear piled on my back, and nobody even noticed when I walked into the locker room with it all. At night, when my last class finished at 11, I hid until the office was locked up at 11:30, then pulled all the bean bags from the break room into my new cozy nook. I slept better on those nights than I had slept at my noisy hostel sharing a room with so many people, so grateful to be wrapped up in that cozy Harvard hoodie.

My plan worked like a charm until the owner found out.

"If I were interested in running a hospitality service, I would be in that business," he told me. "But I run an online teaching company. If I find out that you do this again, you will be banned from stepping foot on our office floor."

The party was over. I asked for an advance on my paycheck so that I could pay rent somewhere close, and he said no. On my lunch break that day, I asked the gym owner if he knew anyone who worked out at that gym looking for someone to rent a room? He said yes, and in that moment, the gym member he knew happened to walk through the door.

He took me to his apartment right then to see the room. His apartment was only two blocks away, right in front of my subway stop, and the available room was beautiful. It had a queen-sized bed with a desk and a big window with an absolutely stunning view of downtown Santiago and the mountains in the background. I imagined what it would be like to live there and walk to the gym and to work every day. While living in the hostel, it took me an hour each way on the subway crammed between people to get to work.

I want this place so bad, but there's no way he will wave the deposit, and no way he will let me wait to pay rent until I get paid. He doesn't know me, and I have no references here.

I figured if I didn't ask him, the answer would definitely be no, and I believe in miracles. What would happen if I did ask him and he said yes?

"I don't get paid until the first week of the month. I can't pay you anything until then, and I can't pay you for a month's rent and a full deposit or else I will be totally broke for a whole month until my next paycheck. I literally have no money to put in your hand right now, but I am working a lot of hours and will have money as soon as I get my check. I literally need to move in after work tonight because I have nowhere else to go."

He studied me, looking really deeply in my eyes, and I let him.

He stuck out his hand. "Deal. I have never done this before, but something about you is different. Full month's rent when you get your paycheck, and I will let you pay your deposit in three payments."

I wanted to jump up and down. I was so relieved. He gave me the key and followed me back to the gym. He said he would be happy to bring my backpacker's bag back home when he finished working out.

When I got home from work that night, I walked in the front door to homemade pizza. He said he always made homemade pizza for his new tenant on their first night. He popped the top of a bottle of imported red wine, and we kicked off my first night in my new home.

Not only were we celebrating my new move, but that day, I received an email from OU congratulating me for passing my final comprehensive exam. I still had a month to get my big final project for Dr. D finished, and the desk and chair in my room were so comfortable I knew I could work those long hours to get it done. As soon as I got my first paycheck, I squared up with Maty and also paid for a month's gym membership.

Just as I knew they would be somehow, things were A-OK.

Chapter 27

Peru-ish

Everything flowed great for a couple of months in Santiago. Then I was notified that my 90-day Visa was about to expire. Chile would let me back in if I crossed the border and came back (maybe), or I could think about crossing borders again and relocating. I was really happy with everything the way it was and didn't feel it was time to go to Argentina yet.

Or, I could go to Peru. I met a guy in Quito I really, really liked, and the intense connection we shared was mutual. He left Quito en route to Santiago, but decided to stop in Lima with no plans to make it to Chile. Then Chile suddenly changed its border laws, making it nearly impossible for him to arrive and find work. I was torn because as responsible as my routine was, it was also boring. The thought of going to have an adventure in a new country with a romantic partner seemed enthralling to me.

I decided to take the risk.

If it doesn't go the way I hope, at least I can say I tried. At least I'll have seen another part of the world, and I can leave doors open here so that I can come back.

I put my two-weeks' notice in at work and worked like crazy night and day so that my last paycheck would be really big. Chilean currency went much farther in Peru than in Chile. I gave Maty my notice so that he could look for a new person to rent my room.

Two weeks later, I showed up in Lima on a one-way ticket, where we spent a romantic week on the beach in

The Other Side of Fear

Miraflores, and we both agreed that the vibe in Lima wasn't the one where we wanted to live. We both needed to find stable work. As we walked through the bus terminal listening to the names of towns being called out, we both heard someone yell out, "Arequippaaaaaaaaaa!" We turned to look at each other and knew that was our new place to go. Off we went on another bus crammed full of people with roosters crowing on board.

We lived with a family who took us in very kindly, and after about a month or so, we both found work. One day, I walked out to the backyard and discovered Napo and his brother skinning the guinea pigs which had been alive on their rooftop. Napo informed me they were preparing their guinea pigs for a big birthday bash, and they had been raising those guinea pigs specifically to offer as a delicacy to their guests at this party. For a week afterward, every time I opened the fridge, I saw a leftover guinea pig on a stick sprawled out on a plate.

The chapter in Peru is important because this is where I got my first job teaching English to students inside of a university classroom. I had the sleeves of my long-sleeve shirt rolled up one day when a student asked what the tattoo in English on my right arm said. *Everything you want is on the other side of fear.*

"Teacher, why you tattooed that?" he asked. "What means other side of fear? What is fear? Fear is like scare?"

I stood there against my desk quiet, every eye in the classroom was on me, and I thoughtfully reminisced about that quote and the frame it came in when my therapist gave it to us in group therapy years before. It reminded me of where I was at that time, the time I held that framed quote in my hands the day before I embarked on this crazy journey and then getting it tattooed before leaving, and all the steps I had taken to get where I stood right there in that classroom of 35 students in Peru. I told them my story, and it was the first time that I had ever really shared it with anyone. My students were enamored, and so was I, and from that moment on, we used storytelling in the classroom to learn English. We became a family.

A couple years later, a student from that classroom sent me a photo of her ankle, where she now had that same quote tattooed. She said, "Thank you for sharing your story, miss Jenni. It inspired me to push forward out of a dark place and keep reaching. I also wanted that tattoo, to remind me to always face my fears and push past them." That showed me the powerful ripple effect that can occur when we have the courage to tell our stories.

Nothing in Peru went as I imagined, but I learned some valuable lessons, and I don't regret any of it. The university would not commit to a contract for me to work there long term, and they kept pushing off paying me, so I found an online teaching job working for another Chinese company where I taught kids. The Wi-Fi wasn't consistent enough for that, so it was stressful to constantly try and make things work. The relationship I was in had served its purpose; we parted on mutual terms, and I left with a broken heart after five months of nothing flowing smoothly.

When I knew it was time to go, I first went back to Colombia to my beloved Jardín where I could cry in the mountains. I also decided it was time to go back to the states for a few weeks, not only to get some legal paperwork done, but something told me that it would be my grandma's last holiday, and, of course, I needed to see my Gracie Ann.

***

After Jardín, I went back to the northern coast of Colombia to see Carlos in Santa Marta for one week. On the rooftop of that hostel, I crossed paths with Juan Karlos and his friend Pandita. We spent hours on the rooftop rocking back and forth in hammocks, smoking fat doobies, and having the deepest conversations I have ever had with strangers, although it felt like we had known each other for lifetimes, and we were finally meeting in this one.

I had already been to Santa Marta a few times at this point, but something else that made this specific trip memorable was when an older gentleman came into our bunk and dumped his bag on his cot. He shared with me that his name was Pablo, he was from Spain, and he was a professional, published writer, having recently retired and gone through a divorce.

"For years, everything I did in my life was for my career and my family. When I got through my divorce, I decided that life is too short not to do everything my heart desires, so I bought this backpack and a one-way ticket to Colombia. I'll travel south for a few months until I feel like I've seen everything in the countries I want to see." He had literally just arrived for the first time, making this his very first hostel experience. I remembered the gift that Or gave me at my first hostel experience in Medellín, and I paid it forward to him. We sat out on the rooftop drinking ice cold beers as I shared some of my travel stories, and he took notes on things he should see as he trekked south.

From there, I went back to Oklahoma for a couple months, saw my grandma and Gracie Ann, saw my family a bit, and taught any online classes that came my way. I discovered that I loved teaching English and was good at it, but I felt like I didn't know how to do it well. I found an online master's degree program in linguistics with a minor in ESL teaching, and applied for it last-minute. While still in the states, I got the notice that I would start my online classes in January the following year.

My short trip back in the U.S. confirmed something I had already known for a long time: life in the U.S. was not for me, and I wanted to keep drifting across borders. Something really big was happening inside of me, and I had to continue on the path I found, so I decided to pick up where I left off in Santiago. I discovered once I got back to Santiago, Chile, that the room I had rented from Maty the first time I was there would be available by the time I arrived. I was able to have the same amazing view, back in the same spot where I already had a routine with Maty. However, I discovered the door to my previous online job teaching ESL was no longer open. The owner had made some business shifts that didn't allow for my full-time position.

It was super expensive to live in Santiago compared to anywhere else in South America. I had inconsistent part-time hours teaching adults in China through an online company based out of Beijing, but that would hardly be enough to cover expenses, let alone save for later travels.

This was how I got my first job working for a company that would send me all over the city to people's business offices or homes to give 90-minute English lessons. It pushed me out of my comfort zone to learn how to navigate the public transport services, sometimes taking two or three buses just to get to one place. The job paid little, but the experience was enriching, and I built friendships with students who will be life-time contacts. My most memorable students at the time were Alejo and Aleja, originally from Bogotá but living in Santiago for work. It made me so happy to connect with people from Colombia. Twice a week I gave them private lessons at their kitchen table, and Aleja always shared her Colombian pastries and coffee with me.

Another highlight of my week was going to a fancy office in the ritziest area of Santiago to give private lessons to a fashion designer. She needed to learn English to do business with colleagues in China who sold fabric for her clothing line. It was cool to invest my talent in the lives of other individuals who would then use it to go pursue their paths around the world.

I ran myself ragged all over the city giving private lessons, taught online classes as they flowed my way, and pushed through an extraordinarily difficult first semester in the field of linguistics, which was the hardest thing I had pursued academically thus far. I returned to my workouts at the same gym a couple of blocks away to keep up my weightlifting routine, and one day I met a guy named Roger. He was an American who began a rogue bicycling adventure in Argentina with a friend and made it all the way to Santiago when their bikes needed maintenance.

I was grateful for his friendship because I often was alone at that point. Lisa had married and moved to Brazil before disappearing completely. Jose and Orlando were doing great but were busy with their new lives. Orlando had a great job and was able to start bringing family members over from Venezuela. Jose had two jobs and was pursuing his dream in modeling and fashion.

All I did was work every day, and at night, after everything was done, I would chain-smoke menthols out my window, pour myself a cup of red wine or pop the top on a liter of Chilean beer. I felt tremendous, aching sadness in the depth of my soul. It had been there for so long. I hurt a lot, but I kept myself so busy that I didn't pay mind to it until nighttime came around.

Right before my semester ended, I got the phone call that Grandma had passed, but I already knew. I felt it. Her spirit had her body a day or two before her physical body stopped. We'd had our last videochat a month or so before that, when she told me that she was proud of me, I'm beautiful, and she loved me. I still have all her travel stories tucked away in my heart. They were on my mind every time I got on a bus to go to a new place.

The morning after I finished finals, I thought about what I would do with three months of break between semesters. The thought of using the time to run myself ragged roving the city and sitting behind my computer begging for online students made me cringe. My life was starting to feel like it had in the states.

If I were meant to stay in one place forever, I would be a tree and grow roots. But I don't have roots. My wheels are my feet and I have wings to fly as high as my heart desires to go.

I looked out the window at the view of the mountains behind the city; I'd looked at them for months.

"Maty!"

He came in from the kitchen and peeked around my door frame. "Yenny!"

"What's behind those mountains?" I asked him.

"Argentina."

Argentina. I had three months of freedom before focusing on four months of very difficult work for yet another university.

"I'm going to work as much as I can for two more weeks, and then I am leaving. It's time to have more experiences, and I'll start with seeing what's on the other side of the mountains," I announced.

The following weekend, Roger and I went to the theme park Fantasyland in Santiago. I had not ridden a roller coaster in years, and I laughed so hard that day riding the rides over and over and over that I swore I peed my pants at least once. It was the first time that I saw a lookout point view over a foreign city from the height of a roller coaster.

Afterward, we walked a couple of miles to go spend time with Jose next to the pool back at the hostel, and I was so overjoyed to run into Pablo, the retired man I met at the hostel in Santa Marta who had just started his adventure! What were the odds that out of all the hostels in all the countries between where we met and where we were, that we would be there at the same time in the same place? He was so excited to tell me all about what he'd learned about himself while traveling, and I was ecstatic to learn that he had taken the time to see some of the things I'd recommended, including spending a week in my beloved Jardín.

Then, one night, after a long day of teaching classes, I decided it was the perfect moment to pack up my belongings. It was time to go see Argentina.

Chapter 28

Argentina

What would be on the other side of those mountains? Before I left to find out, I wanted to see something new in Chile. Gosh, I'd been there a total of eight months and only saw bits and pieces of Santiago.

Once I left Santiago, my plan was to go south eight hours to spend time in a town called Pucón, which I had heard was beautiful with mountains, and a litany of outdoor activities such as rappelling and white-water rafting. I figured I would have great experiences there before deciding where to cross the border into Argentina. It felt so good to be on the bus leaving there after months of doing the same things over and over like a hamster on a wheel. I was melancholic because of all the wonderful things I experienced, but joyful about closing the chapter so I could open a new one.

However, the universe threw me a curve ball upon arrival in Pucón. I traveled overnight from Santiago and arrived mid-morning to discover it was freezing cold, so foggy that I couldn't even see buildings around me, and rain was coming down in torrents. All I had on was my cotton Harvard hoodie with a long sleeve t-shirt and other t-shirts underneath. It all got wet, and nothing I had was waterproof. While walking to find my hostel, everything else I had got soaked, including what was in my suitcase. I was frozen to the bone before I even got to my hostel. When I got there, the owner told me all the tourism offices were shut down for a few days since the winter storm was blowing through, so basically if I stayed, I would just be hanging out at my hostel around the wood stove with the three other people who were guests there. I would not be able to go do anything in town.

Fuck that, I thought. I decided I would just find a way to get to Argentina. I wanted to get away from the cold. Before committing to pay for tha night, I found a bus terminal selling tickets to Argentina. It was a bus ticket kiosk inside a little convenience store. The ride would be on a small bus running just across the border into the first little town on the Argentinian side, Junín De Los Andes. It wouldn't leave until early the next morning.

That bus ride to Junín de los Andes was only three hours, and it was one of the most beautiful border-crossing experiences I've ever had. Our bus was full, maybe 20 people, and the driver chained our tires as we entered the snowy, icy Andean mountain. My God, as if the mountain scenery wouldn't have been beautiful enough, I felt blessed by the honor of seeing the view during winter with all the foliage disguised in ice and snow. It was like riding through a winter wonderland. Halfway through the mountain pass, the bus stopped on the side of the road. We were instructed to get out and follow the driver with our documents. We crunched through the snow together for a few yards to a little wood cabin with a border patrol inside to issue passport stamps.

I was entering Argentina! I was entering country number five. There I was embedded in this winter wonderland, staring up at the blue sky. I opened my arms wide and let out a rooster crow that rang through the voluptuous surroundings while I waved my passport at the sky.

"I'm in Argentinaaaaaaaaaa!" I laughed. The people from my bus probably thought I was crazy. No, they were crazy. I was normal. I was living my life. I was born to live all these experiences.

When I got to Junín, the bus terminal was tiny because the population was only 10,000 people, making it a bit smaller than Jardín. This was my first impression of Argentina. I took off on foot to find a bed for the night. I really wanted to shower, get a good meal, and rest for one night instead of plowing forward on a night bus. I didn't even know where I wanted to go next. I finally found a local person who told me where to find a bed for the night.

After I got there and paid for my bed for that night, the owner informed me that there would be no running water for a couple of days while they fixed a plumbing issue. I felt like I had a seafood buffet in my pants, a half a roll of toilet paper stuck in my ass, and an onion farm growing beneath the layers of shirts I had on, but a shower would have to wait again. I walked back into town to find a diner that served local food. What would my first experience with Argentinian cuisine be?

I got a bottle of Malbec, which was divine, and tried three different desserts I had never seen. They were exquisite. When I left, the snow was coming down so hard I could barely see around me, but I had so much fun sucking down the rest of the wine right from the bottle, soaking my shoes (once again) in the snow that was piling up, and catching snowflakes on my tongue. These weren't your normal snowflakes. These were Argentinian snowflakes. I pretended that each one was arriving just to welcome me along my new path, and I stumbled through the streets until I found my hostel again.

My only option to get back north was to take an eight-hour bus to Neuquén. On the bus, I sat next to another angel who'd been placed in my life for a moment. Katrina shared stories with me about her life, her experience being a teenage mother with no support from her family or the father of her daughter, and how that had pushed her into a life of entrepreneurship. She gave me the lowdown on Argentinian slang, shared her snacks, wrote down famous dishes for me to try while I was there, then she fished out an extra sim card she had in her purse, and even helped me get it into my phone so that I could use my phone in the new country.

Before we parted ways at the bus terminal, we gave each other a tight hug goodbye, promising we wouldn't ever let the hard stuff detour us, but instead allow it to be a step to go higher in life and become who we were born to be.

I was delighted to discover that at my hostel it was rare for tourists to stay. It was full of local Argentinians and Venezuelans who paid a monthly rate to stay there while they worked for the booming oil and gas industry. I was relieved to finally take a hot shower and get warm. I had been chilled to the bone with wet shoes and feet since I left Santiago.

I made friends with the guys in my hostel, and they were kind enough to host a no-shit Argentinian grill out on my last night. It was my first night to try fernet, the liquor that locals drink, and soon we all went somewhere to play pool until the sun came up.

I literally ran back to my hostel to grab my bags, and showed up drunk as a skunk to catch my bus. As soon as I boarded the bus, the driver was able to pull out so we could begin our journey. I watched the sun come up as we pulled out onto the highway, and before my eyes slammed shut, I laughed about how much my cheeks hurt from laughing all night long.

My next stop was 15 hours north, a place called Mendoza which is a famous destination for wine-drinkers on the west side of Argentina. I arrived at Hostal de los Artistas, and as soon as I walked into the front door, I ran into an American guy named Mark who I had met before at the Red House Hostel back in Santiago. I set my things on my bunk when a girl walked in our room and said, "Sarah and I rented a car to go spend the day in the Andes. We're going to stop for pictures along the way, and our end goal is to make it to a lookout point for Aconcagua. Do you all wanna come?" She looked back and forth between me and the girl across from me in her bunk, who I had not yet met. *You should watch your expenses until you can do online teaching.* My thought process started, but it got interrupted by my mouth saying that I would love to go.

I wanted to say yes to everything because I knew I only had one chance to live this experience. I had no winter clothes, but Mark was kind enough to loan his layered windbreaker.

We were Jesse from Canada, Sarah from New Zealand, Simone from Germany (who shared my room), and crazy, beautiful me. The places we stopped for pictures were beautiful, beyond anything I could have imagined. It was a totally different beauty than the mountains I had drank up in Colombia. Once up into the mountains, we hiked through the snow until we got to the lookout point to see Aconcagua, its elevation of nearly 7,000 meters making it the tallest mountain in the Americas. The wind was just ripping through those snowy mountains. I couldn't imagine *not* having the windbreaker from Mark.

We were on a long, paved road back to where we had parked when I said jokingly, "Imagine how invigorating this arctic wind would be if we were naked!"

The girl from New Zealand said, "I want to find out. Who wants to join me?" We all just looked at her like she was crazy. Without skipping a beat, she started stripping down completely naked except for her tennis shoes, she cupped her mouth to let out a loud, happy cry, and she took off sprinting buck-ass naked right into the roaring winter wind as fast as she could, our tears, laughs, and whistles pushing her forward until she threw herself onto the snow to make a naked snow angel.

We laughed so hard all the way back to the hostel, and as soon as we got there, Mark and his New Zealand friend Caine got the grill ready for a huge cookout. The owner joined with a box of assorted Argentinian wines, and we ate and drank like it was *The Last Supper*.

The next morning, Simone and Jesse suggested that we go on a wine-tasting tour. I didn't feel up to making decisions and was happy to go along for the ride. The three of us went bus-hopping until we found our stop on the outskirts of town where there were dozens of vineyards. We knew we had struck gold when at our very first stop, we discovered that $7 USD each covered a three-course meal made from scratch by the chef, along with our very own wine flight. Each of us ordered different foods and wines so we could try it all. We sat there long after we were through with our food, our bare, pedicured feet on the ledge of a table, passing wines back and forth, taking in the view of the vast vineyards with the snowy Andes behind them and sharing our travel experiences. The sky was clear blue that day with the warm sunshine, which made us peel off our sweatshirts. It was perfect.

We did this on repeat at two more wineries until we were so sloshed we couldn't keep track of our stories or which language we were speaking, and then we hitchhiked back into town. I ended up staying there for a whole week, cooking out every night with my group of friends, and exploring together in groups to see new things during the day.

I knew I would eventually make it to Buenos Aires, the capital located on the east side of Argentina, but I decided to spend a month in a place called Córdoba--the halfway point to the capital from where I was in Mendoza. I asked the owner of my hostel, Danny, if he had any connections for a place where I could rent a room in the Córdoba area. It turned out he had several family members that owned a big property in a town called Carlos Paz about an hour away from the big city of Córdoba. He made a phone call and said his family would have a place ready for me with everything I needed and would be happy to pick me up from the bus terminal when I got there.

After an overnight, 12-hour bus ride, his sister-in-law and cousin were there waiting to welcome me with open arms and take me to where I would stay for the next month. You can imagine my surprise when, after entering their gated property, they led me to a cabin behind their house that they usually rent out to travelers during high-peak season, but which was vacant now in winter. For $200 USD a month I had the whole cabin to myself. It was fully furnished. I had a big bed with blankets and pillows, a kitchen and a big table in the bathroom all for me. I had Wi-Fi, so it was a perfect place to be able to teach online for a month while I explored the area.

I spent a month in this cozy, wonderful place. It was so quiet I could hear the neighbor's cows moo close by every morning while I drank my coffee. A ten-minute walk from the big iron gate took me to a little store where I got all the groceries and toiletries I needed. Right behind that store was an entrance to a passageway that led to San Roque Lake, where I walked on my days off. I sat by the blue water while I read books or journaled. I made friends with Paola, a family member who lived on the property. She was a hardworking single mother who loved to invite me over for homemade empanadas and fernet.

When I first got to Colombia, I had met an Argentinian lady while hiking in Salento the first time I saw the Colombian mountains. We stayed in touch as I continued traveling, and it turns out she lived only an hour away from where I was, so she came to see me one day. She told me she had many memories of spending summer vacations in the little town where I was.

One day, I got a text from Simone, the German girl who I had explored with in Mendoza. She came to stay with me for a week. She was a nature person, very quiet, and it was a perfect setup for her to share the other half of the cabin. We had so much fun making delicious vegetarian dishes, and at night we drank wine while she taught me German. We went paddling in a canoe one day and got lost on the lake. We paddled for hours looking for the dock where we had rented the boat. It was really cloudy that day, and the way the mountain's foliage peek through the fog reminded me of a scene from Jurassic Park.

Her last full day there, I woke up really sad. I told her I was going to stay in my room all day teaching English online, but she insisted I go with her on a long hike to Cerro de La Cruz, a small mountain whose peak offered a lookout over the whole city and surrounding geography. She had already made us snacks, and everything was ready for our fun day hiking.

We introduced ourselves to the others on the summit once we finished the hike and had a great conversation with one of the guys named Leo. We ended up making the descent on that path together, where I found out he currently lived in Buenos Aires, but had left to travel for a few days. He gave me his number and told me to contact him whenever I got to Buenos Aires if I felt like it.

The Wi-Fi at the cabin faded in and out, so I was only able to make enough to cover my expenses for rent and a bus ticket to get to my next spot. I knew I had to find a place with better Wi-Fi where I could make more income fairly soon. I had been in contact with two families that planned on receiving me when I got to Buenos Aires, but when I showed up in the big city, I couldn't get ahold of either of them. I was truly alone in this new big city, different than any I had seen yet. The first night at my hostel, I looked for a cheap room on Airbnb where I could go for a month to work as many hours as I could. I had no idea that the room I chose was in a really, really bad neighborhood. The Wi-Fi also cut in and out there, but I'd already paid for a full month of rent, so I had to push through. I struggled with a lot of darkness and despair inside of me, not even realizing to what extent.

It rained a lot, and it was so cold. There was no heater in my room, and my window opened up to the main street where there was always noise. I left my room once a week to get groceries from the supermarket three blocks away, and I bought economic things like pasta that would last me for a few days. All I did was teach online, drink wine, and eat pasta in my room. The only time I came out was to use the bathroom or shower. There were two other people renting rooms on that floor, and we all shared the bathroom at the end of the hall. One of the people was a kind young woman from Brazil, who ventured out to join me while I cooked pasta. We had broken conversations, with her practicing her basic English and me practicing the Portuguese I had picked up in my travels. I discovered that since Portuguese is in the same language family as Spanish, she could talk to me (slowly) in her language and I could understand most of what she said.

I always drank wine out of a coffee mug while I taught. I kept the bottle within arm's reach so that I could refill my cup without anyone seeing. One night, I got so sloshed that I really messed up my classes. After I finished that class, I started singing karaoke by myself in my room and decided I wanted to go find some beer. It was a terrible drunk decision to wander out so late at night to find a kiosk, and it was a decision that got me robbed. A couple nights later, I heard loud noises and watched a knife fight between two guys on the street right outside my window. I lay there night after night, shivering and drunk under blankets, crying myself to sleep.

One morning, it dawned on me that I never texted Leo. I was not, indeed, alone in this new big city. I was scared to open myself to someone new; my nerves were shaken from the bad experiences I'd had thus far in this new place. Still, I decided to give it a chance.

The first day we hung out, I met him at the bus stop down the street from my room and his first words were, "What in the hell are you doing in this neighborhood?" All we could do was laugh about it.

We started laughing that day and never stopped. I don't think I have ever had so much fun hanging out with someone. He was kind, pure-hearted, and respectful, and he was a traveler pursuing the same path I'd already been traveling for some time since I'd left the States. He helped me find a new room in a better neighborhood. The day that he came over to help me pack and move my things, he gasped when he walked into my room and saw so many empty wine bottles lined up against the wall next to the desk where I taught.

"Is this your stash from the past month that you've stayed here?" I was ashamed to tell him that all those wine bottles were from just the past few days of drinking alone in my room. My routine there had been to fill my mug with wine instead of coffee during four hours of early teaching, eat some pasta and take a long nap, then open a new bottle for my night classes.

"Are you sure you're okay?" he asked. He genuinely cared, and something about his sincerity reached me very deeply. At that point, I realized maybe I had not been so okay. His sincerity helped shine light when I needed it the most.

Leo and I spent our time having so much fun while he took me all around town, showing me every part of the big city. He took me to the port where we played pool, drank beers, and ate street food on the coast by the river. We went to Tigre for a day and had a blast drinking local liquor on a boat, hootin' and hollerin' across the water like we owned all of it. He took me to a place to sing karaoke, where I felt brave enough after several drinks to sing Adele songs in front of a bar full of people. I learned that it didn't matter how many mistakes I made singing. When I sing in English in a place that doesn't speak it, the people think I am the best singer they've ever heard.

One weekend, we caught a last-minute bus to the beach town Mar de Plata so that I could say I visited the ocean on the east side of the continent, and a couple of times I took a ferry over to the coast of Uruguay just to say that I'd been to that country.

My new semester was in full swing, so my weekly schedule was a blur of intense coursework and trying to get as much work online as possible. On the weekends, Leo and I would find something fun to do. After a couple months of this, Leo said, "I'm bored with the routine. I want to go see my cousin in northern Argentina. I want you to come with me." I decided that everything I did for school and work was online, and I could do it there, so I said yes! We were hungry for travel and had to answer when it called us. Leo found an announcement from a truck driver who was heading 17 hours north to Salta and had a spot for two people to ride along. The next day, we were stuffed inside the back cab of the truck and began our overnight haul.

Time at his cousin Celi's house was a delight, where we spent so much time around the dinner table eating home-cooked food. We explored the area until Leo saw a post on one of his travel pages from a French couple looking to share car rental expenses on a four-day adventure to see a common tourist loop through surrounding small towns. Off we went to practice our French with strangers.

This was the first time I had traveled so much with another person, and although we had moments that were wonderful, we had just as many that were not. While we had many things in common, we both acknowledged that neither of was able to open up to the other in a deeper way for a potential relationship because we both needed to heal first. There was something about Leo that made me look at my self in a deeper way. There was something about him that made me think about *everything* in a deeper way.

He told me he wanted to go to Brazil for at least three months by himself so that he could heal, and he hoped I could meet up with him again whenever I decided to backpack up the eastern coast of the continent. I agreed that I would go forward alone, too, at least for a while, and the feeling was mutual about a desire to journey together again in a different chapter. Before he left, we went out on the town with his cousins and their friends. It was Halloween night in Argentina, and they wanted a night out.

What could it hurt? It's just one more party.

Chapter 29

Getting Sober

"I finally understood alcohol was not a cure for pain; it was merely a postponement."

Sarah Hepola, <u>Blackout: Remembering the Things I Drank to Forget</u>

Drinks flowed all night long, and being the 20-year-olds they were, the cheap mixed drinks on special were the ones flowing. They danced like that night was the last night they would see. *You're used to drinking heavily, but you can't mix all this cheap alcohol,* some inner voice of wisdom kept beckoning.

Hours on the dance floor ended when the lights announced closing time, and we were ushered outside to discover that it was almost 6 a.m. The faint light on the horizon let us know the sun would soon be upon us. Our drunk group wandered to the plaza where we drank more beer before deciding to go to one of Celi's university friend's houses to grill out and keep the momentum going.

When we got to the house, the only thing I wanted was to lie down, so Leo took me to a quiet room where I could sleep peacefully. I remember lying down in my clothes and fading off to sleep as I heard everyone else having fun outside.

A few hours later, with the sun fully up and cloaking the town in its 100-degree heat, I woke up drenched in sweat in a strange room, alone, with no fan and no AC, vomit and food caked in the corners of my mouth. My left temple was throbbing so hard I swore the side of my head was going to explode. I felt like I had sandpaper in my throat, the room was spinning, and I had no idea where to find water or a bathroom.

Then, I remembered. *Fuck, it's Sunday.*

Not only was Sunday my busiest day to receive non-scheduled calls from students looking for teachers online, but I had several hours of reservations with regular students. I'd already missed several at that point. I would miss all of them that day, and I had no way to notify my students or the company I worked for that I wouldn't be there. Not only was I out the money for bar tabs, but I would be without the money from that day's classes, and my online teaching account would be frozen for a week as punishment for not showing up that day, meaning I would also lose income for the whole week.

I lay in that bed so furious with myself, and for the first time looked directly into the mirror of my relationship with alcohol.

"If they'd never invited me out, none of this would have happened," I thought, beginning to finger-point.

I called myself out, and it was time to be painfully honest after years of lying to myself. Nobody made me mix all those cheap drinks. In fact, nobody put a gun to my head and made me go out at all! For years, I'd been angry at others for their relationship with alcohol. For years, it was everyone else's fault.

"If people didn't offer to pay for bar tabs, it wouldn't be so easy to drink."

"If alcohol wasn't around every corner, in every convenience store, at every restaurant, and in every fridge, I wouldn't drink so much."

"If that person wouldn't have made me so angry, I wouldn't have ever opened that bottle."

"I would've closed my tab after those two beers and just gone home if that person hadn't started buying shots for everyone."

"I never drank heavily until I dated someone who had a real problem with alcohol. It's the influence of that person that made me choose to binge on tequila."

"They have a problem, but my relationship with alcohol is nowhere as destructive as theirs."

But, the truth of the matter was, I was the common denominator in all those relationships.

In all the work I had done with myself, I hadn't ever taken ownership of my relationship with alcohol and the damage it did to my life and the lives of others. Alcohol steals, and it had been stealing from me for years. My choices stole thousands upon thousands of dollars that could have been invested in creating security and wellness for my future.

Drinking was the foundation of hundreds of toxic relationships I otherwise would have not been involved with. I would've never have taken oxycodone or Lortabs alone; it was only when I was drunk that the thought crossed my mind. I never would have experienced the cocaine detour had it not been for my marriage to alcohol. It was my true blue, my rock solid, the homey hanging out on my shoulder, keeping me company no matter who came in and out of my life.

It made me a lazy gatekeeper of my life for as long as was attached to it. Things that I normally would not accept suddenly seemed okay after drinking. I went places I never should have gone, I put myself in extremely dangerous, life-threatening situations with people I had no business being with, and I wouldn't have if it weren't for being under the influence of alcohol. It had been my normal for so long. I couldn't imagine my life without it.

I lay there in the sweltering heat, my tears adding an extra salty layer to the sweat dripping from my body, furious at the truths staring back from the mirror in front of me.

I am powerless against alcohol, I acknowledged. Nobody was holding a gun to my head forcing me to do this, so why did I choose this misery? I was still enough to finally hear my soul, something else that alcohol had been drowning out for years. My soul was screaming bloody murder. It begged for something new. It begged to be explored. It begged to let something out, to grow, to heal, to release something huge.

The thought of being totally sober for a long period of time paralyzed me with fear, but why?

Why would anyone choose this misery? Why did I choose to wake up like this on a regular basis? If you were looking at yourself as a different person on the outside, would you treat that person how you treat yourself? *No way.*

Then why do you do this to yourself? *Because I'm scared of feeling good.*

Why? *Because I'm scared of my potential, and I'm scared of what would happen if I let myself grow and expand without self-sabotaging consistently.*

Why? *Because I'm scared of what truths will surface when I stop numbing everything.*

Why am I so scared to give up something that is destroying me? What is alcohol giving me that makes it so hard to let go of? *It protects me.*

It protects me from what? *Being seen.*

Why are you scared of being seen? *Because then I would feel vulnerable.*

These were powerful truths that came out as I was finally honest with myself, and BINGO, I found the root of my fear. I was scared to be vulnerable.

If I don't hide behind alcohol, who am I really? I'd only ever known myself through the lens of alcohol my entire adult life. How much was there to discover underneath all these layers?

What if I get sober, and I live the most authentic version of myself that I can possibly be, and it's not enough? *What if I'm not enough?*

I marveled at how many obstacles I had overcome at that point. Who faces rape trauma in a therapist's office to conquer fears, buys a one-way ticket to a foreign country, and then drifts from village to desert to beach to big city and back again through six countries? I was courageous to do that, but I was doing it all with my crutch of booze, so how courageous was it, really?

Real courage would be stepping out beyond that and truly allowing myself to feel the fullness of life, living out loud as the most authentic version of who I was born to be, embracing all my fears, and allowing myself to feel vulnerable, which meant starting to sit with *all* of me, even the parts that booze had been stealing. Not just pieces.

Everything you want is on the other side of fear.

For years, I'd hoped that romantic partners along the way would fill the abyss I had inside, but it gave way to codependent relationships every time because I never learned to fill my own cup. How could I expect someone else to understand me if I didn't understand myself? How could I expect someone else to love me, listen to me, and learn about me if I wasn't willing to? Alcohol robbed me of that, too.

Nobody was going to swoop in and save me from my misery, just like they couldn't when I hit rock bottom other times. I'd waited for someone other than myself to intervene during times of destruction and give me permission to be free. I now realized, just like the times in my life that I'd been at rock bottom because of drug addiction, I could not wait for someone else to come free me. I had to save myself. I had to decide to change the standard for myself. I was responsible for creating the life of my dreams, for finding my own happiness.

How could I stop drinking in a world where alcohol is everywhere? Well, I thought the same thing about coke, and I came to the conclusion that I could not ever escape it; drugs will always be around, and I can't stop living my life just to avoid them. I had to choose where I stood without regard to what anyone else did around me. It can't matter who chooses to drink in my presence. That is their relationship with alcohol, and none of my business.

The fear of being sober was crippling. It didn't matter how many "sobriety" challenges I took. If I didn't find the root of what made me want to drink, my cycles would never change. That meant embarking on an internal journey that was more intense than the twists and turns of the adventures I'd had across so many borders.

Forgiving my rapist wasn't enough. My pain was still there. It was deeper than all of that. I had to find the root of my pain, and as long as I was consistently numbing my emotions with alcohol, I would never be able to move forward to align myself with the life that my soul begged to align with.

I had drank heavily for nearly 15 years of my adult life! What would life look like on the other side of that fear, the fear of facing life head on, sober, stepping into a new world and opening up myself in a deeper way? I listened to the lies start flowing, and I let them because I wanted to see honestly what my belief systems were. A list of my "just"-ifications commenced:

"Just control it; no need to give it up completely."

"Just stick to a plan, like only beer and no hard liquor."

"Just save it for special occasions and make it off limits besides that."

"Just have a two-drink limit and never drink more than that."

"Just drink socially, but don't allow it in your house."

"Just say no to shots."

"Just save it for the weekend, and during the week be sober."

I had to be honest about the fact that I'd made those negotiations for years, and not one of them ever worked. After one drink, my rationale was rendered powerless. My way was not working. It never had, and it was time to do something radically different. It was time to go through a divorce with alcohol. It was time to get sober, not as a temporary challenge, but as a permanent life decision. It was time to take my journey of learning to love myself to the next level, and it was time to find the root of my pain.

Leo went his way to the beaches of Brazil, and although my initial plan was to travel across the border of Brazil and backpack north to meet up with him, that decision was not resonating in my soul. Instead, I listened to my soul. It didn't want Brazil quite yet.

I wanted to go back to Colombia. I booked a flight from Buenos Aires to Medellín and used the two weeks in between to explore new places along the way. I spent a week in Esteros de Iberá where I canoed along the banks of swamps to take pictures of alligators sunbathing and saw animals I had never seen. In fact, I got to see an alligator even closer when it jumped into the outside pool for a night swim at the place I was staying. The owner said that was a nightly occurrence, so everyone knew not to get in the pool after a certain hour.

I got back to my little studio apartment in Jardín in the nick of time to finish my final semester projects, see my beloved Sebas, and go on long hikes through banana fields and coffee farms. It was different this time, though. Everything was different sober, and alcohol was everywhere. Around every turn, I was invited to partake in bottle service from the locals to welcome me back to the village. But I'd expected this to happen and had prepared for it this time.

On long hikes, I was able to reflect on the version of me who hiked there during previous trips to Jardín. I felt divinely empowered to see how far I was now from the Jenni who fled the destruction she caused to herself and those around her. I offered amends to those I had harmed. For some, it was received and strengthen the foundation for our friendship. For others, the door was closed, which I grew to accept as a consequence of my former poor decisions.

I celebrated my 34th birthday there, and I felt like I truly celebrated my existence for the first time ever. In previous years, I'd always experienced deep sadness around my birthday and spent days in phases of drunkenness, hungover, or some stage in between. The sadness was still there, but I was able to be fully present with it and still experience joy at the same time.

I made my first vision board of things I wanted to attract to my life in the following year. I took all my art supplies and poster board up the mountain to the big Jesus statue. There were covered tables there, and I sat and drew out my vision board, looking down over the village and the mountains surrounding it.

After village-hopping in the area, I knew it was time to make the transition from Jardín to Medellín so that I could have more stable Wi-Fi to teach online. A friend in the village connected me to her mother-in-law, who had a room to spare in her apartment in a Medellín neighborhood off the tourist trails.

It was while living there that I began writing this book. I would go sit at tables outside of hole-in-the-wall coffee shops or bakeries, tucked away on side streets of that Belen Rincon neighborhood, and write for hours until my soul said it was done, and I would hike up the long hill back home. I did this for a little over two months until one day my soul said it needed the kind of inspiration that only traveling give me. I packed my essential items, secured the rest in my rented room, threw my bag on my back, and took off, not having a clue that within a few days, the world would be engulfed in the COVID-19 pandemic and I would be stuck in strict lockdown for months.

Chapter 30

Unhidden Heroines

After two and a half months of strict lockdown in Bogotá, Colombia, it came time to get everything ready for my humanitarian flight back to the United States. I knew I wouldn't have room for everything in my suitcase after I got goodies to bring back to friends and family, so I started thinking about anything I could donate from my small collection of belongings. I got a creative idea about making a sweet care package for another woman, a woman whose presence I felt in my soul, but whom I had not yet met. How could I nurture her? What could I give that would bring warmth to her soul, for her to feel cherished, celebrated, and fortified by the love of another woman during this crazy time we were all living? I had an image of a woman holding the hand of a little girl, and in my spirit, I understood that as, "The person I needed to make this package for was a single mom of a little daughter."

I found a big reusable grocery bag from the kitchen and put together this love package, letting my heart tell me what to put in it. I stuck in two nice blouses I'd been given but hadn't worn because they were way too small. I put in one of each color of my colorful hair ties, hoping that it would bring joy to her daily routine in some way. I had several extra pairs of little pearl and diamond stud earrings from a jumbo pack I'd found on clearance in some market borders ago, so I found a little baggy to put hair ties and earrings in together.

I thought about what she would feel on her heavy period days because I know mine are really painful and heavy. What could I give her so she could feel connected to her body during that time of reset, and what could bring her relief? I dug in the bottom of my backpack to fish out the quart-sized Ziploc I'd always kept hidden there just in case I needed to waterproof my valuables in a pinch. It was the perfect size for feminine products, a sleeve of 800 mg ibuprofen, the last big chocolate bar out of my own period-munchy stash, a snack-sized bag of my favorite plantain chips, what I had left of my herbal teas, and the last four tealight candles I had left.

I found an extra journal that said, "Be Your Own Hero" on it that I wouldn't have time to fill before I left, with a pen that said, "Cousins" on it tucked in the spiral binding. I found some extra antibiotics I'd saved in case of an emergency, as well as other toiletries, nail polish and polish remover, and some non-perishable food items.

After I got this all put together, I wanted to include a financial blessing hidden somewhere in it that would hopefully come in the moment she least expected and when she needed it the most. I folded a bill and hid it between the maxi pads in her feminine bag. I was eager to let my heart show me who needed to be the recipient of this care package I had put together with so much love.

The next morning, with my heart leading my footsteps, I made my way toward the center plaza of Bogotá with an open spirit and a big smile beaming behind my mask. Our hearts always have all the answers to everything we want to know. The tricky part is learning how to listen. So, I was walking down 7th Avenue for a while, when a guy with a goody basket yelled at me, "Viva Colombia!" He flew me a thumb's up sign, and in spite of the mask covering his face, I could tell he was grinning ear to ear. He was telling me that he loved my Colombian soccer jersey, so I went over to make small talk with him.

We chatted for a few minutes when I noticed a quiet young woman standing a couple feet behind him watching us. I invited her to come join us. I noticed that she had a pull-behind basket with coffee thermoses in it.

"Here, have a coffee!" the guy offered me.

"No, I want her coffee," I responded. She eagerly sold me a cup, and I could tell she was very kind and very shy.

"Where are you from?" I asked her in Spanish. "Venezuela?"

She nodded.

"This girl is out hustling from dawn till dusk," the guy told me. Her gentle eyes lit up when she smiled, a smile that came from an authentic place in her soul. *Ping ping ping.* My heart told me that she was the one.

"What do you have in the bag?" the guy asked.

"I'm returning some items to their rightful owner," I responded. Then, I asked this young girl if she would take a walk with me.

I didn't want anyone else to hear our conversation. Once away from the group, she asked if we could walk and talk so that she could still sell her coffee. As we strolled down 7th Avenue, she told me her story. Her name was Luxbetsy. Because of the crisis in Venezuela, she migrated to Bogotá a little over a year prior in desperate search for work. She had a couple of family members already there, but once she arrived she was forced to find her own way to survive because her family wouldn't help her. She had to find a way to make money, toting her one-year-old daughter on her hip, and find some way to make enough to keep shelter over both of their heads and have food, formula, and diapers. She only had enough to buy one thermos and a stack of cups to sell coffee in the street, so she walked the streets all day with her baby on her hip selling little cups of coffee day after day until she finally had enough for two thermoses. Then, she eventually found a way to get her pull-behind basket, which could hold more thermoses and free up her hands.

Her baby caught pneumonia being exposed to the cold, rainy Bogotá climate, so thankfully she worked out an agreement with her landlord to watch the baby during the day so that the young mother could sell coffee. She hustled hard enough to expand her business to four thermoses and add a mini basket to the side of her cart that held different brands of cigarettes to sell in addition to coffee. She said the more product available to sell, the better, because she takes the same number of footsteps every day regardless. She told me that her next goal was to upgrade her basket to a four-wheel cart that would hold up to eight thermoses on the bottom, and a cooler on top with different compartments to hold pastries and homemade Venezuelan food, all of which would greatly increase her sales revenue per footstep.

She had done all of this herself with a one-year-old baby and as a migrant worker in a country that did not welcome her. I watched the glow all around her face as she told me her story. She was so proud of it. The suffering brought her to a point that she had no choice but to reach down into the deepest parts of herself to make her own way when things seemed impossible. I was so inspired by her, and I found myself relating to her in many ways, although our lives, cultures, nationalities, native languages, and skin color were so different. What we suffered through hadn't made us bitter; it made us *better*, and we saw infinite possibility to keep growing and creating, all thanks to hard times. It made us relate to each other at a soul level that transcended borders.

I explained to her what my love package was and offered it to her with every ounce of pure love from my heart, and then we hugged and hugged. We knew how to love from a deep place, the one that only those who have suffered and then healed know about. Every little bit of it had come at the most perfect time in a pandemic, when sales were at an all-time low and the streets were a ruthless reality, full of hungry people fighting for their own sales to feed hungry mouths at home. She hadn't been able to do fun things with her daughter or buy any gifts, so she was excited to paint her fingernails and put in those little pearl earrings. My heart was beaming as wide as it could, imagining her finding that secret bill stashed away once she got home and really went through the bag in detail.

I went to sit in Plaza Bolivar, just totally floored that it was empty except for me and all the pigeons. I took in the beauty of the architecture of the government buildings. I thanked Colombia for starting and ending this three-year chapter, I apologized for any harm done on my part while she allowed me to have such a powerful journey, and I let her hold me there while I cried and released so many things. It was time to tell my story. It was time to talk about what made me have that moment with Luxbetsy.

I felt the bliss of pure joy surge through my body, ruminating on the experience that had just taken place, and I thought about how happy I would be if I could dedicate my next chapter of traveling to documenting stories of people just like her everywhere I went. If her story inspired me, maybe it would inspire countless others. Maybe it would inspire something big in just one person, and maybe that person would let their inspiration lead them to a place where they'd be empowered to inspire ten more people in a big way. What if it snowballed into a bigger movement where women all over the world were empowered by sharing their story, and they all found unity by healing together and continuing to rise into new layers of greatness? Before we parted ways, she gave me permission to make a video with her telling her story, and that was how I launched my YouTube channel right before I closed the chapter of traveling in South America.

Nearly 20 years later, my life had turned full circle to what I'd sensed as my life purpose in my teens. The epiphany left my jaw hanging wide open, sitting right there on that cement block on the edge of Plaza Bolivar. It brought me full circle to the soulfire I first experienced when I was 15 years old, the first time I walked into a formal Spanish class. It had brought me full circle to the soulfire I had experienced at 19 years old on an island the first time I traveled to a foreign country. Not one single step along the way had been a mistake. I had to live through all these chapters to fulfill my purpose in the most powerful way now.

Having been on-the-go so frequently around another continent for three years, being back in Oklahoma was quite an adjustment. I had assumed that I could scratch my itch for traveling by taking road trips in my jeep. I got on my volunteers' website (the same one where I found the opportunity building a bamboo house in Ecuador) and found ten different places here in the states that, in spite of the covid crisis, were looking for a single volunteer to stay long-term to come house sit, work on their farm harvesting food, or take care of animals. It was no coincidence that in less than a month after getting back to Oklahoma City, my jeep broke down and none of the ten host families to whom I had written about coming to stay as a volunteer responded. What was I going to do stuck in Oklahoma with no job, no vehicle, and no money? I searched deep within for the answer.

For the first time in my life, I was void of distractions. I had worked so hard for nearly 20 years, ever since I had my first job at 15, and being in a constant emotional state of surviving had gone on much longer than that. I had never been so still for so long, in Oklahoma, and *sober*, all at the same time. Sobriety was the key factor, though, because it allowed me to truly feel. I wanted to drink so bad.

My soul started to pour over onto paper as I hand-wrote every chapter of this book. I never had time to really sit with any of the parts of my story, and so many months of doing this work showed me how many wounds from my life I still needed to heal. Penning out my story gave me the opportunity to also sit with myself through each of those chapters in my life, from the age of 20 until now, to love myself, and to analyze my life in a different way. I was able to see that I had cycles. I didn't write about Jose to demonize him, but to show one example of what my relationship reality looked like. Jose was just one, but in reality, there were dozens, one right after the other, with similar endings. The common denominator was me. I kept myself in cycles of financial insecurity and woundedness. I was able to count how many times I noticed red flags about what I was walking into--nearly every time--yet disregarded them.

It made me look deeper. These things didn't start after the kidnapping and the rape. They were already there. I kept asking, "Why?" and, "But how did you get there?" to keep backtracking earlier and earlier into my life to find where these patterns started. That was how I found the root of my pain.

The root of my pain is my father. My father began a sexual relationship with me when I was 3-years-old and it continued for eight years – until he got me pregnant at 11 years old (I miscarried). Right after that is when that mysterious psychotic breakdown happened followed by my first suicide attempt when I was 12. Actually, it was not just my dad, but also his dad, who sexually abused me, and there were a total of four men in my childhood who raped me before my breakdown landed me in that mental asylum. I can't even count on one hand how many different men have raped me in this lifetime. Why is it important to go back and sort through it? Because it impacted everything after that, and still impacts me. Actually, I am just now opening this chamber, the deepest one within me, and it requires much hard, painful work. This kind of soul work fucking SUCKS! It hurts, its hard, it feels like anguish, but why is it necessary? Because it still impacts several areas of my life today and impedes me from living the life of my dreams. I now know that I deserve to live the life of my wildest dreams. I will face every demon and every monster within me until there are none left.

I realize I have many things related to my family that are a big mess inside of me. It will take a lot of work to figure them out, not for anyone else, but for me. While I began sorting through some of these things, I read a big stack of books related to broken family relationships, the impact of sexual abuse in one's childhood, how these things impact relationship and money cycles, and how to break the cycles. At the end of this book, I am including a list of books that have helped me tremendously in working through all these chapters. If anything I shared about my traumas and healing process resonates with you and you desire to do your own inner work, my hope is that some of these books can help you like they helped me. My next book will be dedicated to telling the story of the first half of my life, how it impacted my belief systems going forward about everything, and how to heal it so that I can live the fullness of the life I deserve. This is why its important to heal.

Coping with these powerful tribulations wasn't and isn't easy. I wanted to drink so bad. The pain that is still there from that chamber, the deepest chamber yet, is so great that it made me want to reach for anything to not feel it. This is what my soul had been screaming to let out, when I heard its cry the day that I lay miserably hungover in my sweat before I left Argentina. I had told myself, "If I can make it through my 34th birthday sober in Jardín, I can make it sober through anything." Then, the world caught on fire when the pandemic hit, and I told myself, "If I can get through lockdown in a foreign country sober, surrounded by others drinking, I can get through anything sober," and I did. I told myself, "If I can get through doing this level of healing while in Oklahoma, with no job, no car, or money, sober, with the person who terrorized me more than anyone still alive and living in town, I can get through anything." I celebrated my year of sobriety from alcohol on November 1st, and I don't plan on ever looking back. Drinking so much alcohol for 15 years of my adult life never let me feel. It is imperative to feel in order to heal. There are no shortcuts to that.

✳✳✳

While I wrote this book, a friend with whom I hadn't spoken in years gave me a surprise visit one afternoon. She emotionally confided in me that she was secretly surviving an abusive marriage, and although she wasn't ready to leave it yet, she watched the YouTube video of Luxbetsy sharing her story at least a dozen times. Every time she watched it, she felt inspired by the strength of another woman and it gave her hope and courage to keep choosing to face life every day. I was once again re-aligned with my life purpose. Gosh, the local people in the streets of Bogotá looked at Luxbetsy down their noses, just one more meek unwelcome Venezuelan refugee fighting for her space to sell coffee for coins, but look at her power to inspire a woman on another continent, by having the courage to share her story in a 12-minute unedited YouTube video!

Her sharing her story made her unhidden, and I knew that me sharing mine would make me unhidden as well. I was ruminating on one of my favorite quotes by Nora Ephron, "Above all else, be the heroine of your life, not the victim," when the name "Unhidden Heroines" came to me. *This.* This would be the name of my book series, with my memoir being the first book, and books afterward dedicated to documenting stories of women like Luxbetsy and others who came into my life. What if our stories could inspire women across borders, and by learning how the world looks through the eyes of another human, we could love and accept each other instead of being so judgmental?

As I sat with my story, I relived the joy of my travels, and realized how many women inspired me along the way. When I wrote about my hostel experience in Salento seeing the mountains in Colombia for the first time, I relived the inspiration that Ruth gave to me, the girl who'd made a comment about my leggings and how I shouldn't care what people think. Why would I wait on someone else's permission to feel okay in my body? "I wish I could create my own leggings designs," I thought. I heard a faint whisper inside of me say, "Why can't you?" I had never considered such a thing.

I figured out how to make a pair of leggings that were a collage of all the world's flags, born out of the joy I experienced in my first language classroom where I was enamored by vibrant flags. I imagined aligning with the energy of the women in all those countries, how exhilarating it would be to cross borders to meet them later in perfect timing. I created another legging design with the translation of "Love Conquers All" in sixty-four different languages sprawled all over them, the tattoo I had gotten in Arabic on my left arm from the first time I visited Bogotá. What unites us all across borders is love, our ability to love others. Creating this pair further inspired me to make leggings and matching products in other languages, as well, such as Chinese, Arabic, Hindi, Russian, Mayan, Egyptian Hieroglyphics, sign language, and multilingual messages about love and peace.

Writing about Colombia made me go back to look at all my travel pictures, and I thought, "How cool would it be to make a pair of leggings that has a collage of the pictures of artwork I photographed around Colombia?" So, I did. I wanted to connect to joy by wearing them no matter where I physically am, and to give the same gift to women all over the world, especially to those who may not ever have the chance to go on the same adventure I did. Writing my story also reminded me how the universe always showed up and was always working in my favor, even when it didn't seem like it, so I made a universe collection to wear as a reminder to always trust.

As I worked through my story and realized that life had brought me full circle to what I always knew I wanted to do, I made another legging design out of my favorite quote, "Live life by a compass, not a clock," with the quote on one leg and the world map of countries and oceans surrounding it on the rest of the pattern. That pattern brought to mind the dreadful flight back to the states from Cozumel years ago, when I begged my grandma to let me stay on the island, asking her why I would force myself to do something I didn't want to do, trying to fit myself into a box, waiting to live the life of my dreams until later in life. I wanted to create income for myself doing work I absolutely love to do, which is writing and travel.

What if I could find a way to set up an online store where I can sell these leggings, and when traveling, I can create new legging designs? By selling them, I can fund my travels. So, I did, and then came the birth of my online business, also called Unhidden Heroines. I found a way to make my leggings available from sizes extra small to 6XL because, like Ruth said, "Why don't I deserve to feel beautiful and confident just as I am?" I make the coolest leggings in the world, and they should be available to women in all sizes.

Once I figured out how to upload my leggings for sale on my official business page, I learned to design other apparel with my favorite quotes on them so that they can inspire other women as much as they have me. I used quotes like, "Above all else, be the heroine of your life, not the victim," "Everything you want is on the other side of fear," "The world is yours," "I needed a hero, so that's what I became," "Nevertheless, she persisted," from the tattoo on my arm when I escaped that bus driver who threatened to kidnap me, "Empowered women empower women," "What's your Why?" and "Keep Rising," "Make Love, Not War," among several others. I put them on products such as t-shirts, tank tops, tote bags, hoodies, pillows, and drawstring bags perfect for traveling. These are quotes that have inspired my whole journey, and I hope they do yours, too. They are created from a deep place of joy within my soul, and you can find your favorites at www.unhiddenheroines.com

***

Before I sign off, I want to share these words to the younger version of me who needed them:

You are worthy. You were born worthy. Your worthiness is not earned; you were born with it. It is not based on your waistline, the love or validation that others give you (or don't give you), the money that you earn (or don't earn), the good deeds you do (or don't do), or how productive you are (or aren't). Make sure to know what your inner belief systems about worthiness really are. When you try to create something new and wonderful but you subconsciously believe you aren't worthy of it, it's like picking fruit to put in your basket with one hand but gauging a hole in that basket with the other.

Don't be afraid to start over as many times as you need to! Each time you try again, you aren't starting from scratch, but from experience. Each time you try, you learn something new, and applying it is wisdom. Have fun with your adventure and never get tired of exploring every avenue.

It doesn't matter what hand of cards life deals you. Your power is to choose to play them however you want, and you can make anything work in your favor.

It wasn't your fault, not as a little girl, not as an adolescent, not ever in your adulthood. Your abusers didn't take anything from you that you can't get back. Those pieces are yours. Doing the inner work to get your power back is hard, but worth it, and *you are worth it*.

You are not dumb, dirty, damaged, or destined for doom. It is not your divine fate to suffer. You were not born to survive. You were born to thrive.

You deserve to live the life of your dreams, whatever that looks like for *you*.

Don't wait on anyone to create the space for you that you desire. Blaze your own trail. You weren't born to be like anybody else. When you march to your own beat, people may not understand you, and they may even hate you for it, but mostly, they'll wish they had the courage to do the same.

Everything you need is already inside of you. You are magic, baby, pure magic.

It is wonderful that you have a heart of gold and desire to do so much for others, but you should always give to yourself first. You cannot pour from an empty cup. That is not selfish. That is self-love, and you will be able to give from a place of true love to others when you first love yourself.

I love you so much, just as you are. You are worthy of being unconditionally loved, no matter what anyone did to you and no matter what you did to anyone else. You deserve to be loved and be in love with life, always, every day, no matter what.

Fear is your friend. It exists to show you where you need to grow and go to those places outside of your comfort zone. That's where all the magic is.

Your words are so powerful. Use them to plant seeds that will be a harvest of love and abundance in your life and the lives of others.

Well, it's time to go. It's time to pack my suitcase for my next chapter. I have more healing to do, more things to discover about myself, more books to write, stories from myself and others waiting to come alive on paper, languages to learn, tattoos to get, leggings to create, and places to explore all over this beautiful world.

I will be headed back to my beloved Colombia on another one-way ticket, but this time, I'm not running. Telling my story has aligned me with my life purpose, and I plan on living it as authentically as I can. I am so excited to find new ways to create the life of my dreams, and I wish the same for you on your journey, whatever that looks like for you. Now that you know why I started traveling, you will know why I do what I do going forward, my heart in the palm of my hand leading the way. I beckon you to follow my journey.

I love you,
Jenni.

List of Books I Recommend for Further Reading:

Personal Memoirs and other inspiring works:

The Night Trilogy: Night, Dawn, and Day by Elie Wiesel
I Know Why the Caged Bird Sings by Maya Angelou
The Only Girl in the World by Maude Julien
Man's Search for Meaning by Viktor Frankl
I Am Malala: the girl who stood up for education and was shot by the Taliban by Malala Yousafzai
Girl in the Woods: A Memoir by Aspen Matis
Wild: From Lost to Found on the Pacific Crest Trail by Cheryl Strayed
Men We Reaped: A Memoir by Jesmyn Ward
Whip Smart: The True Story of a Secret Life by Melissa Febos
Blackout: Remembering the Things I Drank to Forget by Sarah Hepola
Getting Off: One Woman's Journey through Sex and Porn Addiction by Erica Garza
Wasted: A Memoir of Anorexia and Bulimia by Marya Hornbacher
Quit Like a Woman: the radical choice not to drink in a culture obsessed with alcohol by Holly Whitaker
The Glass Castle by Jeannette Walls
Love Letters: My personal journey towards healing by Eunice Jones-Mitchell
Shadows Before Dawn: Finding the Light of Self-Love through your darkest times by Teal Swan

From Living to Legacy: Beyond the Barriers of Mediocrity by Donelle Cole
As Muses Burn: A Poetry Collection by Mira Hadlow
The Story you Need to Tell: Writing to Heal from Trauma, Illness, or Loss by Sandra Marinella

Spiritual

The Completion Process: the Practice of Putting Yourself Back Together Again by Teal Swan
The Intender's Handbook: A guide to the Intention Process and the conscious community by Tony Burroughs
The Abundance Code: How to Bust the 7 Money Myths for a Rich Life Now by Julie Ann Cairns
The Law of Attraction by Ether Hicks and Jerry Hicks
The Astonishing Power of Emotions: Let Your Feelings be Your Guide by Esther and Jerry Hicks

Self-help & Psychology for family and trauma

Toxic Parents: Overcoming their Hurtful Legacy and Reclaiming Your Life by Susan Forward
Men Who Hate Women and the women who love them: When Loving Hurts and You don't understand Why by Susan Forward
Emotional Blackmail: When People in Your Life use Fear, Obligation, and Guilt to Manipulate You by Susan Forward
Mothers who can't love: a Healing Guide for Daughters by Susan Forward
Money Demons: Keep them from sabotaging your relationships – and your life by Susan Forward
Betrayal of Innocence: Incest and its devastation by Susan Forward
Obsessive Love: when it hurts too much to let go by Susan Forward

Will I Ever Be Good Enough? Healing the daughters of Narcissistic Mothers by Karyl McBride

How Can I Forgive You? The courage to forgive, the freedom not to by Jani Abrahms Spring, Ph.D.

The Inner Child Workbook: what to do with your past when it just won't go away by Cathryn Taylor

The Journey from abandonment to healing: Revised and Updated: Surviving through and recovering from the five stages that accompany the loss of love by Susan Anderson

Healing from the trauma of childhood sexual abuse: the Journey for Women by Karen Duncan

The Rape Recovery Handbook: Step-by-Step Help for Survivors of Sexual Assault by Aphrodite Matsakis

How to Find and Follow me on Social Media

Follow my author page on Facebook: Jenni Reavis, Multilingual Author

Subscribe to my YouTube channel here https://www.youtube.com/channel/UC-rwIxQAqAvpu2hWwGm6tKw

Find me on Instagram! www.instagram.com/fearfacer528 and www.instagram.com/unhiddenheroines

Check out my author page, blog, and e-commerce store and travel blog at **www.unhiddenheroines.com**

If you or anyone you know has survived trauma and tragedy and would be interested in sharing it with women across the world by having a chapter published in my book series, *Unhidden Heroines*, please let me know! Your story can be completely anonymous if you desire. Please email me at **reavisjenni@gmail.com** if interested. Sharing stories saves lives!

www.ingramcontent.com/pod-product-compliance
Lightning Source LLC
Chambersburg PA
CBHW071805080526
44589CB00012B/691